DEEP TRIVEDI

Deep Trivedi is a renowned author, speaker and pioneer in spiritual psychodynamics who writes and conducts lectures with an all-pervasive perspective, guiding an individual towards the achievement of his full potential. Till date, he has led thousands of people onto the path of success and happiness through his works.

In his voluminous works, Deep Trivedi has extensively explained Nature, its laws, its behaviour, its psychology and the effect it has on human life. No aspect of life and human psychology has been left untouched by him. He states that the lack of psychological knowledge and understanding is the sole reason for all the sorrows and failures pervading human life.

An author of numerous books, he is known for his special ability to touch upon the deepest aspects of life and explain them in a very lucid language, leaving no scope for any ambiguity.

His command over the biggest psychologies of life can be gauged by the fact that he holds the Record for 'Maximum Number of Quotations on Human Life (about 12038) on subjects such as Soul, Human Life, Psychology, Laws of Nature, Destiny and much more. He also holds the record for 'Maximum Lectures on Human Life', 'Maximum Lectures on Psychological Aspects of Tao Te Ching', 'Maximum Lectures on Ashtavakra Gita' and 'Maximum Lectures on Bhagavad Gita', which is 168 hrs, 28 mins, 50 secs in 58 days in different national and international record books. These lectures have been delivered in front of a live audience across India.

The distinct spiritual-psychological language and expression in his writings and lectures, begins to have an instant effect on the mind of the reader or listener, which makes Deep Trivedi a pioneer in this field.

To know more about Deep Trivedi,

D0503461

DEEP TRIVEDI The Speaker

Deep Trivedi uses a unique combination of psycho-spiritual content, voice, language and expression which effectuates an instantaneous transformation in his viewers and listeners. Innumerable lives have been transformed just by listening to him. This is the reason why he is known as a pioneer in spiritual psychodynamics.

Deep Trivedi sheds light on every subject related to life. There is no aspect of human life that has been left untouched by him. He has spoken on numerous topics such as Bhagavad Gita, Tao Te Ching, Ashtavakra Gita and:

● Laws of Nature	● Involvement	● Concentration
● Time and Space	● Expectation	● Joy and Happiness
● Religion	● Partiality	● Wealth
● DNA-Genes	● Acceptance	● Good-Bad
● Path of Life	● Natural Intelligence	● God
● Day-Sleep	● Power of Transformation	● Ego
● Mind and Brain	● Marriage	● Anger
● Personality	● Freedom	● Self-Confidence
● Complex	● Future	● Love
● Phobias	● Hypocrisy	● Confusion
● Guilt	● Creativity	

I am The Mind

The Master Key to achieve anything you want

Once I am Set - All Set...

By the Bestselling Author
DEEP TRIVEDI

Also available in Hindi, Marathi and Gujarati

From the Author's Desk

Who does not wish to understand and unravel the mysteries of the 'Mind'? For, it is the mind which governs a human being round the clock. Human beings are rendered helpless when pitted against the might of the mind. However, those who have been wise enough to master their mind go on to scale the peaks of joy and success. But unfortunately, they are few in number.

I have written this book with only one aim - to increase the number of people who are the masters of their mind and thus increase the percentage of happy and successful people in this world. The mind follows a simple rule; if the mind is your master, it wreaks havoc in your life and if you become the master of your mind, the same mind transforms into an extraordinary power centre.

Nevertheless, the biggest concern here is that surprisingly most people aren't even aware that the 'brain' and 'mind' exist separately. Whereas the fact is, both their areas and systems of functioning are radically different. However, it is due to sheer ignorance on the part of humans regarding the difference between the two, that both of them keep interfering repeatedly in each other's domain. Honestly speaking, it is this interference which is largely responsible for the current sorry state of human lives.

So, with the help of many interesting stories, anecdotes and parables, I have not only shed light upon the difference between the 'mind' and 'brain' and the system of functioning of the mind, but have also suggested the ways of dealing with them in this book. I am optimistic that this book will accomplish its purpose of providing a new, unprecedented direction to your life. And it is with this hope that I present this book to you all.

DEEP TRIVEDI

INDEX

01 My Introduction

07 My Existence

13 My Shenanigans

19 My Composition

31 My Power Centres

50 My Correlation with Others

60 Repercussions of Suppressing me

83 Remedies to dispel Sorrows and Worries

84 The Present

97 Personality

114 Complex

137 Involvement

150 Expectation

159 The Keys to Success

160 Intelligence

183 Creativity

196 Concentration

219 Curtail your Ambitions

230 Self Confidence

242 Contentment

247 The Summary

Sixth Edition: 2018
Price: Rs 295/-
Printed in India

Concept, Illustration and Design:
Aatman Innovations Pvt. Ltd.
Place of Publication: Mumbai

ISBN 978-93-84850-09-8

www.aatmaninnovations.com

My Introduction

I am the 'Mind'. My existence is as old as the Universe. I am the sole 'witness' to the advent of human existence and the subsequent ups and downs of human life. It is only because of me that human beings even exist today. It is solely 'I', who governs every human being round the clock. I am the primary and most significant reason behind all the ups and downs of his life, all his successes and failures, and even all his joys and sorrows. However, the irony is, despite my being in existence for aeons, the human being is still completely ignorant about 'me'. And truly speaking, it is this ignorance, which is the root cause of all his sorrows and failures. Today, after so many years, my compassion is compelling me to discuss my existence, my system of functioning and my influences. But before we proceed any further, I would like to draw your attention towards a thought-provoking and profound subject.

Think...! What is the purpose of human life? If stated in one line—Happiness and Success. I have observed, and certainly even you must have noticed that everyone is toiling day in and day out only to achieve joy and success. And this practice is not a present day phenomenon; it has been prevalent ever since human beings came into existence. It must be acknowledged here that human intelligence has been developing with every passing epoch. And I am not making a baseless statement; the results of the consistent efforts of human beings to improve their life are there for us to see. Humans, who earlier satiated their hunger by consuming wild fruits, roots and raw meat, have concocted thousands of delectable and nutritious delicacies today. Living in forests, humans who earlier braved the wrath of every season, have now constructed concrete houses that offer effective protection against the heat and cold. Similarly, humans who covered their modesty using leaves in primeval times, have now created myriad colourful garments to enhance their beauty and appearance.

Not only this, man, who lived a secluded life in the early ages, has now effectively developed the concept of society as well as a socially relevant way of thinking. Today, with his untiring efforts, man has united the whole world and transformed it into a global village. The greatest outcome of this development is that the sphere of his care and concern, which was earlier confined only to himself, has now been expanded to include mankind at large. At present, millions of people and thousands of social service organisations are relentlessly working towards the betterment of human life. Hundreds and thousands of orphanages, homes for the challenged, hospitals and parks have been established for the benefit of the underprivileged. Several laws have been framed and judiciaries have been set up to prevent people from falling prey to injustice. Simultaneously, various religions and religious scriptures have also been created to help human beings eradicate their sorrows and lead a happy and joyous life. In keeping with the beliefs of human beings, thousands of saints and incarnations of Gods have taken birth on this earth for the sake of human upliftment. And if their belief system is considered to be true, they will keep descending in the future too, as and when the need arises. Moreover, for the upliftment of human beings, thousands of rituals, various forms of prayers and worship and religious practices have also been prescribed by the different religions of the world and their religious heads. Human beings, who have anyway been yearning for their upliftment, soon succumbed to these rituals and as a consequence, entire mankind became religious and ritualistic.

Then came Science which took charge of ensuring a happy and joyous life for human beings. A legion of intellectuals engaged themselves in this noble cause and ushered in such a remarkable revolution, that the infant mortality rate which was almost fifty percent two hundred years ago, has been drastically brought down to around two percent. Not only blood tests, but medicines and treatments have also been invented to diagnose and treat most of the diseases, in order to ensure the health and well-being of humans. Complex medical procedures, ranging from heart surgeries to knee and liver transplants have also been made easily accessible to all. In a way, it is these remarkable efforts of Science that have drastically transformed human life.

Science has worked its marvel in other areas of human life as well. It has not only concerned itself with the health and well-being of humans and longevity of human life but has also gone a step ahead and taken great pains to ensure a life full of comfort, prosperity and progress for them. Having advanced from creating means of survival to those of comfort, Science has not only designed comfortable houses, but has also thoughtfully invented air conditioners, cars, elevators and many such conveniences. For the luxury and entertainment of human beings, Science has invented the movies, television, DVDs and much more. At the same time, to lead man onto the path of progress,

The secret behind all the successes and failures of a human being is hidden in the deeper recesses of his mind

Science has brought about a revolution in the field of communication and transport. From airplanes and radio to mobile phones; a host of machines have been invented for people to stay connected. In other words, Science has brought the entire world within the reach of all human beings. While I am acknowledging Science for its remarkable feats, how can I forget, that it is due to the efforts of Science that children these days are being provided education right from childhood. Undoubtedly, it has ventured on this path with the sole aim of fulfilling the primal desire of human beings to be happy and successful. I, 'the mind', sincerely appreciate and commend the efforts put in by human beings for the collective upliftment of human life. I agree that religion, society, science and education have made tremendous efforts to fill the lives of human beings with joy, peace and happiness. However, with utmost humility, I would like to draw your attention towards the end result and ask you; despite all the efforts, is human life truly filled with joy, peace and happiness?...I do not think so. Even today, I see anger, ego, sorrow, failure, stress, anxiety, boredom and violence reigning in their lives as it had during primaeval times. If you observe your life as well as that of the people around objectively, you will surely find this reality manifesting in every other person's life.

Indeed, it is extremely unfortunate that even after thousands of years of efforts, human beings are still besieged by sorrows and worries to this extent. That being the case, this ground reality cannot be ignored any longer! Even after scaling the heights of prosperity and progress, if human beings are still living in such a pitiable state, dying each moment, then is it not deplorable? Well! However agonising it may be, but this is the harsh reality, which gives rise to the obvious question, is there only pain in human life, irrespective of what one does? Have religion, science and society, completely failed to make human beings happy? Has Nature's most marvellous creation, the 'human being' come into this world only to face sorrows, tension and anxiety? No, that cannot be the case! To be happy, successful and joyous is the first and foremost right of a human being. Nature has not bestowed this privilege upon any other creation on this earth.

If this is true, then why can't we be happy? Where is the problem? Is it in the scriptures or in God? Is it in Science or in society? Or is it in our way of being?

To find an answer to these questions, observe carefully; the entire functioning of human life is driven by emotions, and all the emotions arising within a human being are directly related to me, 'the mind'. So from this perspective, am I not the supreme authority governing human life? Of course I am! For, it directly implies that it is because of me that human beings experience joy and success, and I am the only reason behind their sorrows and failures. Religion, science, society or education have nothing to do with it whatsoever. Surprisingly, human beings have striven hard and have left no stone unturned for their upliftment. But they have never made any significant effort to understand the functioning of the mind and recognise its power. Let me clarify here that without understanding me and utilising my powers correctly, neither can human beings ever become joyous nor can they achieve success.

I am not saying that efforts have not been made at all to know, understand and explain me...efforts have certainly been made, but those attempts have proved to be inconclusive and superficial. Hence, today my compassion has compelled me to reveal everything about myself in detail, so that in future, human beings can always stay happy and joyous.

Let us begin with an anecdote from the life of the great scientist, Thomas Alva Edison. You may very well know that in order to illuminate the world, Edison was in search of a fibre that could light up the bulb. He began with his experiments and started testing various fibres, one by one. Edison segregated all the fibres that were unable to light up the bulb under the category of fibres that 'cannot light the bulb'. Only after testing over six thousand fibres, did he finally discover the 'carbon filament' which could successfully light up the bulb.

Similarly, you too have been yearning to illuminate your life and have been experimenting with numerous fibres (solutions) since ages. But success is still eluding you. Why? Because, you have been consistently experimenting with the same solutions that have failed to enlighten your life not just once, but a thousand times. The same old temples, mosques and churches, and the same prayers and rituals. The age-old reliance on the brain, and the same old teachings; the same societal norms and religious scriptures; the same stories, principles and the same old run-of-the-mill drills. Why do you not understand that despite experimenting with these solutions umpteen times, you have still been unsuccessful in bringing happiness into your life. Now the time has come for you to understand this and do something new. After all, you are a human being and you ought to bring an end to this vicious cycle one day. And bringing an end to this cycle will not be possible without an in-depth understanding of me i.e. your mind. Know for sure that without utilising my 'filaments', i.e. my 'powers', your life will not be illuminated. Hence, it is for this very purpose that today, I have myself come to your help, to tell you in detail about my composition and system of functioning.

My Existence

Having introduced myself to you, let me enlighten you about my existence. I am present in all human beings in equal measure. If you broaden the horizons of your understanding a bit, you will find that it is 'I', who hold the reins of the entire human life. At the same time, if I were to talk about my influence, then no aspect of human life is left untouched. And as for the system of my functioning, it is so complicated that it will not be easy to explain it to you right away. For, despite being the supreme controlling power of your life, I am still an unknown entity to you. Even the greatest of intellectuals have miserably failed in comprehending me. So, first of all, I would like to shed light on my existence because in spite of making such remarkable progress, as far as my existence is concerned, Science is still in the dark.

However, there is a reason behind this; Science deals with the discovery of the system of functioning of 'visible' objects by observing and analysing them. Science is essentially the discovery or study of results effected from the fusion or collision between different things. To spell it out in plain words, Science is the discovery of the system of functioning of things that exist within the realm of 'Time and Space'. Science does not recognise the existence of anything that cannot be brought to the desk of a laboratory, and rightly so, it should not either. For, the progress of Science rests on its disbelief in the 'invisible'. The very basis of the progress of Science is, its conviction that one day, owing to its relentless efforts, it will be able to unravel everything. Science rests on the faith that a day will arrive, when there will be no mysteries left to be unravelled in this world. Science must certainly be commended for its conviction and efforts. The strength of its determination is the reason, Science has not only set its foot on the Moon and Mars, but has also discovered the Black Hole and billions of galaxies. Not only this, it is also conducting a series of advanced experiments on 'The Big-Bang Theory' by using the 'Large Hadron Collider'.

Coming back to the subject of my existence, the efforts, experiments and the conviction of Science are acknowledged, but in reality, let alone the mysteries of the Universe, Science can never even fathom my existence. Because in spite of being present at the navel of every human being with my complicated mechanism and all my frequencies, emotions and powers, I am entirely independent of the limitations of Time and Space. If I were to speak scientifically, then I do not have any physical existence in your body which is the very reason why Science has never accepted my existence. As a result, Science has always upheld the brain as the primary centre of a human being. Here I wish to make it clear that the brain influences only ten percent of your life. The rest of the influences exerted on your life are solely mine, and mine alone. However, I will explain to you the difference between the brain and me at the appropriate time as we proceed further. For now, let me explain how my presence and my existence are beyond the purview of Science.

At the onset of this discussion, I would like to give you a simple introduction of myself. I am the centre of your good and bad emotions, as well as the powers that are a thousand times more effective than that of your brain. And because 'I' am invisible to Science, all my emotions and numerous powers are also invisible to it. Happiness, sadness, jealousy, remorse, anger, tension, anxiety, euphoria and several other moods are all emotions generated by me, and it is solely because of me that you experience these countless emotions and are bound to endure them. Now if you observe carefully, what is a human being, if not an embodiment of these various emotions? What is the reality of human life, if not an interplay of these emotions?

Nothing! There is not even a single moment when he does not live in either a positive or a negative emotion. In fact, even when he does nothing, he ends up living in the 'bored' state of mine (mind). This means, your life is nothing but me, me and only me.

Now the problem is, Science does not believe in my existence. It is also true that there have never been more intelligent people born in the history of this world, as the scientists born in the last 500 years. I definitely have no reason to doubt their intentions as they have greatly concerned themselves with the happiness, peace and progress of human beings. These scientists are aware that physical pains and hardships make human life a living hell. They have also realised that peace and happiness are the primary desires inherent to each and every human being. But the problem that arose was, Science, with its limited understanding, linked peace and happiness of human beings to their physical comfort, progress, and entertainment. As a result, Science, with its relentless endeavours, invented several means and machines for the comfort, luxury and entertainment of the people. Certainly, Science made all these efforts to progressively elevate the living standard of human beings. Agreed, that progress, comfort, enjoyment and entertainment are the primary needs of human life. And these means and machines have elevated the living standard of human beings to a large extent. Yet, Science will have to accept that all these factors have only had a superficial effect on human life. You must have experienced that the happiness quotient offered by even the best of means and machines of Science has been limited to physical comforts. At my level i.e. at the level of the mind, in spite of all these means of comfort and luxury accorded by Science, human beings have still remained besieged by sorrows, worries, anger, frustration, etc.

When Science realised that all these means of comfort and luxury were of little help in providing a happy life, it initiated experiments on the functioning of the 'brain'. Science endeavoured to discover the type of chemicals released by the brain and the types of hormones secreted by different glands in the body under stress, and it achieved partial success too. The conclusion that Science drew from these experiments was, human beings experience the impulses of different emotions because of specific chemicals released by the brain. Science hastily arrived at the conclusion that it is the brain which is responsible for the several highs and lows of various emotions experienced by human beings. But here, let me make it clear; this conclusion drawn by Science is absolutely wrong, as it is 'I' who sends the emotion and the brain simply reacts to it. Now, irrespective of the quantum of research on these reactions carried out by Science, it will not be able to taste much success, as it will never be able to invent any medicine or injection that could stop the brain from secreting a particular chemical or prevent a human being from getting worried.

Nevertheless, when even these efforts proved to be ineffective, Science discovered 'DNA' and 'genes'. Science surely deserves to be commended for this path-breaking discovery. This significant accomplishment of Science has unravelled many mysteries relating to human life. Yet, in the context of sorrows and stress, things were at a standstill, because while DNA and genes are definitely the primary determinants as far as a person's physique, age, skin colour, etc. are concerned, they are incapable of exerting any influence on anxiety, stress, anger, etc. However, Science must be applauded once again for its research initiated in the field of decoding and re-engineering DNA and genes. Certainly, these are milestones achieved by Science for which mere words do not suffice. But the question is, even after all this, what have you gained? Of course, some human diseases have been eradicated, the life span of human beings has increased; but what about the emotional highs and lows experienced by them? In short, all these efforts of Science can only be applied to man's longevity and health, but not to the emotions emanating from me.

You may say, "You are saying so, but how do we believe it?" I very well know that I am unveiling the mystery surrounding me in this scientific age; therefore whatever I state, will have to be proven and I have come prepared for the same. But my predicament is, since I do not have a physical existence, I cannot prove anything about myself in a scientific laboratory. In fact, had I been existent within the parameters of Time and Space, Science would have analysed me long back and successfully eradicated worries, stress and anger from

" As far as the mind is concerned science too is absolutely in the dark "

human life. However, this does not mean that my existence cannot be proved in any laboratory. A human being is my 'living laboratory'! Anyone who applies even a little intelligence, will in no time realise and acknowledge my existence. Just absorb all that I say and experience it within, because I exist within you, and what and how you feel is my laboratory.

Now, if I take the discussion forward in the same vein, then you will definitely agree that major discoveries relating to the human body have already been made by Science. Science has now become competent at accurately detecting the abnormalities in different parts of the body with the help of just a few drops of blood. Science has formulated innumerable types of medicines to deal with various health issues. Not only this, it has even become adept at treating your body, by performing various kinds of surgeries. But then, just see the helplessness of Science; even though it denies my existence, it has to inevitably accept all my emotions. Even scientists have to experience joy, sorrows and worries. Is it not ironic that on one hand, Science denies the existence of invisible things and on the other, scientists themselves have to endure these intangible emotions on a daily basis. So if not today, maybe in the future, but one day, Science will definitely have to accept the existence of the 'invisible'.

After all, for how long can Science turn a blind eye to that which is existent? Even if the principle of the invisible does not concur with the scientific principles of the visible, one day, the scientists will have to recognise the invisible emotions as invisible entities, because despite all its efforts, Science will never be able to find them in your body. Apply your intelligence and think; can Science ever discover a test that can reveal the measure of anxiety in human beings, like they have in case of cholesterol and blood sugar? Can Science ever invent a measuring device such as a thermometer that will be able to reveal whether anger has crossed its threshold or not? Will Science ever be able to formulate tablets to control fear and insecurity of a human being as it does in case of blood pressure and uric acid? Can Science foretell from someone's genes or DNA, the extent of anxieties and the number of problems that he or she is going to face in life? Will Science ever be able to conduct a surgery that can eradicate the sorrow hidden in a human being? No! It is simply not possible. Because these matters are beyond the realm of Time and Space, and far from Science's reach.

Hence, firstly, using your intelligence, recognise my invisible existence and my invisible world. Thereafter, experimenting with me, you can definitely get rid of worries and miseries from your life. If you are successfully able to recognise me, the one who is inconspicuously present within you, then joy and success can become your destiny. In short, your life can definitely become a blissful journey if you acquire the intelligence to experiment with me.

My Shenanigans

Now before I describe my powers and the ways and means of my functioning in detail, I would like to tell you something about my shenanigans i.e. my mischievous antics. As such, all of you are not only aware of my shenanigans, but have also been greatly troubled by them. And since you have had to deal with my shenanigans in one way or another on a daily basis, it is not difficult for you to identify them. Now think, would any of you like to prove yourself a moron or harm your own interests? No... So can your foolishness be controlled just by thinking thus? Are you able to protect your interests, just because you desire so? No...because you think about all this with your brain, whereas, these shenanigans stem from my depths.

Let me elaborate my point with an example. Once, a 22-year-old man was relaxing in a park. He was in a very peaceful state, when one of his friends, a habitual prankster, happened to pass by. Perhaps, the prankster could not bear to see his friend in a relaxed state. He went running to him with a concerned face, and in a serious tone he said, "You are sitting here, and there, your wife is out on a stroll with someone else!" Upon hearing this, the relaxed friend lost his temper and blurted out, "I shall not leave that wicked woman alive!" Incensed, he began to hurl abuses at her, but the very next moment he realised that he was not even married yet. However, it was too late. He had already exhibited his gargantuan stupidity.

Well, you can laugh at him and his predicament, but you too are sailing in the same boat. Quite often, each one of you encounters similar situations. However, I shall discuss the reasons behind this later, because at present I am only discussing the impact of my mischief

13

in your life. In this regard, you must realise that you fall prey to my mischievous antics on a daily basis only because of your sheer ignorance about my system of functioning. Further, let me elucidate on my point with another example. Once upon a time, there lived two very close friends. One belonged to an ordinary household while the other hailed from an affluent family. However, this disparity in wealth had never been a hindrance to their friendship. But for how long?!...when I exist.

One day, it so happened that the poor friend was in urgent need of a bike. Some guests were expected at his place and he was in a hurry to procure some grocery. Since his rich friend owned a bike, he thought, *"Why not borrow it for a day?"* With this thought in mind, he immediately set out for his friend's home. He had barely walked a few steps when it suddenly occurred to him, *"What if he refuses to lend his bike to me?"* But then a counter-thought immediately reassured him, *"In so many years of our friendship, I have never asked him for a favour, then why would he refuse?"* But since I am naughty as ever by nature, I induced another thought, and he began to think, *"No, no, I am sure he will refuse. He is not as innocent and straightforward as he appears. He will certainly give excuses like...there is no fuel in the bike. No worries, I shall tell him, 'Give me the keys and I will fill the tank'."*

With this thought, he once again rallied his confidence. But as he had walked a few more steps, his mind was up to a new mischief again... *'Your friend will come up with scores of excuses to not lend you the bike; his friendship is all superficial. He might just say, "Today, it is not possible for me to spare the bike as the tyre is punctured" or "Some guests have arrived at my place as well."'*

While all these thoughts were flitting through his mind, the poor friend became angry. Around the same time, he reached his friend's house and in an enraged state, rang the doorbell. His wealthy friend opened the door. As the poor friend was already furious, now seeing his rich friend standing in front of him, he lost his cool and began to yell, "To hell with you and your bike! I have seen enough rich people like you. You people can never be true friends. That is it! I end this friendship today." The rich friend was stunned!

He was taken aback by his friend's behaviour. Neither could he comprehend the situation nor the reason behind the strange behaviour of his friend. Bewildered, he asked, "Which bike and what rich people are you talking about?"...But his poor friend had already left after venting out his anger.

In short, what I mean to say is, I am the factory that produces such erratic impulses. Most human beings, having no control over me, are compelled to bear the brunt of my mischief. They end up committing such madness, even though they do not wish to. In spite of them not wanting to, my mischievous antics strain their interpersonal relationships. All in all, despite everything being in order, thanks to me, human beings keep getting trapped in new troublesome situations.

Now, let me narrate another very interesting incident related to this topic. The story dates back to around two hundred years. In a small village, there lived two young lads called Akram and Salman. Both of them were around fifteen-sixteen years old and their friendship was the talk of the town. For over a decade, they were constantly in each other's company. They never had a single altercation, but one day suddenly, there was a bitter fight between them, which turned so fierce, that they beat each other up black and blue. Fortunately, around the very same time, some villagers who happened to pass by the area intervened, and pulled the fighting friends apart. But by then, the situation had already taken an ugly turn. So the villagers thought it wise to present both of them before the village elders. Hearing about the incident and seeing the state that the once inseparable friends were in, even the village elders were speechless.

It did not take time for this news to spread like a wild fire through the entire village. The incident was so shocking that people wondered, "How can two inseparable friends fight so bitterly that they draw each other's blood?" Whoever heard the news, rushed to the meeting place!

Stunned, the elders asked both the friends what had happened between them which led to such a violent brawl. But both kept mum. What could they even say? The elders repeated the question a couple

Essentially a human being is nothing but the mind

of times, but the two still did not utter a word. In the end, when the elders sternly asked them to reveal the details about the incident, they started nudging each other to narrate the course of events that had led to such a bitter fight.

Fantastic! The two friends, who had not felt ashamed while beating each other black and blue, were now feeling embarrassed while revealing to the elders what had actually transpired between them!

Seeing the situation, the elders sternly asked Salman to divulge the details of the incident. Feeling extremely embarrassed, Salman finally spoke, "It so happened that we both were sitting peacefully beneath a tree, just chatting in general. Suddenly, in the midst of the conversation, I told Akram, "I was wondering for how long we will depend on our parents' money. Why not start a business so that we can pay our school fees and earn our pocket money ourselves?"

The elders could not find anything remotely provocative about it, as it was a good thought; but then, what had led to such a fierce fight? When prodded further, Salman narrated the incident in detail. "Hearing my proposal, Akram readily agreed. He said he too was thinking on similar lines for some time now.... Thus, our conversation proceeded further. After pondering upon it for a while, I said, "I am thinking of purchasing two buffaloes. It will take merely two to three hours to milk the buffaloes and sell the milk". Hearing this, Akram said, even he was contemplating upon buying a patch of farmland. He was confident that three to four hours of hard work a day in the field, would yield him enough harvest to pay off his school fees and have a decent amount of pocket money. Upon hearing Akram's plans, I exclaimed in excitement, "This is a really good idea!"

I said, "I will not have to take my cattle far for grazing now; I can bring them to graze in your field." The moment Akram heard my plan, he vehemently objected to it. In a harsh tone, he clearly warned me, "Don't you dare send your cattle to my field for grazing."

Hearing this, even I lost my cool and challenged him in an unrelenting tone, "My cattle will certainly graze in your field, come what may!" When he heard these words, Akram became furious and threatened me, "If your cattle happens to enter my field for grazing, I will break their legs." Hearing this, I too was incensed and warned him, "If you touch my cattle, I will break your head!" And then, both of us lost our temper and came to blows."

Did you see the amazing impact of my shenanigans? The cattle were not yet purchased, the farm was not yet bought, and yet, a simple conversation had led to such a violent fight between the two, who were good friends for over a decade. With this example, all that I wish to suggest to you is, search for similar incidents in your life as well. You will find that I, the one who resides within you, i.e. your mind, coerce you to indulge in similar mischief. If you notice carefully, you will realise that when I get down to my mischief, all your wisdom and intelligence gets locked away. Prodded by me, you are invariably driven to indulge in madness.

Now, if you accept that you do not have any control over my shenanigans and it is because of them that your intelligence gets corrupted on different occasions, then I shall discuss the solutions for it...because only he, who genuinely accepts that he is ill, can be treated. Obviously people, who, for no reason assume that they are healthy, cannot be held and administered treatment by force. In the least, you will have to accept that neither have any of your measures been able to control my mischief nor has your intelligence been able to save you from the tumult created by me. At the same time, even your education and society have miserably failed in finding and providing a solution for it. Here, you will also have to accept that neither your religion nor your philosophies have succeeded in finding or providing a concrete solution to this problem because I am a much larger, independent and unique entity compared to them. So, 'I' am the only one who can offer you the solutions to save yourself from my shenanigans. But my suggestions will work only on one condition. You will have to look for ways to save yourselves from my shenanigans only in the solutions provided by me. Otherwise just think, what is the use of the progress and the numerous comforts gifted by Science, when your mind is unhappy and gripped with madness? However, before I begin with the solutions, it is imperative for you to understand my composition.

———————■———————

My
Composition

Now, if you accept that you are suffering, I shall tell you about my composition. This will not only help you understand me, but will also help you safeguard yourself against my shenanigans. However, before initiating the discussion on this topic let me once again remind you that I am present at your navel in an invisible form, with my entire complicated mechanism. And because I am invisible, I am beyond the comprehension of Science. Speaking of my mechanism, based on the variation of my frequencies, I can be categorised into seven major states. Some among these states are tempestuous while others are brimming with unique and astounding powers.

My Tempestuous States:
1) Conscious Mind
2) Subconscious Mind
3) Unconscious Mind

My Power Centres:
4) Super Conscious Mind
5) Collective Conscious Mind
6) Spontaneous Mind
7) Ultimate Mind

The inherent nature of all my seven states is absolutely different and such is the beauty of my mechanism that whenever you are in a particular state of mind, your attitude automatically reflects the behavioural traits of that respective state. Now, if I recapitulate my different states, though some of them are unruly and dangerous, there are others brimming with extraordinary powers too. What it implies is, it is solely the state of mind you dwell in, that decides the ultimate outcome of your life.

However, before I expound upon my seven states, you will have to understand the mind of children. Only then will it be easy for you to comprehend my various states, their influences and their system of functioning. Also, let me make it clear that in terms of potential, all children are born with almost the same mind, which means, at the time of birth, there is no difference among children at the level of the mind. Whatever differences exist between them can be attributed to their DNA and genes and it is an established fact that all these differences are only limited to their physical appearance, health and brain.

Returning to the discussion about a child's mind, children primarily understand only two languages - Love and Anger. And these two are the most powerful energies in the world. If you view it in the context of the Universe, energy is created either when two objects unite, i.e. Love, or when two objects collide, i.e. Anger. For example, if you want to bring about a positive change in someone, you can either do it by expressing love towards that person or by expressing anger. Likewise, if you wish to bring about a change in yourself, you have no other option, but to communicate with yourself in these two languages. And unfortunately, it is these two energies that everyone lacks in today's world. However, I shall discuss later as to why these two supreme energies, anger and love - responsible for the progress of life - have faded away from human life. For now, let me make it clear that a child is born with the supreme presence of these two omnipotent energies which provide him with all the potential to achieve success in life.

If you observe carefully, you will see, when a child gets hold of an object of his fascination, he becomes so engrossed in playing with it. On the other hand, if any of his favourite objects is taken away from him or if something is not done as per his wish, he becomes angry and resorts to mischief. The child just does not understand any third language...this means that a child is essentially born with an unbounded pool of energy.

As for other distinct qualities of children, they do not possess much knowledge; at the most, they recognise their mother. They are just not concerned with any other relationship. They play with whoever they like and steer clear of the people they dislike. Differentiation between mine and yours or superior and inferior does not exist in them; futile information is far from their radar. At the same time, they are unaware about their religion, caste, society and nationality; and you must have noticed that these things do not make an iota of difference to them or their life in any way. If you apply even a little intelligence, you will understand that all the above-mentioned qualities are the very secret of their abundant joy and exuberance, and this is the prime reason why children are loved by one and all.

Another quality peculiar to children is, since they possess only love and anger, the two most powerful energies of the world, they are always brimming with exuberant energy. Hence, do as you deem fit, but do not ever make the mistake of underestimating children. You must have definitely observed that despite being incorrigible mischief-mongers and playing innumerable pranks, children rarely get tired. Irrespective of how much they have already played, no sooner do they find the slightest opportunity to play again, than they are ready in an instant. The extent of their mischief making is such, that even if four adults take turns to tend to a child in a day, all of them would get tired after a while, but the child would not. Even if an athlete is asked to perform the activities of a child in a day, he will get exhausted in a matter of a few hours, but not the child! The child will go underneath a chair and come out on the table. And stairs! He will climb the stairs nearly twenty to thirty times in a day with great ease. Finally, the athlete will surrender and confess that it is easier to win a medal in the Olympics, than to keep up with the child. The essence of this discussion is, love and anger are the two most powerful energies of the world. A human being, who has lost these two energies, becomes enervated i.e. energy less.

Speaking about the intelligence of children, they are extremely intelligent as well. They precisely know...what they want and when, and how they can get it. This is the reason why they manage to get whatever they want at any cost. They will smile ever so innocently and speak in such an endearing manner that there will be no scope left for refusal. Even then, if they do not get what they want, they always have anger, mischief and stubbornness to resort to. They will bring the entire house down and make your life miserable, but they invariably manage to get what they desire.

At the same time, what can one say about their charm? Is there anyone who does not love children? Is there anyone who does not want to give children their best? The magic of a child's charm is such that even the cruellest person is unable to cause them any harm. Many a times, parents who have been trapped in life-threatening situations with goons or thieves, have been saved because of their children. Seeing a child along, one is compelled to show mercy.

Besides this, innocence, simplicity, playfulness, and concentration are their other intrinsic qualities. As for concentration...? Oh! What can I say about it! Their concentration is supreme. Even you must have observed the incredible concentration with which children play. Think, if adults could have that kind of concentration, would they not be capable of achieving great success in life?

The child also has a phenomenal ability to forget the past, so much so that he would lovingly play with the same child, he may have fought with just a couple of minutes ago. As for their enthusiasm, children are so zestful that irrespective of the number of times they fall, they get back on their feet again in an instant.

In contrast to them, look at adults; they cannot concentrate even on one thing! This in turn gives rise to the question that, where did the concentration which they once possessed as children, disappear to? And as for the level of enthusiasm in adults, do not even ask about that! No sooner do they face a couple of failures than they become so despondent that they even contemplate suicide. This being the case, it is useless to even talk about their innocence, simplicity and energy.

" Nothing in this world is more complicated than the mind "

However, the subject of contemplation at present is, where did we falter that we have landed in such a grim situation?

It was in order to make you understand this very point, that I was explaining the difference between your mind and the mind of a child. Basically, the state of mind in which a child is born is called the Super Conscious Mind. As this mind is suffused only with love and anger, it is a powerhouse of energy. Wittingly or unwittingly, all those who have become happy and successful in the world, have at the least been living in the Super Conscious Mind. To give you a detailed explanation, if I point out a few of its special qualities, then most importantly, there is no dearth of energy in the Super Conscious Mind. It is completely devoid of any useless information, and at the same time, it is brimming with enthusiasm, concentration and an intense desire to constantly try, innovate and learn something new. To top it, as this state of mind is suffused with energies of anger and love, it is capable of accomplishing anything it desires. To summarise, there lies a striking similarity between the traits of successful people and children, because both dwell in and around the Super Conscious Mind. Indeed, if this is the case, then the question that arises is, why and how does the child born in the Super Conscious Mind reach the other states of mind? Which are those states of mind and what are their attributes? I shall definitely tell you, as it is with this objective that I have created such an elaborate background. And it is imperative for you to understand it because this is going to be the turning point of your life. If due care is taken and caution is exercised at this juncture, nobody can stop you from becoming happy and successful.

Returning to the main topic of discussion at hand, as the child starts growing up, parents as well as other members of the family start imparting various kinds of information and teachings to the child. Next, the child is made aware of his religion and caste; a differentiation is created in his mind with regards to who is his own and who is not; futile objectives are then thrust upon him with the aim of propelling him to become something in life. This is how a child's Conscious Mind begins to form. But this Conscious Mind is very weak. It experiences fear and insecurity at the drop of a hat. And needless to say, upon contracting fear and insecurity, the child's enthusiasm and concentration begins to recede...meaning, it is from here on that he begins to get trapped in a vicious cycle and the chances of him living up to his potential become bleak.

The matter however does not end here; burdened with the goal of accomplishing something great in life, the child is then sent to school. The child, who initially lived in complete freedom is now forced to go to school encumbered with a heavy bag and is taught against his wishes. Not only this, the child is then pressurised to score good marks too. And what do I say about schools? ...The child who desired love, the child who wanted to play, is harassed in school in the name of discipline. His condition becomes so pitiable that he does not get any love from his school teachers, and as he grows a little older, he stops receiving affection at home as well.

Thus, a child, a smiling-budding flower is left with no choice but to wither away under the pretext of 'studies'. Under pressures and impositions, the otherwise iron-willed child begins to give in to the compulsions imposed upon him by others and his firmness* begins to weaken. As the child's firmness weakens, his fighting spirit also begins to wobble. Leaving his much desired fun, freedom and playing, no 4 to 5-year-old child in the world would prefer being restrained in the shackles of discipline. This is the reason why most children, except a few enervated ones go to school crying. And the funniest part is, the parents whose children go to school smiling, boast about their children not crying! In all likelihood, the child must be dumb. They should consider themselves fortunate if their child on growing up, does not become an obedient clerk. Here, I am particularly referring to kindergarten, first and second grade children. However, once they make friends and the desire to know and understand the world kindles in them, perhaps even they may enjoy going to school.

Then we have parents, family and school teachers who start tutoring children about good manners and ways to behave. *Do not get angry, always listen to elders, do everyone's work*...so on and so forth. Now the child, who is a powerhouse of energy, and wants to live spontaneously according to his own wishes, is coaxed for no reason to become a stereotypical, obedient servant and lead a banal life. Initially, the child does not find it interesting, but with the help of various temptations and plaudits, the child is enticed to comply with it. At times if these tactics also fail to work, he is compelled to follow their diktats either with reprimands or by the use of threats. Here, an interesting point to note is, in this process, two very important energies of children...anger and love, keep getting suppressed.

And it is this suppression that begets the most grievous results which demands an in-depth understanding. In fact, the more a child's love is suppressed, the more sentimental and emotional he becomes. The child begins to get engulfed in numerous emotions such as disappointment, pity, sympathy, etc. And then, all these emotions lead to the formation of his Subconscious Mind. In short, if I explain

---

* Firmness - In this book, the word firmness is used to denote the quality of persistence and determination in a human being for his natural instincts or liking.

this phenomenon in the language of psychology then, the measure in which a child's love keeps getting suppressed, in the same measure, he becomes emotional and his sentimentality keeps getting accumulated in his Subconscious Mind.

Unfortunately, the tale of the child's plight does not end here. He does not wish to go to school – but is forced to. He likes to play and indulge in mischief – but he does not get an opportunity to do so. Being the master of his own mind, the child likes to be free, but is compelled to live in the shackles of discipline. As a result, on several occasions the child's anger keeps getting suppressed. This suppressed anger gradually gets converted into life-destroying emotions such as anxiety, distress, fear, jealousy, and begins to get accumulated in his Unconscious Mind.

Well! You all are aware of the story that follows. As the child grows, along with anger, he starts losing his vital life energy. Gradually, important qualities such as concentration and enthusiasm also begin to dissipate from the child. In effect, he starts becoming a storehouse of dangerously negative emotions such as sadness, anxiety, fear and disappointment. And then, all through his life, whether the situation calls for it or not, he keeps venting out this accumulated sadness, tension, fear and disappointment on several unnecessary occasions. Do not be under the impression that you are worried just because it is a matter to be worried about; actually worries are stored in your Unconscious Mind and they are only finding a reason to be released.

But I know you will not believe it so easily. So, let us understand it with the help of an example. Once, a person read in the newspaper that a few million years from now, the sun would cease to rise. Now it is obvious that if the sun ceases to rise, the earth will also cease to exist. So what? But here, this person was gripped by anxiety. Now forget millions of years, even if the sun ceases to rise after hundred years, what difference was it going to make to him at present? But the anxiety accumulated within, is always on the lookout for a reason to surface. He is not the only one, due to this repressed anger, you all are also sailing in the same boat.

However, the story of the downfall of human beings does not end here! Firstly, you bombard the child born in the Super Conscious Mind with unnecessary information and objectives, which in turn, leads to the formation of his Conscious Mind. Then, by suppressing his love and anger, you strengthen the Subconscious and Unconscious minds of the child, and burden them with emotions such as anxiety, sadness, fear, sympathy, attachment, etc. But even then, do extra-intelligent people such as you ever feel satisfied? No! You further advise him to restrain the expression of emotions, as a public display of emotions does not always serve one's interest. 'Others should not come to know, what is going on in your mind.' And the poor child falls for it! As a result, he not only begins to suppress his worries, sorrows and fear, but also his emotions and feelings in general. And then, all his life he goes on repressing his anger and love. This brings out yet another disastrous result, for, not only the suppressed anxieties, fears, sorrows, attachments and sympathies get firmly rooted in his Subconscious and Unconscious minds forever; but lying dormant, their intensity multiplies manifold. Then, the poor human being, thanks to the 'contributions' of his fellow human beings, is never able to get rid of the impulses triggered by these negative emotions! Living a life of tensions and sorrows becomes his destiny. Here, you must understand clearly that anxiety, sorrow, fear, insecurity and other such negative emotions, manifest only because you have these emotions lying within you. Do not think that you are gripped by anxiety or are forced to live with these negative emotions because your life or situation calls for it.

I shall elaborate on this point later as we progress further. For now, the reality that we are faced with is, why does the potentially prosperous life of a child turn into a terrible disaster? The main reason for this is our inability to provide children with the correct upbringing and knowingly or unknowingly strengthening their Conscious, Subconscious and Unconscious mind. And that is why, only one among millions manages to escape this vicious trap, and become happy and successful...and that too, only the one who has been able to keep his Super Conscious Mind intact. This is possible in two ways: either the child himself is so firm and powerful that he refuses to fall prey to anyone's instructions or set of guidelines, or if the parents and teachers are wise enough to not unnecessarily force the child. Let my words be carved in stone for posterity that, "No child in the world can become happy and successful without preserving his Super Conscious Mind. At the same time, no one can stop the child who has retained his Super Conscious Mind from being happy and successful."

Even Science tells you more or less the same thing. If scientists state that eighty percent of the development of a child's brain occurs in his childhood, then they have not arrived at a wrong conclusion. What they are stating is absolutely right. Kudos to them for arriving at this conclusion! This is precisely what I have explained to you; the talent of any child depends on the extent to which he has been able to safely preserve his Super Conscious Mind. Certainly, the entire responsibility for this, lies on the shoulders of the family and school teachers of the child. They ought to learn to respect the child's desires and his independence. Under all circumstances, they must refrain from teaching the child any kind of discrimination and should not impose any senseless and unnecessary discipline on him. Most importantly, they must keep the child away from futile and mindless teachings. A child...is a child, do not unnecessarily make him serious. Make the environment at school so conducive for children that they should enjoy being at school more than being at home. Only if the child never misses his home, can he be saved and his potential retained. If being at school gives the child a feeling of discomfort, then it is in the interest of the child that he does not attend such a school.

Otherwise let me warn you, by the time the child grows up, he would have lost all his vital qualities. The current state of human beings is a strong affirmation of the truth of my statement. Irrespective of the progress achieved by human beings, they have still not been able to improve the ratio of successful people, which they ideally should have. Even today, barely a few people manage to become successful amongst millions, and the sole reason for this is the inability of human beings to provide a conducive upbringing for their children; as barely a few among millions possess the art and capability of enhancing the inherent potential of children.

Well! This was the discussion as far as the mistakes committed by you are concerned. In the same vein, there is one more thing related to my nature which is extremely important as well as imperative for you to understand. And that is, I am absolutely free and independent by nature. If an attempt is made to unnecessarily suppress me, I invariably make human beings suffer grave consequences for their actions. In fact, my independent nature has earned me a bad reputation, as for ages, human beings have held me responsible for the various difficulties faced by them in life, whereas, I have already made my stance very clear. I am independent by nature and I do not like any kind of impositions levied upon me. Hence, commit to memory that you will have to bear the consequences of any kind of compulsion thrust upon me. And most importantly, my nature will never change; it is the manner in which you deal with me that will have to change. Hence, if a child falls from the level of the Super Conscious Mind to the level of the Conscious and Unconscious Mind, then it is the family, society and education that ought to be blamed, not me. If you so earnestly want to improve the ratio of people who are happy and prosperous, then bring about the necessary changes in your education system. Teach parents and families the upbringing they need to provide to their children...but do not ever blame me. If you try to kill my nature, I will surely activate my defence mechanism. Well, everyone in this existence has the right to safeguard their nature. Hence, do not ever unnecessarily tamper with me.

If you have grasped this, you will not allow my three weaker states - Conscious, Subconscious and Unconscious Mind – to strengthen within you. With regards to this, I have already explained to you that the Conscious Mind is created by the accumulation of futile information, whereas Unconscious and Subconscious Mind are formed and further strengthened due to suppression of anger and love. If not for these reasons, why else would a human being be gripped by the frequencies of sorrow, anxiety, jealousy, frustration and so on? Neither is any child born with them, nor are human beings forced to live in these emotions because of me. It is because human beings choose to be ignorant about my nature that they are compelled by me to suffer the adverse consequences of their actions. Otherwise tell me, have you ever seen a child getting worried? Hence, if you have to blame anyone for the pains, problems and failures of your life, then blame yourself. And also understand well that you happen to commit all these mistakes because you fail to comprehend my system of functioning.

———◼———

My
Power
Centres

Here too, see the wonderful feats I can pull off! I could not mend my mischievous ways even while revealing details about myself. Did you see? I sought to discuss about my mischievous forms even before I initiated the discussion on my other powerful and useful forms. Nevertheless, I had already made it clear that these are not my primary forms, but they have been brought into existence by your ignorance. As far as I am concerned, let me tell you, I am the source of numerous incredible powers. In this existence, I am the sole entity that is not only connected to Nature in its entirety, but is also capable of performing all the efficacious tasks that essentially lead to the growth of your life. This means, your communication to the supreme power of Nature is possible only through me and you are entirely dependent on my power centres to achieve success in life. To shed more light upon this last sentence; without activating my power centres, a person can never become joyous and successful. Moreover, the extent of happiness and success a person attains in life, is also directly related to the percentage in which my power centres are active in that particular person. Externally, you may resort to thousands of solutions, acquire immense knowledge or put in a great deal of hard work, but neither will you be able to achieve lasting happiness, nor will you be able to achieve any remarkable success in life. Otherwise, there is no dearth of education, hard work or determination and for that matter, even religion, society, family or friends that one has. But then, why are barely a few among millions able to make their lives worthwhile? It is solely because only a few out of millions are able to activate my power centres in themselves.

Now, before I discuss my power centres in detail, let me tell you that they get activated only in accordance with their natural laws. Neither does Nature discriminate nor is there any partiality done with anyone at my level, i.e. at the level of the mind. The sole reason for the innumerable failures of human beings is nothing but their ignorance about my power centres. In that case, to be able to activate these power centres or to know the laws that activate them, seems to be a distant reality. However if you wish to achieve success, you have no other option but to activate them. So now I will tell you about my powers. Well! You cannot even imagine what amazing powers lie dormant within me! If you carefully sift through the history of mankind, you will find that I am the sole reason behind each and every success. All those who have become great, happy and successful have knowingly or unknowingly used my powers abundantly.

Please understand! A person is not successful and joyous, because he is virtuous. At the same time, a person is not happy and successful because he leads his life following a code of conduct decreed by the society. Neither is man happy and successful because of his educational qualification or hard work. Man is not successful because of his visits to temples, mosques or churches either. If this was the case, then would the world not be flooded with 'successful people'. After all, ninety nine percent of the people visit their respective places of worship. But no! Giving success or keeping a man happy falls under my purview and I have no relation whatsoever with any of the factors mentioned above. In accordance with my laws, I am active in all human beings in equal measure. Either utilise my powers or be prepared to become a victim of my destructive forms. The choice is yours! Either scale the peaks of success or keep wandering hopelessly in the dark and deep abyss of difficulties for your entire life. There is no midway as far as I am concerned.

It must be reiterated here that a child is primarily born in the Super Conscious Mind, which is naturally the centre of my extraordinary powers. If families, schools and society learn to recognise a child's desires, intelligence, talents, his nature and his pertinacity, and support him accordingly, then at a tender age itself, the child will begin to delve into my power centres. However, if he is suppressed in the name of discipline and extraneous knowledge, or ignoring his potential, if he is forced to act contrary to his talents, then the poor child will soon become a victim of my destructive forms. Meaning, the upbringing of a child is the determining factor, which decides both the condition and the direction of his life. Hence, encourage the child, recognise his potential and talents, and respect his desires. Yes...whenever necessary, do guide him. Teach the child the ways and means of the world. But please ensure that in this entire process, his love and anger are not suppressed. Even if the child is stubborn or is a brat who is always up to some mischief, do not label him as useless; on the contrary, if the child is mischievous, it is a sign that he is very powerful and brimming with energy. Just channelise his energy in the right direction i.e. the direction of his innate talent and then see for yourself, how his power centres become active in no time.

In short, while interacting with the child, you must exercise due caution and care, and ensure that the child's anger and love are not suppressed in any manner. If they are suppressed beyond a point, then not only the child's Conscious Mind, but his Subconscious and Unconscious Mind will also begin to develop. And remember, these three states of mind are the reservoirs of negative emotions and impulses. Once these minds have developed, then for the rest of his life, the child will have to bear the repercussions of what emerges from these reservoirs. That is why science states that a child grasps all that is worth learning for life, by the time he is 4-5 years old. And this is exactly my point as well; has the child's Super Conscious Mind been preserved or not?

Well, by repeating the same fact, I have once again drawn your attention towards the gravest mistake you could ever commit. Mark my words, childhood is the turning point of a human being's life. Because of your naivety, if you miss the opportunity here, you miss it forever. So, I hope by now you must have understood, why you have to preserve my power centres. At the same time, you must have also understood how you can save yourself from my destructive forms. Moving on, I shall now elaborate upon my power centres and their system of functioning. Primarily, there are four major centres of my powers:

1) Super Conscious Mind
2) Collective Conscious Mind
3) Spontaneous Mind
4) Ultimate Mind

1) Super Conscious Mind

Well! I have already acquainted you in brief with my Super Conscious state while explaining to you about the mind of children. As I had stated earlier; concentration, enthusiasm and self-confidence are the intrinsic qualities of this state of mine. Any person who has achieved great success in life, whether he knows it or not, has achieved it because of his Super Conscious Mind being active.

Let us try to understand this state of mine against the backdrop of the life of the great scientist Thomas Alva Edison, who not only invented the bulb and illumined the entire world but also got a record number of 1,093 patents registered to his name. You all must be aware that 7-year-old Edison was labelled a 'weak student' by his school teachers. They had a problem with him asking numerous questions on each topic.

When Edison's mother, Nancy, a teacher by profession, learnt about this, she could not bear the humiliation of her much loved child. Having complete faith in her son's abilities, she took a brave decision and withdrew Edison from that school. Later, Nancy enrolled him in a couple of other schools, but neither did Edison change nor did the attitude of the schools toward him. So Edison's mother finally decided to home-school him. This one decision made by Nancy changed Edison's life forever. Edison was finally freed from the daily humiliation he was subjected to at school. Needless to say, now little Edison did not have to suppress his love and anger...and certainly owing to this, his Conscious, Subconscious or Unconscious mind did not get strengthened. Little Edison did not face any problem with his mother's affectionate manner of teaching. On the other hand, his mother also did not mind the number of questions her darling son would ask, in fact she admired and appreciated his curiosity to learn new things.

Studying for three-four years under the guidance of his mother, Edison was attracted towards Science and its experiments. But due to the financial condition of his family, he had no option, but to fend for himself. However, that hardly posed a problem for Edison! Faith and immense love were available to Edison in abundance from his mother. So, in order to earn, 11-year-old Edison set up a shop to sell fruits, and sold newspapers in a train. From the money he earned, he set up a laboratory of his own at home, and when the opportunity arose, he set up a laboratory in the train as well. But when a child conducts experiments, mishaps are bound to follow. And that is precisely what happened! As a result, many a times, the shutters of his laboratory were pulled down, either by his father or by the train conductor. But as I said, enthusiasm, concentration and self-confidence are the intrinsic attributes of the Super Conscious Mind. Ultimately, this uneducated but perseverant and determined Edison not only had the highest number of inventions of his time to his credit, but also gave us the most spectacular of his inventions, the bulb, which illuminated the entire world. If you look through the pages of Edison's life, you

At the level of the mind every action has an equal reaction

will realise that all his achievements are nothing but an outcome of his concentration, enthusiasm and self-confidence.

I hope by now you must have understood how important it is to preserve the Super Conscious Mind of the child. Without the Super Conscious Mind being active, even if the child secures numerous degrees or acquires a thousand odd jobs, he can neither attain success nor happiness. This point can best be understood by citing the life of Helen Keller, a symbol of perseverance in this world, as an example. When the lively and vivacious Helen was just about one and a half year old, she caught scarlet fever. Though the fever was treated, it robbed her of her ability to hear and see. But in this hour of grief, instead of brooding over the tragedy, Helen's mother Katherine and father Arthur Keller decided to concentrate on her upbringing. Though Helen's life had plunged into darkness, her parents showered her with so much love that her Super Conscious Mind remained intact. Her caring parents fulfilled all her wishes; as a result, little Helen did not have to suppress her anger and love in spite of the terrible tragedy that had struck her.

When Helen was around seven years old, a teacher named Anne entered her life, who kindled the desire to study in Helen. Very soon, Helen learnt how to form words, read them and also frame sentences with them, which undoubtedly, was a miracle in itself. Deaf and visually-challenged Helen had now started reading. Anne had begun to teach her with the help of letters engraved on cardboard. Now, there was no question that Helen, who had lost two of her primary senses, would find anything more interesting. From then on, there was no looking back. Anne's devotion coupled with Helen's enthusiasm was so well-tuned that by the age of eleven, Helen learnt how to type as well. Thanks to her newly learnt skill, she found a new medium to express her emotions. Meaning, Helen, who was earlier shrouded in darkness, now had her communication established with the world. Thereafter, she felt such a great urge to study, that books with letters embossed in wooden blocks were being made especially for her. With the help of these embossed words, Helen started reading and even memorising entire books. This remarkable achievement drew appreciation and praises for Helen from across the world and overnight she became a world-renowned personality. With her determination and devotion, Helen also secured a graduate degree which indeed was a historical moment witnessed by the entire world.

Helen's remarkable journey did not end here. She then developed a keen interest in Socialism, which in turn, gave rise to compassion in her. The ever-enthusiastic Helen then devoted herself to the cause of improving the state of affairs of the disabled and the physically challenged. For this purpose, she, with sheer determination also learnt how to express different words based on the co-ordination between the lips and the tongue. Then, to spread the message of socialism for the upliftment of the disabled, she began addressing large gatherings of people, which earned her immense appreciation and brought her many accolades. Thousands of people began to flock to listen to her speeches and understand her views. Helen would move her lips and her teacher, based on the positioning of her lips and tongue, would interpret to the crowd what she meant to express. And this is how communication was established between Helen and the world. Helen even achieved the astounding feat of authoring twelve books. Moreover, for the upliftment of the disabled, the perseverant Helen, even at the age of seventy, toured several north-eastern countries for as many as twelve years. This was definitely the height of her concentration, enthusiasm and self-confidence. In all the countries she visited, the president or prime minister of that country yearned to meet her, along with other renowned personalities from various walks of life. So great was her adulation, that when she died at the age of eighty eight, she had communicated with as many as twelve Presidents of the United States of America. Just reflect upon Helen's historic life and her glorious achievements. Does the journey of her life reflect anything but singular-orientation, enthusiasm and self-confidence? Here the point to contemplate upon is, if the Super Conscious Mind can bestow such humungous success on Helen, who had lost her ability to hear and see, just imagine what great wonders it can work in your life!

" The mind and the brain are two absolutely different entities "

The essence of this discussion is, everyone is aware of the fact that in order to achieve great success in life, one needs to have enthusiasm, self-confidence and concentration. In fact, a person himself is desirous of achieving these traits and often, others also advise him and impart the lessons for nurturing such good traits...but the question here is; is your enthusiasm going to soar because you desire so, or because others are pressing you for the same? If these measures were effective, would everyone not have been filled with enthusiasm and self-confidence long ago?

All these qualities are not available in the market or else you would have long purchased them and replenished the deficiency. The fact is, these qualities are nothing but the very nature of the Super Conscious Mind. Without the Super Conscious Mind being active, you may rack your brains umpteen times or resort to numerous solutions, but your enthusiasm and self-confidence, or even your concentration for that matter, is not going to increase. All this is possible only upon the activation of the Super Conscious Mind. And, your Super Conscious Mind can become active only on one condition, that is, your Conscious, Unconscious and Sub Conscious Mind should be weak.

So I hope, leaving the various so-called solutions aside, you will now focus on activating my Super Conscious state lying dormant within you. I would say, at least refrain from unnecessarily tampering with the already active Super Conscious mind of the child and consequently weakening it.

2) Collective Conscious Mind

When this powerful state of mine manifests in its intense form, it automatically connects to the minds of all human beings. Certainly, because of this attribute, the Collective Conscious Mind has the potential to take human life to greater, unprecedented heights. A matter of reprieve for you is, this state is invariably active in every human being, though its degree may vary from person to person. The occurrence of numerous instances and events, wherein, most people are compelled to think alike, is a consequence of my active Collective Conscious State.

Well, understanding this comprehensively will require further explanation and to make it simpler, I shall explain it with the help of a few examples. Many a time, your interest must have definitely piqued when you noticed a song become a chartbuster overnight. You may have also witnessed how a slogan coined by a leader suddenly strikes a chord with the masses and makes him immensely popular within a short span of time. These instances imply that there is a state of mine which leads to most people having similar likes and dislikes. To throw further light on this point, let me explain it with the example of Lady Diana. We are all aware that Lady Diana was always making headlines. Her wardrobe, her sense of style and fashion were always the talk of the town, and her numerous social service endeavours had also attracted a great deal of attention; but her popularity was not enough to bring the world to a standstill. But it did! Astoundingly, the entire world watched her funeral ceremony. The enormous number of people who viewed her funeral on television around the world has created a record which might never be broken. What had happened? It was just that I, in my Collective Conscious state, propelled everyone to react thus. So now I hope, with this example, you must have understood both, the presence of this state of mine and its system of functioning.

Most importantly, here you must bear in mind that merely experiencing and bearing the impulses of my Collective Conscious state is certainly not a proof of this state being positively active in you. Because the person in whom my Collective Conscious state is moderately active, never falls prey to such impulses. On the contrary, he becomes capable of accurately gauging the collective likes and dislikes of people. Using the parlance of today's professionally driven world, such a person becomes an expert in the precise identification of the pulse of the people. And how important it is to gauge the pulse of the people in today's world needs no mention. In order to identify and harness the pulse of the people, millions are being spent on 'market surveys' every year. Which product will sell like hot cakes? Which tagline will strike a chord with the people and make them buy the product? Which slogan will ensure an overwhelming mandate in the elections? Which story-line will make crowds flock to the theatres? In short, be it leaders, actors or even giant corporates; for everyone, everything revolves around the question, "What are the likes and dislikes of the masses?" There is no need to iterate that the person, in whom my Collective Conscious state has become active, gets directly connected to the likes and dislikes of the people. Thereafter, regardless of the field of choice, he is bound to become an overnight success.

However, the ability to identify the pulse of the masses is not the one and only peculiarity of the Collective Conscious state. Just by applying a little concentration, the person with an active Collective Conscious mind can easily discern what the other person might be thinking or intending to do at any given moment, irrespective of the distance between their locations or the amount of time lapsed since their last meeting. This is precisely what you know as 'Telepathy' in today's language. The most advantageous trait of this state of mine is, you will have a premonition of any plan or conspiracy hatched against you. This prior awareness will surely lead you to become cautious as well; in that case, how can you ever be trapped in any problem? Thus, needless to say, peace and happiness becomes your destiny. Not only this, if my Collective Conscious state is functioning at its peak in a person, then with the application of even a little concentration, he can influence anyone to alter the course of their thinking. In short, what I mean is, a person, in whom my Collective Conscious state becomes active, automatically rids himself of numerous problems and scales the peaks of success and happiness in life.

Let me explain this in the language of your interests, as no one can beat you when it comes to grasping the matters of selfish interests. Well! It would be in your interest to know that, the Collective Conscious Mind is active in everyone, but the difference is of it being weak or strong. And because this state of mind is weak in most people, they are exploited all through their life. As a result, in spite of them working hard and putting in a great deal of effort, bliss and success eludes them.

The reason is clear; because of their weak Collective Conscious Mind, they are always trapped in a very ordinary mindset. And that is why, fanning their fear and greed, they are being exploited by one and all. Perhaps you may not have paid attention to this, but do you have any idea about the extent to which you have been exploited in the name of religion by these so-called religious gurus? Be it the birth of a child, marriage or death; you have no choice but to seek their help for performing the rites and rituals. Not only this, on numerous other occasions, either by giving you false assurances or by inciting fear in your mind, they make you perform one or the other religious rites or rituals. And mind you, all this does not happen for free, you have to pay them 'Dakshina'*.

Moreover, these people have deeply ingrained in you the habit of visiting temples, mosques and churches, and donating large

---

* Dakshina - a donation or payment to a priest, or a guru for their teachings or services offered.

41

sums of money. Thanks to this slavery on your part, today as many as fifty million people in the world are living off the funds donated by you. You cannot even imagine the amount of wealth these people have amassed! Have you ever thought about how rich these temples and churches are growing each day? And where is all this wealth coming from? All this is nothing but your hard-earned money. Now think, if someone else is reaping the benefits of your hard work, how will you progress in life? Just think, besides slavery and poverty what are you gaining out of all this? Why do you not think about this from another perspective – in spite of so many people regularly visiting temples, churches and mosques, how many of them have become happy and successful or have had their problems eradicated... None, right? Then why do you expect it to happen in your life?

The answer is obvious...You are bound to suffer such futile exploitation because of your weak Collective Conscious Mind getting easily influenced by everyone. I cannot understand, why are you unnecessarily nurturing fifty million people? Why do you not realise, that how will those who are incapable of doing anything for themselves and are living off your charity, uplift your life? Why do you not make them work hard instead of merely pouring your hard-earned money into their greedy hands? If you collectively compel these people to work in the fields, you will see for yourself how the cost of food grains comes crashing down across the world overnight.

Moreover, it is not only religion or the religious heads who exploit you; the list is long. Instilling fear under the pretext of health, even some doctors exploit you. Medicines and medical tests, vitamins and health supplements; the list is endless! Have you ever given a serious thought to whether you really need all this? Upon a little contemplation, you will realise that in the garb of improving your health or even alleviating your sickness, some people are busy looting your hard-earned money.

And what can one say of large companies and their bizarre products? Regardless of whether you need them, they plant in you a need for the product with their tempting advertisements. Have you ever thought how many useless products they lure innocent children to buy with their enticing advertisements? Do you ever contemplate the necessity of a product before purchasing it? No!!! Owing to your weak Collective Conscious Mind, you are compelled to purchase all these unnecessary products according to your purchasing power.

Likewise, educational institutions too are rampantly exploiting you. In the name of modest facilities and paltry reputation, are they not extracting huge sums of money for your child's education? Well! The question you must ask yourself here is, how many people have prospered in life because of such expensive primary education? But who bothers to even contemplate whether it is good or bad! If it is the question of the parents' reputation, stature and standing in society, children must be enrolled into prestigious schools!

And then how can we forget our politicians! Catchy slogans and long lists of promises! Instigating violence; either in the name of religion, society or caste. As if this was not enough, many a times they play the patriotism card and provoke people to fight in the name of national pride. Do you ever think, what you are achieving by all this? This is nothing but a sheer waste of your precious time and energy. Your servitude and exploitation is only increasing with every passing day. Does involving yourself in the advocacy of such propagandist activities improve your standard of living? And, after squandering your wealth on these people, even if you happen to save some amount of your hard-earned money, there are scamsters who with their dubious schemes to multiply money overnight, loot you of whatever is left. In short, what ultimately remains for you is nothing, but only hard work, struggle, stress and tension.

So, if you wish to save yourself from these numerous forms of exploitations, stop falling prey to false assurances. Take the reins of your life into your own hands; stop seeking any external support to bank on. Your Collective Conscious Mind will automatically be strengthened which in turn, will put an end to you getting unnecessarily influenced by people time and again. And when you do not get wrongly influenced by any person or thing, then how will anyone be able to exploit you?

Just see the pitiable state you have landed yourself in. You toil and someone else reaps the fruits! You earn, and someone else progresses! It is true that because my Collective Conscious state is not active in you to the fullest, you are being exploited to such an extent that your life is reduced to nothing but an endless journey of struggle and hardships. Why are you falling prey to this mob psychology? When you are doing and thinking exactly what everyone else is thinking and doing, how can you even think anything different will happen to you?

Then why do you not develop your own way of thinking? Why do you even choose to be one among the masses or the groups in the first place? How does it matter, whether these groups have been formed on the basis of religion or caste or whether they have been formed on the basis of nation or needs? Irrespective of the group, you will surely be exploited. Bear this well, in your world, groups are always exploited. Only an individual can do wonders, as no one is interested in exploiting a single person, and no one can either. This is the very reason why an 'individual' is saluted by these groups. Needless to say, an 'individual' signifies someone in whom my Collective Conscious state is strong. And a group comprises those, who fall prey to exploitation because of my Collective Conscious state being weak in them.

Hence, if you want to activate your Collective Conscious Mind, the centre of my amazing powers, then save yourself from being a part of any kind of group. Bring individuality in your decisions, likes and choices. Recognise your needs correctly. Do not seek futile support and assurances to bank upon. Never be a part of mob mischief.

Soon, you will not only be able to gauge what is going on in everyone's mind, but will also be able to change the course of their thoughts. And you will be surprised to see, the kind of mastery you will gain over the collective likes - dislikes of people. As a bonus, your exploitation by others will come to an end. Then in that case, who will ever be able to stop you from becoming happy and successful in life?

3) Spontaneous Mind

I hope you must have understood the Collective Conscious

Mind and its influences. Now I shall proceed further and throw light on the existence of my Spontaneous state and its influences.

My Spontaneous state is an intrinsic part of Nature's 'Spontaneous-Consciousness'. The person, in whom my Spontaneous state is active, does not 'think'. He starts making all the decisions of his life as per the directives of this state of mine, and immediately puts the directives of this mind into action. Then he neither thinks of his gain or loss, nor of it being good or bad. This definitely calls for immense faith. Only a courageous person can pull off such an act. And courage...well, that can be mustered, but the question that needs to be answered is, how does this Spontaneous Mind become active and what are its uses?

Now you may say, "Yes, you are absolutely right. Only if we are convinced about its benefits, will we muster the courage."

Well, then! My spontaneous state becomes active in the person, who lives every second of his life in his passion and joy; a person who does not pay attention to anything other than his own field of interest. Persistently leading his life in the pursuit of his passion and joy, suddenly one day, his point of creativity becomes active. This point of creativity is a part of his own Spontaneous Mind, which can suddenly get triggered one day in the field of his interest. The point to note here is, all the great successes of the world are nothing but the result of this point of creativity being active. Then, whether it is the finest poetry or literature, enthralling dance or music, the most beautiful painting or any other piece of art, whether it is an innovative product or concept or an out-of-the-box idea in business, or even a new discovery or invention of science, none of this is attainable without the point of creativity being active.

Here you must note that creativity is Nature's domain; then, how can creativity ever flow without getting attuned to Nature? It is just not possible! No creativity can be accomplished just by thinking, confining oneself to boundaries and limitations, or being determined about it. Creativity simply flows from within in accordance with Nature's laws. Meaning, it manifests on its own in the form of a beautiful creation, once the point of creativity has become active.

And this is the very reason why a poet, singer or any other creative person, cannot decide beforehand as to what creativity he will produce and when; nor can he produce anything creative as per his yearning or need. No matter how accomplished an artist he is, but in order to produce anything creative, he has to wait for impulses to come from within.

This dependence on impulses for creativity is what artists fondly refer to as 'mood'. When they are unable to produce anything creative, they term it as not being in the 'mood'. So what exactly is this mood? You wish to compose a melodious tune, but at that moment, your point of creativity is not sending any impulses for a tune from within. Do not worry, just wait! Once it starts sending out the impulses, wonderful creations will follow, they will just happen. In short, you cannot create something at your will or desire, but it is I who sends it forth as per my laws.

If you glimpse through the history of mankind, you will realise that whoever has achieved great success, has achieved it effortlessly. The moment their point of creativity became active, they created something exceptionally innovative...and when an innovation is exceptional, it is bound to become an instant hit. Its fame is bound to resonate across the oceans, and its glory is bound to be trumpeted all over the world. Besides, you achieve success in life only when you create something new and revolutionary...be it an invention such as a computer or an innovation such as Apple or Facebook. The thumb rule is, 'Innovation rules the world'. I hope, with the above explanation you would have understood the history underlying all the happy and successful people in the world, and also discerned the reason behind their successes. And if you really wish to achieve phenomenal success in life, spare some time and read through the biographies of 50 - 100 great legends...you will understand the facts that I am trying to bring to light all along.

Advancing from our discussion about the point of creativity, I will now tell you about the primary qualities of the Spontaneous Mind. The most important quality of this state of mine is; none of its decisions are influenced by any external powers or factors. Instead of analysing the situation, the person in this state of mind follows and acts according to what his mind suggests at the spur of the moment. To put it precisely, instead of taking the decision on the basis of what is good or bad for him, or analysing the situation to safeguard his own interests, he depends on whatever this state of mine prompts him to do at that particular moment. In such situations, his decisions seem quite shocking. Generally, these decisions are perceived as wrong or inappropriate by others at first, but in the end, these decisions are always proved right, because ultimately, these decisions stem from my spontaneous state.

Here, it is imperative to understand one more thing related to life and that is, which direction your life will head in, depends upon the decisions you take. The greater the number of right decisions, the happier your life will be. Perhaps everyone is aware of this fact too and this is the reason why people take major decisions of their life after due deliberation. However, the results of decisions that were duly taken after much deliberation are evident to all of us. The failures of human beings are not hidden from anyone. It clearly implies that, decisions taken after much deliberation, or decisions taken by the application of the brain have often been proved wrong. This is the reason why I am teaching you the art of taking the right decisions. All the right decisions are always spontaneous and vice versa. And this ability to take spontaneous decisions cannot be achieved without the Spontaneous Mind being active.

To put it explicitly, no businessman can ever become successful without this state of mine being active in him. Spontaneous Mind is the state of mine which has the fundamental knowledge about everything; in fact, this state is interested only in the basics. This mind does not delve deep into the nitty-gritty of matters or get into details. It is simply not interested in elaborate data, detailed agreements, useless inquiries or discussions. Merely on the basis of a few facts, this state of mine promptly takes the biggest of the decisions in the most appropriate manner.

At the same time, neither does it repent after taking such decisions, nor does it backtrack on them. If you ever repent or backtrack after taking spontaneous decisions, then it clearly indicates that your Spontaneous Mind is not fully active as yet, because decisions taken by the Spontaneous Mind are always right. Thus, the question of repenting or backtracking simply does not arise.

Well! It is important to note here that people who analyse or discuss a lot before arriving at a decision, often have to repent over their decisions. Moreover, such people are also accustomed to backtracking from their decisions, which consequently tarnishes their reputation. At the same time, excessive discussions and deliberations before finally arriving at a decision result in extensive wastage of time. Now, how can a wastrel of time who has lost his reputation, ever become a successful businessman? Putting all the above facts together, you will realise that only the people who take all the important decisions of their life with the help of their Spontaneous Mind are able to scale the pinnacle of success. Many people refer to this quality of the Spontaneous Mind as intuition or voice of the heart as well. But in reality, these are nothing but various names given to my Spontaneous state.

4) Ultimate Mind

Now lastly, let us come to the most powerful and the most important state of mine, i.e. the Ultimate Mind. Comprehending its influence and area of functioning is a little difficult, but still, I will try my best to explain it to you in the simplest manner possible. Just think, there is so much drama happening around you; so much interplay between the brain and the mind happening within you; but here is what you ought to be aware of. There is someone who is watching all this drama unfold...that is why you are aware of all that is happening. If you delve a little deeper, you will realise; there is someone on whose screen all this drama is being played. Have you ever thought about it in this manner? Have you ever reflected upon who that 'someone' could be?

I doubt you have. If you were able to think in this manner, you would have marched towards phenomenal progress a long time ago.

For now, I will try to explain this profound subject to you, by drawing parallels to feature films screened at theatres. Who makes the film that is screened in theatres? Definitely the producer, director, actors, etc. Similarly, the makers of the film of your life are none other than your own mind, brain and the external factors and circumstances you are surrounded by. Just as a film made by a producer is exhibited on the screen, your life-film made by your very own mind and brain, is also displayed on the screen. And the screen, on which it is shown, is your Ultimate Mind. In other words, that is exactly who you are! You owe your very existence to the Ultimate Mind and your Ultimate Mind is nothing, but your *prana**. It is because of your Ultimate Mind that your mind, brain, body and heart are all functional. But since it is out of your reach at present, you are ignorant about it.

But the one who is able to delve right up till this state of mind, achieves everything in life. Because then, he remains unchanged forever. After all, how can the screen be affected by the number of ups and downs or sad scenes that come in a film? Similarly, how can the man, who has successfully reached this state of mind, be marred by the numerous ups and downs that come in his life? Meaning, then there is no danger posed to his joy, bliss and peace. And remember, if a man has scaled the height of consciousness i.e. the Ultimate Mind, he has reached it after surpassing all the other powerful states of mind. This means he has reached the Ultimate Mind only after successfully activating my power centres one by one. As a result, he is well aware of the characteristics and the functioning of all those power centres. Thus, as and when the need arises, he can utilise my power centres, whenever and in whichever manner he likes. If you decipher the obvious meaning of this, it means that such a person then reigns over entire mankind.

I have explained this state of mind in brief and in the simplest manner possible. I hope, you must have understood it well. With this, I end the discussion about my various states, their system of functioning and their influences.

---

* Prana - your life-energy.

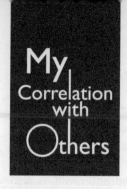

My Correlation with Others

"That was amazing, Mind! You have presented yourself so well that it seems, no other entity is as important as you in our life; as if you are the sole reason behind all our joys - sorrows and success; as if our body, brain and senses hold no significance whatsoever; as if the world, country, society or circumstances exert no influence on our life...!"

Wow! So now you are talking like an extra-intelligent person, huh! I have just begun and have not yet completed what I have to say. But as it is open for discussion, let me elaborate upon it.

The body, brain and external circumstances certainly influence human life. And when human life gets affected by these factors, how can I possibly remain unaffected by them? All these factors definitely influence me in one way or the other; but how and in what manner, is a little complicated. Nevertheless, I, on my part, will try to explain it to you in the simplest manner possible. And for this purpose, I will first tell you about the correlation between your body and me.

(A) The Correlation Between Your Body And Me

Before I begin any discussion pertaining to this topic, you first need to understand the composition of your body. The human body, to a great extent, is dependent on its DNA and genes. At the same time, it is influenced by external factors as well. For example, if you are born as a native European, you will most likely be fair, whereas, if you are born as an African native, there is a high possibility that you will have a dark complexion. Similarly, if you have an oriental lineage, you will most probably have a petite frame. Likewise, your genes and DNA have a strong influence on your health too. In addition, your health is also affected by the place of your birth and the family you are born into.

Now if I were to talk about myself; irrespective of the country, time zone or situation you are born in, 'I', i.e. your mind, remain the same. All the above factors have no effect either on me or my system of functioning; meaning, at the level of the mind, there is no difference amongst human beings.

Well, this was all about my way of being and that of the body. As far as the correlation between us is concerned, i.e. your body and mind, both of us are definitely affected by each other. For example, if a person is suffering from acidity, then I invariably become restless and anxious with immediate effect. Similarly, if I am gripped by anxiety, then it inevitably leads to a rise in the acidity levels of a person. In the same way, if a man's body is afflicted with sickness or pain, then, I too, become sad and anxious.

However, let me clarify here that I definitely get affected by your body, but the extent of the effect is entirely determined by the frame of mind of each human being. People living in the Conscious or Subconscious state of mind get severely affected by the physical conditions of their body, whereas people living in the Super Conscious state and the states higher than that, are scarcely affected by their physical conditions. An apt example for this would be Stephen Hawking. Despite his several physical constraints, he is considered to be one of the few renowned geniuses in the world today. Astonishingly, though he had lost his speech function and complete mobility of the body, by merely learning to express himself by twitching his cheeks, he has attained phenomenal success in the field of science. Essentially, what I mean is, if the mind is strong, physical handicaps or malfunctions of the body are never a hindrance. In other words, the body does not affect me much, but yes, my influence on the human body is significant...so much so that most of the illnesses contracted by a human being are the result of a weak mind. A strong and blissful mind, in itself is capable of conquering a thousand illnesses. Meaning, even in order to keep your body healthy, it is necessary that you pay due attention to me.

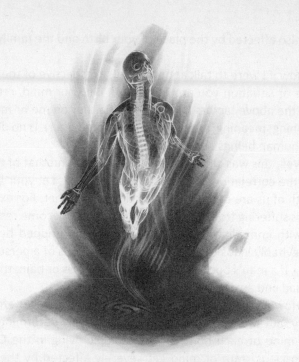

" The mind does not have any physical existence in the body "

Without me, even the sustenance of the human body is difficult; and that is the relation between me and the human body. Although both of us influence each other, here too, I prevail over the human body.

Let me explain this to you with an example. One day, all of a sudden, a mother's right hand got paralysed. In spite of the intensive treatment provided by the doctor, she did not recover. Finally, she was referred to a psychiatrist. The psychiatrist hypnotised the lady and began questioning her about the important tasks she performed with her now paralysed right hand. Sobbing, the lady began her woeful tale, "One day, I had caught my son stealing and had ruthlessly beaten him up with my right hand. But I sincerely repented my act then, and I still do. I mercilessly hammered my poor child as if he were an animal. For inflicting such pain on my child, my hand should be cut off."

The real cause behind her paralysis was now revealed. The woman's right hand was paralysed because of the guilt her mind had contracted. The psychiatrist then reasoned with her, saying that had she not been strict with her child when she caught him stealing, there were chances that on growing up, the child could have actually become a thief. "So whatever you did was absolutely right and necessary. In fact, it was the same right hand that has saved your son's life well in time." Consequently, the woman's guilt vanished, and so did her paralysis.

See the marvels I can pull off! Now, if I talk about your marvellous deeds, then despite the fact that I am so important for your life, you all do not show any interest whatsoever in either knowing or understanding me. Having said that, let us proceed further with my correlation with the other factors and entities.

(B) My Correlation With Circumstances

Without a doubt, the country, surroundings and circumstances in which a person is born, greatly influence his life. And the effect of the influences created by these factors definitely affects a man's life and me, i.e. the mind, as well. A child born into a poor family, living in the countryside, has to toil right from childhood to earn a living. In fact, to become successful, he has to migrate to a city and struggle day in and day out. But still, as I have stated numerous times, irrespective of the external circumstances of a human being, I am always present in everyone in equal measure. I uphold only one principle; keep my Super Conscious state intact, and if you have not been able to, then make every possible effort to rekindle it; and then see, how I will protect you and rescue you from various external factors and circumstances thereby making your life 'happy and successful'. Indeed history stands witness to my claim. Whether it is in the field of music or art, science or business; a majority of successful people have always been uneducated, hailing from poor families. In short, external factors and circumstances definitely affect the life of a human being, but with the support of my power, one can render these factors ineffective and reach the pinnacle of success.

(C) My Correlation With The Brain

This is the most complicated, yet the most important topic of all that we have discussed so far. I have already spoken extensively on topics varying from my composition to my system of functioning. I have also stated earlier that the complicated nature of my mechanism has always rendered it difficult for most people and sections of the society to comprehend me. Here, let me also bring a fact to light that the brain in itself is a very intricate instrument. Yet, the most ironical situation faced by man is, hardly anyone knows the difference between the brain and me. Oh! Talking about differences, most people do not have even the faintest idea about the separate existence of the brain and me. Yes, a few psychologists have definitely accepted and acknowledged my existence. But honestly speaking, in a larger context everyone is completely delusional as far as my existence is concerned. Some people consider me to be a part of the brain, whereas some, on the basis of their new discovery, believe me to be the cerebellum located at the back of the head. However, there certainly are some people who accept me as a complicated mechanism, comprising vibes and frequencies. Today, let me elaborate upon the difference between the brain and me. To be honest, it is not that complicated, because not only our influences and areas of functioning, but both our systems of functioning are also radically different.

Brain	'I' (The Mind)
(1) The brain in itself is a complicated structure, having a physical existence in the body.	(1) I am also a complicated mechanism, but merely a play of frequencies. I have no physical existence in the body.
(2) The brain weighs around three pounds, i.e. around 1¼ kilograms and it contains approximately ten billion nerve cells called neurons.	(2) It is impossible to quantify my frequencies.

(3) The development of the brain varies from individual to individual. Indeed, it depends on factors such as DNA, genes and circumstances.	(3) I am present in everyone in equal measure. No individual or no factor has any influence over my existence.
(4) The brain's focus is always on the necessities of life. And it must be accepted here, that the foundation of human progress is to be solely attributed to this characteristic of the brain.	(4) It is here that the harmony between the brain and me manifests. My powers are abundantly utilised for the fulfilment of the necessities recognised by the brain.
(5) The brain is potent with the power to restrain my weaker frequencies. In fact, it constantly suppresses the weaker frequencies arising at my level; then whether they are those of love and anger.	(5) Without any rhyme or reason, the brain keeps suppressing the frequencies arising at my level, but when my powerful frequencies emerge, riding high in their intensities, they go beyond the brain's control. Irrespective of the brain's efforts to control it, when any intense emotion or fierce anger stems from my depths, it invariably gets released.
(6) The brain is of this particular birth and it becomes sharp or weakens according to its experiences. Additionally, it gets enhanced by energy.	(6) I am fuelled by only one thing - the energy of a human being; I am as old as human existence.
(7) The brain cannot be governed by any rule or law.	(7) I am completely governed by my set of laws, which makes me quite predictable.

(8) Brain is an expert at thinking. Thoughts constantly keep flowing in and out of it.	(8) I am a world of emotions.
(9) To control and govern the body is the function of the brain.	(9) I do not directly control the body.
(10) Brain is an expert at thinking, planning, strategising, analysis and management.	(10) None of these tasks fall under my purview of functioning.
(11) The brain cannot do anything without thinking.	(11) I do not think. I am completely spontaneous by nature.
(12) From society to traditions, everything is the creation of the human brain.	(12) I have nothing to do with society or with traditions and customs.
(13) The brain gets influenced by others and simultaneously, it tries to impress others as well.	(13) I have nothing to do with anyone else. I am complete in my own self.
(14) The brain possesses memory. The function of the brain is to gather and store information.	(14) I have no memory. I function on automation, in accordance with the laws that govern me.
(15) Brain recognises things by differentiating between them. Good-bad, right-wrong, sin-virtue are the distinctions upheld by the brain.	(15) I do not recognise or act upon things by differentiating between them.
(16) The brain has nothing to do with natural creativity.	(16) I am absolutely creative. In fact, it would be more appropriate to say - Creativity is, and will remain solely my domain.

(17) The brain has innumerable needs. It is ambitious by nature.	(17) I do not need anything except my 'mood'.
(18) The brain is extrovert by nature.	(18) I am introvert by nature.
(19) The brain is an expert at leading a life in confining conditions.	(19) I do not accept any kind of bondage or confinement.
(20) All the actions of the brain are calculative in nature. Meaning, selfishness is the intrinsic quality underlying all its thinking.	(20) For me, my joy is supreme. If each moment passes as I desire, I do not need anything else. Then, I do not care about its positive or negative consequences.
(21) The brain is incapable of decoding calculations that are enormous and complex in nature.	(21) I am an expert not only at calculations of the world but also at cosmic calculations.
(22) The brain is always focused on others.	(22) My world begins and ends with me.
(23) The brain is completely ignorant of the structure or composition of the world, laws of Nature and the several enigmatic mysteries that influence human life.	(23) In this Universe, nothing is a mystery for my power centres.
(24) All the tasks executed by the brain are effectuated only after due deliberation, hence, they lack the natural flow.	(24) Whereas, I simply flow and this is the reason, why all the finest creations flow from within me.
(25) The thinking of the brain is limited only to this birth.	(25) I act on the basis of the calculations stretching to infinity and beyond.

(26) The brain is devious by nature. With logic as its weapon, it persistently engages itself in proving itself right and others wrong. Defending and safeguarding itself is the pet peeve task of the brain.	(26) I am simple and straight-forward. I am the way I am. When I do not even think, where is the question of logic? When I do not discriminate between right-wrong or mine-yours, how does the question of harming someone or saving someone arise? To whom do I need to exhibit and from whom do I need to hide?
(27) Since the brain is unaware of the mysteries of existence, it compels a person to live in the shadow of fear.	(27) Since I am aware of all the mysteries, I strongly believe in living fearlessly.

Well! I really hope that after such an in-depth discussion, you must have understood the difference between the brain and me to a great extent. You must have also realised that we both are extremely important and powerful in our respective realms. You would have also grasped that both of us not only greatly influence each other, but are also constantly engaged in the battle for dominance over one another. Such being the case, it is needless to say that our never-ending quest for dominance turns your life to shambles, because just like me, i.e. the mind, the brain too has a positive as well as a negative side to it. Hence, without the appropriate balancing and fine tuning of the brain and me i.e. the mind, it is not easy for you to make your life happy and successful. Hence, it is extremely necessary to grasp the difference between both.

Most importantly, if you are able to differentiate between the good and the bad acts of the brain, you will definitely be saved from several unnecessary problems. To this effect, if I were to talk about the utility of the brain, then it is a very useful tool to analyse, identify needs, imagine and to a certain extent, memorise things. So this is a list of all the life-nurturing activities facilitated by the brain. And the brain must be utilised to the fullest for carrying out these tasks.

On the other hand, if I were to talk about the ills hidden in the brain, then it is equally necessary for you to save yourself from its selfish tendencies and its attempts to suppress the emotions that flow from me, with or without reason. For, I have a world of my own, about which the brain is completely ignorant. The brain steers into action to crush all those emotions which it thinks are not of immediate benefit. And I have no qualms about confessing here that though I am a universal entity, the human brain has the power to decide whether or not it wants to live in the emotions that flow from me. And to tell you the truth...this very power vested with the brain is proving to be detrimental to the well-being of human beings.

In summation, there is no other solution to make your life successful other than understanding the difference between the brain and me. Like me, even the brain has both good and bad influences. Needless to say, only by utilising the positive influences exerted by me and the brain, as well as eluding the negative influences cast by us, can your life be steered onto the path of progress. At the same time, it is also equally crucial for a man to learn to fine-tune and maintain the harmony between these two powerful entities.

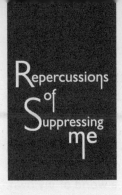

Repercussions of Suppressing me

Now that you have grasped the fact that only the brain can stop the impulses arising at my level, let us also discuss the reasons behind it and its repercussions. It is imperative to make you understand, why I am forewarning you against the brain's suppression of the emotions most natural to me. If you wish to be happy and successful in life, it is crucial for you to understand this in depth. Not only this, once understood, you will also have to persuade your brain to refrain from suppressing my impulses. However, all this is easier said than done, as it demands both perspicaciousness and courage on your part. But I hope after learning about the grave consequences of suppression of my natural impulses by the brain, you will generate the requisite understanding and muster the necessary courage.

So now, first understand, why does the brain suppress the emotions that emanate at my level? Let me explain it to you with the example of anger. If anger emanates at my level, i.e. at the level of the mind, then why does the brain restrict it from getting released completely? That is because the brain finds the anger untimely or fears that the person at the receiving end will get upset or feel offended. Often, there is an apprehension that the person on whom you intend to vent out your anger might cause you harm in the future. And very often, the brain has perceived the said individual as a person useful for the future. Hence, your brain rationalises and arrives at the conclusion, "Why unnecessarily strain the relationship with someone?" Now, regardless of the reason, it leads to a situation wherein you have anger brewing within, but you do not allow it to be expressed.

But think, just by not expressing the anger, does it remain hidden? Can the person you are angry with, not see it? Of course, he can. Either partially or completely, he definitely figures out that there is something baleful brewing within you. However, funnily enough, he too keeps his observations to himself.

Nevertheless, this is the other person's problem, not yours. What you must understand is, when anger arises you have only two options at your disposal; either listen to me, i.e. your mind or to your brain. Now, if the anger is intense, the brain will be rendered powerless. Meaning, in that case, you have no option but to vent it out. At that moment, even if your brain tries hard to make you understand or control the anger, it will invariably be released. Now, in case of mild anger, the brain persuades you to suppress it with the selfish reasoning that releasing it will be against your interest. But then, there is always a price to be paid for each time you get angry. Have you ever thought that the anger you are suppressing can also bear adverse consequences?

Had you ever thought in this manner, you would have never suppressed your anger to such an extent in the first place. Having said that, right now the question is, who will reveal the adverse effects of suppressing anger to you? Obviously, it is I who will explain it to you! And in that context I must say, you are aware of the losses you may have to bear for expressing your anger, but are completely clueless of the damage caused by suppressing it. Meaning, loss is inevitable both ways; whether you release your anger or suppress it; the only choice you need to make is, select the least loss-bearing deal. By now, you must have surely experienced that in the friction between the brain and me, sometimes the brain has an upper hand and at other times, I am one up on it. And, it is because of this constant conflict between us that your life becomes a tumultuous ride.

Rather than talking about trivial matters, let us now discuss the consequences of suppressing your anger. In this context, the first and the most vital point to be noted is, Anger is in fact a proof of my energy. This is the reason it is effective as well as a positive sign for a human being. But, since the time anger has been labelled as evil by the brain and society, the slow and steady degeneration of human beings has begun. Now that is their understanding! But ultimately, it is your life that is at stake, right? So have you ever thought, why do you get angry? You get angry when something happens contrary to what you desire. Hence, anger is a proof of the fact that you wish to protect your desires. Meaning, if something is happening against my wish or I am being compelled to do anything otherwise, it irks me and I send you the impulse of anger.

Tell me...what is wrong in doing so? You are a human being, and you have all the right to fulfil your wishes. If someone is compelling you to do anything against your wishes, you must retaliate. However, religion and society refuse to acknowledge this right of yours. Because if people rebel, how will their businesses run? So these self-professed upholders of religion and society have deeply ingrained in you the conditioning that says, 'Anger is Evil', so that you continue being a slave of religion and society and avoid getting angry. Because anger is energy, they fear that if you get angry today, tomorrow you may also rebel.

But what option is left with those who no longer have energy left in them? Such people begin to lead their lives compromising with situations, which gradually becomes their habit. As a result, they get used to living in this state of suppression to such an extent that either they do not get angry at all, or their weaknesses compel them to become habituated to suppressing their anger. Society terms such people as peaceful, well-mannered and virtuous; and religion proclaims that they are close to God. It is from here on that the situation worsens, which lends the weaklings an excuse to hide their weaknesses. To be honest, the entire human race has become a victim of this conspiracy hatched by religion and society.

Here, I can firmly assert that even suppression cannot really quell your anger. If you suppress it today, it will resurface tomorrow. Today anger has surfaced for a reason, tomorrow it will be vented for no reason. And at that moment, nothing and nobody will be able to stop it. I agree that every expression of anger is not necessarily effective or a sign of energy. In many people, to a great extent, it is also released in the form of frustration from their Subconscious and Unconscious Mind. However, even this frustration lies within you, right? It also has originated from the suppression of anger. And then it is but natural that what lies suppressed within, will surely erupt one day.

Well, let us understand the same with the help of an example. Assume that a few rats have entered your room and you want to get them out. Now, tell me what will you do? Definitely, you will have to leave the door open for them to escape, right? However, if you close the doors of the room, and do not give them an outlet to escape, then??? The number of rats will keep on multiplying! The same is the case with me as well. Any feeling, emotion or an impulse that originates from me can never be suppressed. Whether they are good or bad...you have no option but to express and release them. And this holds true not only in the case of anger, but also in the case of all other emotions that originate at my level. Any emotion you suppress will assume an even more perverse form and keep getting accumulated in your Subconscious and Unconscious Mind.

And this will make the situation even more difficult for you. This means, to rid yourself of this menace, you have no option but to release these emotions. However, we will discuss that later as this is not the right juncture to discuss it.

For now, I will explain to you with a few more examples that how any emotion that arises at my level cannot be permanently suppressed. You must have observed that many people drive their vehicles in such a rash and erratic manner, that it reveals their suppressed anger. Some get so absorbed in watching violent scenes in a movie that the expressions on their faces mirror the violence on the screen. Nowadays, in order to release their pent-up anger, people have found violent games too. Similarly, some people release their anger by watching wrestling matches.

All this is nothing but your suppressed anger finding an outlet to release itself. And trapped in this vicious circle, you are compelled to resort to many such foolish acts. You will often notice that if a fight begins to brew on the street, a crowd instantaneously gathers at the spot. High hopes and great expectations that today they will get the opportunity to witness a violent fracas can be clearly noticed in the people gathered. And funnily enough, when both the quarrelling parties seem to be calming down, the crowd, under the guise of making peace, further provokes them and prods them to fight. Moreover, amidst the ruckus, if a wise person mediates and stops the quarrel, the crowd gets disappointed. Feeling let down, the people return home. What is this disappointment all about? The disappointment is; your repressed anger did not find a release. Just see the level to which you have stooped in an attempt to suppress your anger; you are now deriving pleasure from the fight between two strangers! Then you must ask yourself, how are you virtuous and your society, civilised? The irony is, you have reached such a state because you have been suppressing your anger in an attempt to portray yourself as civilised and virtuous. Think about it! Is this the brain you are so proud of?

Well! For now, let me tell you, your repressed aspirations also get revealed in a similar manner. Why only aspirations? Every now and then, your other emotions also get inadvertently released slowly and gradually, in the same manner. The time and again release of these repressed feelings proves nothing but the fact that they are being accumulated in the Subconscious and Unconscious Mind. This is also a proof of the fact that any feeling arising at my level can never be suppressed permanently. If you are suppressing it today, you will release it tomorrow, but you will definitely release it.

To bring further clarity on the point that nothing can be suppressed at my level, let me cite an example. An elderly man is walking on the street, when suddenly his bag falls on the ground. A Good Samaritan not only lifts the bag and hands it over to him but also helps the elderly man cross the street. After crossing the street, the old man, lost in his thoughts, forgets to thank him and walks away. This is where the fun begins! Suddenly, the Good Samaritan begins to feel bitter. He thinks, "What kind of a person is this old man? He did not even thank me!" Surprisingly, he had no such expectation in his mind when he was helping him. Then where did it come from? Obviously, it lay repressed in the Unconscious Mind and on finding an opportunity, it raised its hood and manifested itself.

Similarly, many a time you might have experienced that when a person in need approaches you, benevolently, you help him out. The matter is soon forgotten. Yet, when you meet the person the next time, without even realising it, you tend to expect an expression of gratitude from him.

Now, this was not your intention or expectation at the time of helping that person. Indeed, such strange desires and expectations manifest because they are suppressed in your Unconscious Mind. But the question is, how do these desires and expectations creep into your Unconscious Mind? It is because you have been suppressing your anger time and again.

I shall explain the same point to you with a few more examples, as I want you to have a thorough understanding of the fact that no emotion emanating at my level can be suppressed permanently. When suppressed, not only do these emotions assume a destructive form, but they also start manifesting on inappropriate occasions... How? Let us understand this with an example. Once the owner of a well-established company had a quarrel with his wife over a trivial matter. But as he was in a hurry to reach office, he left the argument midway. Now, even though he had left the house, he was unable to cast his anger aside. However, his wife was not in front of him, so who could he vent it out on? Thus, compelled to suppress his anger, he reached the office. But upon reaching there, his suppressed anger immediately found an outlet. He reprimanded the manager by deliberately finding few errors in the reports submitted by him. The poor manager could not comprehend his mistake, but what could he say to his boss? Hence, suppressing his anger, he quietly stepped out of the boss's cabin.

Now as the manager was already fuming, the moment he stepped into his cabin, he summoned the accountant. He skimmed through a few accounts pages and reprimanded him unnecessarily. The accountant was aghast. The behaviour of the manager was beyond his comprehension, but how could he retaliate against his superior? So, he kept quiet and left his cabin. The moment he returned to his cubicle, he called the office assistant. Now did the accountant even need to think of a reason to scold the office assistant? The poor man was at the receiving end of a tongue-lashing. Having no option, the office assistant quietly swallowed the insults from the accountant. But he could not hold his anger once he reached home. He released the anger he was nursing against the accountant, on his wife, which left her utterly stunned. But what could she do? Well, she in turn, scolded her kids and gave them a sound beating. The children were left dumbfounded too. In the evening, when they went out to play with the other kids in the neighbourhood, they unnecessarily picked a fight with them. So, the quarrel that had remained unfinished between the company owner and his wife finally ended in a violent fracas between the children of the office assistant and that of the neighbours.

Just think, whenever you get angry with someone, is that person really at fault at that time? Do you think, you are venting on him the anger of that moment only? No...! His mistake may warrant minor reprimanding; but the anger you vent out on him is a lot more severe than needed. Now the question is, where did this surplus anger come from? Definitely, it was suppressed within you, and it just found an outlet.

Now, let us discuss one more point about anger. Very often, most of your repressed anger tends to be released on the same person against whom it is repressed...but only, at the wrong time and wrong place, and that too, when the concerned person is not at fault. Owing to this unreasonable behaviour on your part, if nothing else, you are definitely tagged as insane! The funny part is, when you vent out your anger on someone for no reason, you later repent it too. This repentance, in turn, gives rise to more anger. At that moment, why do you not accept that whatever happened, has happened. If you accept it and think in this manner, your anger will subside to a great extent. But no, your brain convinces you that if you repent, you are absolved of all your ill-doings. In reality, absolution is not possible, as my system of functioning is radically different. On the contrary, at my level i.e. at the level of the mind, by repenting, you create another space for venting yet another unnecessary bout of anger. For, by the act of repenting, your score is never settled with the person in the first place. At my level, every action not only has a reaction, but every reaction also induces a chain of actions. You can liberate yourself from this vicious circle only by realising the fact – **"Whatever is there, express it and whatever has happened, forget it."**

Let me elaborate on my point with the help of another instance. There lived two brothers who were brought up in a joint family; they had an age difference of fifteen years between them. Since the elder brother was a working man, he would return home tired in the evening; on the other hand, the younger one, who was still naive, was always up to some mischief, when he returned. The elder brother would get infuriated by his pranks but fearing the elders in the family, he would suppress his anger and not scold his brother.

But one day, the situation panned out differently. When the elder brother returned from work, there was no one at home except his younger brother. Realising that no one was home and the elder brother had just returned after a long day's work, the younger brother promptly asked, if he wanted some water to drink. However, there could not have been a better opportunity for the elder brother's repressed anger to surface. He hit his younger brother, the moment he asked him for water. Why did it happen so? Because, the anger, that had been suppressed for so long, had finally found an opportunity to release itself. And this is exactly what I am trying to explain to you; your anger is bound to be released on the very same person against whom it has been suppressed. But at the wrong time and for no reason...which means it will manifest itself in a monstrous form. So then, what is the use of suppressing your anger? These untimely spurts of anger are the very reasons for rifts to erupt, and bitterness seeping into your relationships.

You must have understood this clearly, but the question that still remains is, why do you have to suppress your anger? It is because

**" The brain is located at the apex of the human body
whereas the mind, at the navel "**

you see only the immediate loss or harm that can be caused by
venting your anger. But what about your interpersonal relationships
that have been put at stake by these repressions? Have you realised
that? No! Perhaps, you have become habituated to these things and
accustomed to living in this manner. Why do you not understand that
your plight does not end here; this suppressed anger is taking a toll
on you in several other ways too. The most alarming among them is,
this repressed anger keeps changing into various negative emotions
such as anxiety, fear, jealousy and so on, and these are the causes

that eventually ruin your life. That is the reason why anxiety about trivial matters which should have subsided in a couple of hours or days, stretches for months at times. Why do you have to live in such excessive worry? Because using the loss caused by trivial ups and downs as an excuse, the anxiety suppressed within you is getting an opportunity to release itself.

Why do you not observe it for yourself that when you are upset or angry with someone, does suppressing the emotion eliminate it or abate it? No...on the contrary, changing its forms, it manifests itself every now and then. Sometimes in the form of pointing out mistakes, and at times by disparaging someone, sometimes by back-biting, and at times in the form of sarcastic comments. This means, the suppressed anger first mutates into anxiety, fear, jealousy and gets stored in the Unconscious Mind, and when continuously repressed, the same accumulated fear, jealousy and anger become all the more destructive and keep manifesting in the form of ludicrous acts... And then eventually, a day comes when you end up becoming a caricature of worries and the epitome of frustration.

But then the worst tragedy occurs when your suppressed anger starts manifesting collectively in the form of a mob - sometimes in the name of religion and at times in the name of country, society or politics; sometimes in the form of agitation and at other times, as an unnecessary revolution. As if this was not enough, the crafty religious heads and politicians lure you with attractive propaganda and use this anger repressed in you, to achieve their selfish goals. Otherwise, tell me, what is the need for a human being to harbour enmity against other human beings?

Well, the psychoanalysis of a historic event will help you understand this better. I am sure everyone knows how India achieved independence in the year 1947. Certainly the British had perpetrated severe atrocities on the common people of India. After such a long spell of slavery and so much of ruthless carnage, it was but natural for the common man in India to harbour anger against the British in their minds. But like a civilised nation, India attained independence on the principle of non-violence preached by Mahatma Gandhi. But what was the psychological implication of these non-violent movements? Did the anger suppressed in the minds of Indians against the British dissipate? No...at my level i.e. at the level of the mind, it is simply not possible! After the country was freed from the hands of the British and the independence celebrations were over, everyone came back to their senses. Now that the British were gone, on whom would they vent out their anger? So, this suppressed anger surfaced in the form of enmity and riots between the Hindus and the Muslims. It is difficult to describe the horrendous violence and the bloodshed that followed thereafter. The sense of brotherhood that prevailed among the people for centuries was strained. Brothers of the same soil fought amongst themselves and became each other's enemies. Therefore, you need to understand that I have nothing to do with the good thoughts and the high morals preached by the brain. I function according to my own laws, as per my discretion with no exception and total freedom. At that time, had India attained freedom following Bhagat Singh's ideology, then maybe, these Hindu-Muslim riots would have never occurred in the first place. The interesting point to note here is, had Indians displayed the same amount of violence against the British which they did against one another, the country would have been freed much earlier and with much lesser violence. Meaning, if the minds of Indians had been seething with anger and they were determined to attain independence, they could have attained it much earlier. At least the unnecessary animosity and distrust between Hindus and Muslims could have been avoided.

All in all, bear in mind that anger can never be suppressed. The question is not of violence, uprising or anarchy; neither is it a question of good-bad or cultured-uncultured; the question is of my law, according to which suppression of anger is bound to yield disastrous results. No matter how many or how good the words or thoughts you cultivate, or how firmly you have embraced them, it will not make any difference. If human life is in such jeopardy today, then the one and only reason for it is the so-called high moral thoughts which the brain has created without understanding me. What is more, the common man also gets drawn towards these thoughts. These naive people, owing to their ignorance, even try to implement these thoughts; and this is where they get ensnared in a trap. If a man implements these thoughts, I, i.e. the mind create chaos in his life; and if he does not, then his brain and the society make him feel guilty for not doing so. Poor human being! What should he do? I will tell you – muster the courage to keep the brain, society and the world aside, and just take care of the mind, and make every effort to protect it. By following this principle, if not for others, at least for you, everything will definitely fall in place.

Let me explain this point to you by drawing parallels to your inter-personal relationships. As inter-personal relationships are an intrinsic part of human life, you have enough experiences of them and you can easily relate to them, which in turn, will help you grasp my point quicker. In life, you must have often experienced that eventually, it is our friends who end up becoming our foes. It is our near and dear ones who turn strangers. A foe never comes from outside, he thrives on our warmth and affection. On the same lines, just think, when there is so much of warmth in a family, why does one brother end up becoming the other's enemy? Similarly, think, why barely after a few years of marriage, the husband and wife grow to resent each other? ...and the bitterness in your inter-personal relationships does not end here. The relationship between a father and a son gets strained. Grudges begin to develop between relatives. So much transpires and yet your brain – the transmitter of so-called wise and high moral thoughts is unable to do anything about it...and to be honest, it cannot do anything about it either. For, there is a reason behind all this disharmony and rift; a human being is conditioned to not hurt or disrespect anyone, maintain relationships, uphold lofty principles, and hence, he ends up suppressing his anger. *Choose your words wisely, so that no one feels bad or gets hurt. Do anything you want, but be careful enough not to disturb the people and disrupt the familial environment.* Following numerous such impositions, no one expresses the anger they harbour against each other. This repressed anger assumes a perverse form and gets accumulated within. Then one day, even if it's a trivial matter, the pent up anger gets triggered and erupts at once. This causes enmity of humungous proportions and strains relationships forever. Imbibe it well – "The greater the discipline imposed on a family or the greater the amount of freedom curbed, the greater will be the measure of turmoil, fights and rifts that the family will face in the future." A revolt inevitably erupts against a tyrant. Let us take the example of The Mughal Empire. The regime was prospering for a long spell of time. But, along came Aurangzeb! He ascended the throne, tyrannised the people and brought doom upon the Mughal Empire. The mighty Mughal Empire that reigned with such splendour was shattered into pieces by the storm of tyranny!

What this implies is, each and every suppression will invariably result in an adverse reaction! It has to, and it definitely will. That is why I assertively state: In a family where there is full freedom to speak and express one's anger, there will be differences of opinions and arguments on a daily basis, but there will never be a major dispute. Their love for one another will never fade. The same principle holds true in the case of rulers and leaders as well. The country that provides complete freedom of expression will never face a violent revolution. Because when there is freedom to express the anger brewing in one's mind, what is the need and where is the scope for violence? The same principle applies to the relationship between two individuals as well. If both of them openly express themselves, then their love for each other will last forever. Now, I need not reveal the truth of inter-personal relationships to anyone. You all are aware of the amount of resentment, you are harbouring against each other.

Here a point to ponder upon is, why does religion or society not come to your help, when it is owing to them preaching suppression of anger that your inter-personal relationships are bitter and strained? When they have taught you these lessons, why do they not stand by you, while you are enduring the grave consequences of their preaching? Let us not even discuss it...all they know is to impart unfounded lessons; and how it affects you, they are least bothered about it. Anyway, they will only impart the lessons that will enervate you. And this is the reason why, despite walking the path shown by them, when your life is in a complete mess, you cannot even muster the courage to question them.

Well, leave them aside! If you have understood everything clearly and really want to get rid of all your problems, then the only solution is, accept my supreme authority. If the insanity of anger stems from my depths, then it is in your best interest to vent it out. If you really want to save yourself from the insanity of anger or its destructive forms such as worry, sorrow, fear, etc., then let the insanity of anger be transformed into the energy of anger. And there is only one solution for this, release your anger in its entirety, whenever and on whomsoever it arises. As such, what is wrong with that? It is not that you are getting angry at your will. Since anger is accumulated within, it manifests outside; you are just releasing it. And when the person who is getting angry is not responsible for the outburst, then why should the recipient of the anger feel bad about it? If an entire family or a group of friends cultivate such understanding, there would not be any problem at all. If everyone understands that anger is just the mental bank balance of a person and he simply wishes to spend it, then why would anyone object to it? Let the person be angry... why should you be bothered?

And then you will see! Whenever any of your family member gets angry, the other members shall understand that it is not his

Nothing can be more mischievous than the mind

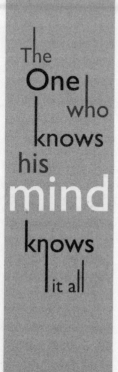

The
One
who
knows
his
mind
knows
it all

fault; the anger is pent up in him and he is just releasing it, with or without a reason. Let it be released. Endure the person's outburst and see for yourself, whether the person calms down in some time or not. Then some day, it will be another family member's turn...let him also release his pent-up anger. With this exercise, the family's bank balance of anger will soon be wiped out. The family will experience a transformation that will bring them personal as well as familial peace and serenity forever. I hope you must have understood and also learnt about the consequences of your attempts of tampering with me. And by now you must have also grasped how to deal with my destructive forms; meaning you will also have to allow anxiety, sorrow and other such negative emotions to be released.

Take the example of a young child. By nature, children are naughty and mischievous, and that is the way, they ought to be. Children usually have fights and disagreements among themselves, which too, they must have. But, because they are innocent and naive, they do not know how to express their anger with the help of words or sarcasm for that matter, hence they directly resort to mischief and physical brawls. Well, that is not a major problem; at least their anger gets released. And when the anger has been released, how can there be any room for dispute or quarrels? Hence, as soon as their anger is vented out, they once again start playing with each other. This is the process which makes them what they are – the most natural – wherein there is no scope for enmity. Children quarrel amongst themselves hundreds of times, but their friendship remains completely unaffected.

Unfortunately, the so-called intelligent people, instead of recognising this nature of children as their quality or virtue, teach them that fighting and quarrelling are the acts of children belonging to uncultured families. Children of cultured families do not indulge in such actions. But then, does that change this natural attribute of children? It is because of the teachings of suppression of these innocent childish fights that violence is rising in children. Just have a look at the video games available in the market today; the quantum of violence in the games is perennially on the rise. Moreover, it is the children of these so-called cultured families who play these violent video games all day. This is nothing but the manifestation of their anger in its perversely mutated form.

Have you still not realised that in reality, anger is a proof of friendship, not of enmity? You get angry only with those, whom you consider as your own. No one ever gets angry with strangers. And, as the children of the so-called cultured families do not fight much among their friends, their bonds of friendship too never grow strong. This is the very reason why they do not have many true friends as well. And then, in order to hide their loneliness, they party with people whom they barely know. But does it help them sweep their loneliness under the rug? Not releasing their anger as children and being brought up in the so-called cultured society by extra-intelligent people, is the reason for the growing frustration in today's generation. In the name of safeguarding culture, society has curbed the need for free interaction amongst human beings and pushed them into the dark valley of alienation and loneliness. Owing to this, man is left with no one whom he can call truly his own.

To summarise all that I have stated, the brain and I are the two most important, immensely powerful and extremely complicated instruments. You must have also come to understand that on one hand, we both have the powers to nurture lives and on the other, we can precipitate actions that can destroy lives. You must have taken note of the fact that both of us are incomplete without each other. Probably, you must have also realised that without striking a proper balance between the brain and me, happiness and success cannot be achieved in life. I need not mention here that though our systems and domain of functioning are very different, we both influence each other completely. Simultaneously, the body and external circumstances also exert their influences on both of us.

Now the question is, how do you establish a synergy between me, i.e. your mind and your brain? How do you save yourself from the inherent traits of your mind and brain that leave a human being weak and vulnerable? How can you effectively utilise their powers to make your life meaningful? ...I will give you a few remedies, but before I discuss them, let me assure those, who have missed the opportunity of safeguarding their 'Super Conscious Mind' in their childhood, that they need not be worried.

Even if their Subconscious or Unconscious Mind has become very strong, there is a solution for it. Because whether it is me or the brain, at both our levels, "It is never too late to set things right". Moreover, the remedies that I am about to discuss now, are exclusively for the ones whose Super Conscious Mind has become weak...else a child whose Super Conscious Mind is active does not need any guidance, for he will find his path on his own.

The problem mainly arises with those, whose minds have been tampered with during their childhood. They are the ones whose Conscious, Subconscious and Unconscious Minds have become strong; and this is not the case with just one or two, but with almost everyone. At present, this is the basic problem faced by one and all. However, this problem exists at my level i.e. at the level of the mind. But to add to your woes, you are faced with another problem; your family, society and educational system have wrongly conditioned your brain during childhood itself. And before I elaborate on this further, let me first define the word 'conditioning'. Years ago, an extremely important experiment was conducted on a dog. Now, it is but natural for a dog to salivate on seeing a bone. In this experiment, they gave the dog a bone in front of a church at a particular time every day, and cleverly, at the very same time the church bell was rung too. Well, in no way, was there any relation between the bone and the bell, but by repeating the same sequence again and again everyday for over a month, a connection between the bell and the bone was established in the dog's mind. Then after a month, the bell was rung at the same time, but no bone was placed in front of the dog; despite that, as soon as the dog heard the bell, he began to salivate.

And this is exactly what is being done to your brain also, since the age of four. You were very happy and satisfied playing with paper toys, and even mud for that matter, but the world around you ignited the fire of high aspirations in you. You were born as a human being, but were reduced to being a machine. You were living a life of freedom, but you were forcefully fed the knowledge of when, what and how to do things...and you began to run the rat race! The journey that begins with your school continues into college and then...goes on and on, and does not end till your last breath.

So if you understand carefully, at my level i.e. at the level of the mind, your problem is the formation of the Conscious, Subconscious and Unconscious Mind; whereas at the level of your brain, it is the conditioning, which is your problem. And in both the cases, the solution is the same. What is the solution? The solution is called 'Psychology'. And now I am going to

The human mind is the mOst complicated mechanism in the world

The mind is the sole Controller of human life

discuss a few psychological treatments which will not only help you weaken your Conscious, Subconscious and Unconscious Mind, but will also help you undo the wrong conditioning of your brain. Here an important point to bear in mind is that Psychology will be effective only when you let it sink into the depths of the mind, rather than understanding it with the 'brain'. Therefore, I humbly request you to begin your day by reading through each and every solution I have suggested in the next chapter and consistently make an effort to implement it in solitude, solely with the help of your mind. Spend half an hour doing this exercise and then, see, how your life gets on to the path of happiness and success, how all your problems come to an end and how you are freed from worry, fear and frustration. So, I hope in order to transform your life, you will diligently follow this exercise.

Moving further, it is important for you to know yet another fact. I have already stated earlier that the brain is located at the apex of the body; whereas I am present at the centre of the body, i.e. at the 'navel'. In a manner of speaking, the distance between the two is three feet, but in reality it is quite long. And in order to cut this distance short, you will have to learn the art of reading from your mind, rather than your brain. To cultivate this art, it is imperative that at the time of reading or listening, you let the point be absorbed 'as it is' into my depths, instead of trying to understand it with the help of the brain. At the depths of your mind lies a computer, a million times more effective and faster than your brain, which can process all the calculations, in a fraction of a second and arrive at the right decision. Else understanding and memorising is the domain of the brain and merely understanding with the help of the brain is of no value as it does not yield any effective result. You must have experienced this; in spite of having strong ethics or moral fibre, are you able to put your convictions into practice? Do they yield any results? No, they do not! At the eleventh hour, something invariably goes wrong. A disruption of even a small magnitude lands you in the grip of worry. You know that the matter is not indeed worrisome, but does that stop you from worrying? ...No! But if the same fact has penetrated deep into your mind, then you would not contract worry for the same.

I am sure you have grasped that without letting a point sink deep into your mind, you cannot expect any change to take place. So now the question that arises is, how do you know whether the fact has been understood by the brain or has sunk into the depths of the mind? Oh! That is so simple! I have already explained to you earlier that the brain lies at the apex of your body whereas I am present in the centre, i.e. in the navel of your body. And the distance between the two is long enough for you to know as to which one is active. Let us understand this with the help of your personal observation. You may have noticed that when you are trying to remember or understand something, your focus shifts to the brain as thinking and analysing is the function of the brain. Upon close observation, you will realise that all these activities are taking place in the upper section of your body. On the other hand, when you are at peace or extremely anxious, you will realise that all these activities transpire in the region between your heart and the navel. If your anger is at its peak, you will immediately realise that it is rising from deep within. Right from happiness to tension, this applies to all the other emotions as well. If the feeling or emotion is intense, you will experience it emanating from your navel. And if a feeling or thought is shallow or superficial, you will clearly find it arising from your brain. With practise, you will invariably realise this distinction right at the rise of any emotion or thought. Summing up, first of all, try to sense my presence near your navel, and you will soon begin to realise the difference between the brain and me. And once the distinction is clear, start reading and understanding everything significant using your mind, rather than your brain. With the vital facts sinking deep within, the necessary changes will soon begin to take place in you.

In short, what I mean is, not only with psychology, but whenever you read, observe or mull over something, you must learn to let it penetrate into the depths of your mind rather than analysing it with your brain. The mind, on the basis of the assimilated facts, will soon start breaking the barriers of the brain's conditioning. And once the conditioning is undone, you will never repeat the same act or mistake again. If I were to state it in simpler words, then in order to progress, you will have to backtrack. You will soon have to regain the state of mind and brain that you once possessed as a child. Meaning, you will have to begin the process of unlearning all the thoughts that have been ingrained in you while growing up, as that world of thoughts holds no significance. No one can ever translate all their thoughts into actions. Only when something is absorbed in the depths of the mind, can it be implemented in actions... But, people with their Super Conscious Mind intact, need not retract as they have not changed or donned any guise due to conditioning. The problem is with those, who have embraced all the thoughts that came their way and have conditioned their brain accordingly. It is they who need to break the barriers of this conditioning, so that they can reactivate their Super Conscious state of mine.

However, re-attaining the state of mind and brain of your childhood in order to let everything fall into place is not going to be as easy as it sounds. Because the strongest conditioning done to you is – "If you desire to progress in life, you must always forge ahead". And the desperation to progress in life has engaged the entire world in an insane rat race! But you tell me, how many have actually progressed?

Then why do you not just understand what I am saying? In the race to forge ahead, you have already fallen from the Super Conscious

Mind to the level of Conscious mind. Now without regaining the former state of your mind, nothing worthwhile will ever happen in your life. And since your quest to race ahead has veered you away from the path, the right path can be found only by backtracking. It is so simple! The right direction can only be found from the point where you had gone astray. For instance, you lose something in London and by the time you realise it, you have reached New York. Now you have no option but to return to London to get it back. In this case, you can take a flight and return to London. However when it comes to life, the problem is, neither are there any teachings available to help you return, nor is any encouragement provided by anyone for the same. Everyone is just too engrossed in the race to forge ahead, and that is where they are faltering. Here, the important fact to be noted is, in spite of innumerable examples of successful people, neither have you brought about any change in your educational system, nor has the mindset of your family or society changed. And the dire consequence of such a mindset is, to progress in life everyone has adopted the same mediocre, stereotypical approach. But yes, the one who has been spared this run-of-the-mill process has truly progressed in life. Even a great scholar like Vivekananda had acknowledged the futility of knowledge and later emphasised the significance of the process unlearning as well. If you wish to succeed, even you need to tread the same path.

Trust me, a happy and peaceful life is eagerly awaiting you with open arms. Because here, I am discussing with you the remedies to 'uncondition' your mind and brain; on the other hand, science, after successfully decoding DNA and genes, is engaged in their reengineering to provide you with a long and healthy life. Just look at the magnificent missions science has embarked upon for the betterment of mankind! Imagine what your life can eventually be transformed into, if you follow the remedies suggested by me and uncondition your mind and brain accordingly. On one hand, thanks to Science, your body will become healthier and your life longer, on the other, owing to the un-conditioning of your mind and brain, you will be freed from all kinds of worries and fears. Then, would you not be on cloud nine? For the past millions of years, no one has had an opportunity to lead the privileged, luxurious life which a modern day man is blessed with, and I hope you will take full advantage of this opportunity now.

With this hope, I shall commence the discussion on the perversities emanating at my level and their causes. I will discuss this topic in two parts; firstly, I will tell you the remedies which can help you lessen your sorrows and worries along with the ways to enhance the quotient of your happiness and bliss. And in the second part, I shall suggest the ways and means to scale the peaks of success in life. As per my understanding, you have only two major concerns:

1) To lessen sorrows and worries and fill your life with peace and bliss!
2) To achieve success!

So, let me begin my discussion with psychological remedies to lessen your sorrows and worries.

———————■———————

Remedies to dispel Sorrows and Worries

So far, I have revealed everything that is important and worth revealing about myself. I have also made it explicitly clear that I am the most influential force in your life and it is I, who gives rise to all the sorrows, worries and tensions you endure. Hence, only I am in a position to suggest to you the remedies that will dispel your sorrows and stress. Only I can tell you how to transform this arduous journey of life into a happy and joyous one.

So, let me straightaway initiate the discussion about the remedies, which can help you replace sorrow with happiness, and stress with joy in your life.

83

The Present

'The Present', is a very effective remedy to reduce sorrows and worries. But before I elucidate on this topic, you must understand that just as every single particle of the Universe exists in three dimensions, so does Time. Even time has three facets; the past, the present and the future. What is the past? ...Something that has already elapsed; and the past has no value, as it never returns. Yet, the ridiculous part is, not only do you cherish your past, but also persistently react in accordance with your past impressions. You very well remember when and how someone behaved with you in a particular situation. But then, what do you gain out of it? Unnecessarily, not only do you undermine the capabilities of your brain, but also muddle your mind.

You deal with the future also in the same manner. What is the future? It is the facet of time which has not yet arrived; and a moment that has not yet arrived, is always uncertain. Still, for no reason, you remain engrossed in thousands of desires and millions of worries of the future. In fact, you gain nothing out of it, but you definitely lose something, and that is your precious energy meaning, it leaves you enervated. Upon careful reflection you will realise, the entire human race is being pulverised between the grinding wheels of these two facets of time i.e. the past and the future. And in this grind, you lose the golden opportunity of experiencing the most beautiful facet of time, 'The Present', in which one can truly live, and achieve something worthwhile. After living for eighty years, when death knocks on the door, the realisation dawns upon man that entangled in the past and the future, neither could he live wholeheartedly, nor could he accomplish anything significant in his life.

Please contemplate over what I have just stated. Realise the worth of the present, because, the present is a magic that is capable of eradicating all your problems in no time. Have you ever thought that the root cause of a majority of your sorrows is in the past, and the reason for most of your worries is the future! What if a particular thing happens? What if something does not happen? How will it happen? But I say, at least let it happen! Why are you unnecessarily bothering yourself thinking about it right now? The biggest problem with you is that you do not learn even from your past experiences. Have you ever realised that from the thousands of things that you have been worried about till now, barely a few have actually occurred? Thinking and deliberating about the rest, you have just wasted your precious time, energy and life. Why do you not understand that life can only be lived today, in this very moment! And you extra-intelligent people are squandering this opportunity of living your life in the present... either by remembering the sorrows of the past or by worrying about the probabilities in the future. Bear this in mind that even the most intelligent person on this earth cannot live more than a single moment at a time. And this is the reason why, by living each moment, you can spend your entire life happily, but in that one moment you cannot mend your entire past and improve your future. Therefore, if you have spent your present moment in happiness, then you have truly lived your life, and if you have frittered away that moment in worry or anger, then you have killed that precious moment...a beautiful opportunity to live has slipped away from your hands.

Do you know what the joy of living in the present is? Let me tell you; suppose if someone is falling from the hundredth floor and when he is on his way down, a person standing at one of the windows asks, "How are you?" To this, the person who is falling, replies, "I'm fine at least till now. Will see what happens when I touch the ground!" Tell me, can such a person ever be unhappy? Can even death dampen his spirit of living? And the important point worth understanding here is, how can worries, fears and sorrows be encapsulated in this one single moment of the present? Their very existence rests on the premise that you have digressed from the present.

If you reflect on your life, you yourself will notice a thousand losses you had to suffer on account of straying away from the present. The biggest loss of straying away from the present is, whatever you possess becomes or rather seems insignificant to you, because you begin to seek happiness in what you do not possess at present, or in that which you have already lost. However, while committing these follies, you tend to forget that you can derive happiness only from the things that you have at your disposal. Funnily enough, the trail does not end here. The height of your foolishness is such that you do not enjoy what you have at present, but when the same is lost, you endlessly mourn over it well into the future! Ironically, this is your attitude not only towards objects, but also towards the people in your life. For example, a husband perceives his wife to be ruining his life, but when the same wife departs from his life, he finds his life in shambles. In old age, parents are perceived as a burden by their children, but if they die, the children are saddened by their loss and endlessly grieve over it... Is this the way to live? Why have you become the enemy of your own life?

Let us try to understand this with the help of a few examples... Once upon a time, there was a woodcutter, who was almost seventy years old. Neither did he have a family, nor any savings. His health was also not in his favour; it was slowly deteriorating. Still against all odds, he would have to go to collect timber every day. He would then have to go to the market every evening to sell the wood he had so painstakingly cut. After a hard day's labour, he would barely be able to earn enough money to feed himself a morsel or two in the night. Indeed, his life was filled with drudgery. The poor man's woes would worsen in the monsoon; often, the rains would dampen the wood he had so painstakingly cut, making it unsaleable. As a result, many a times the poor old man would be left starving for two or three days at a stretch. Due to his increasing age and such a strenuous life, the old man was extremely distressed. Often he would pray in grief, "Oh, Lord of Death! Why do you not kill me and end my misery? Why are you so angry with me? When you can take away people much younger, why not me? What enmity do you harbour against me?" His prayers echoed the pain and hardship that he was suffering.

Suddenly, one day, an astonishing incident occurred. In the same distressed state of mind, the old man was sitting under a tree, and again praying to the Lord of Death to free him from a life of hardships. He repeated the same question umpteen times, "When will you take me away from this world? Why do you not end my life? Please take me away!" As he was praying, he felt someone's hand on his shoulder. The old man was startled! He turned around and noticed a gigantic man standing next to him. Shocked, the old man asked him to introduce himself. The man said, "I am the Lord of Death! I was just passing by when I heard your prayers filled with agony. Actually, your time is not yet due, but I am deeply saddened on seeing your plight. So come, I will take you with me." As soon as the old man heard this, he came to his senses. Since he had an experience of over seventy years with him, he soon realised that he had committed a folly. He immediately changed his tune and said to the Lord of Death, "Well, since I was hungry for the last 2-3 days, in sheer desperation, I had uttered those words. I am very happy and I do not wish to die. I blurted out those words in a fit of anger. Honestly speaking, I thank you for visiting me today, but please do not pay me a visit in future. I will make sure, never to call out for you again, but even if I do by mistake, please do not come to my rescue".

"As you wish!" said the Lord of Death, and off he went. The moment he left, a wave of realisation swept over the old man. The old man not only breathed a sigh of relief, but was bouncing with delight. Astonishingly, thereafter, he never experienced the feeling of struggle or pain again. His life and thinking both had changed for the better. Looking back at the situation, you will notice that everything was just as it was before; everything was the same; still, how everything had changed! Why was it so? Because, the moment he saw death face-to-face, he realised that if nothing else, he at least had his life with him. And when his feelings and sense of existence were still alive...why would he need anything else?

So, recognise the worth of this life and understand its importance. Value it! Think, what exactly human life is all about? And in order to comprehend it, take a look at the Universe and realise its enormity. Can you even fathom its infinite expanse? In fact, it is expanding with every passing day. In such a colossal Universe, what is the significance of this speck called earth, on which you live? It is akin to an ant living on the earth. And if this is the position of the earth in such a vast Universe, then of what consequence are you?

Let us do a similar analysis in relation to time. Time is... expansive! It has a history of billions and trillions of years; or perhaps more...and maybe even much more than that. According to the scientists, light from the known stars, despite travelling at a whopping speed of 1,86,000 miles per second is still not reaching the earth, even after 2,00,000 years... This means that many of the stars that we see today are, in fact, a mere reflection of their existence over 2,00,000 years ago. Now in such a vast Universe and in the world of immeasurable time, what is the significance of your six feet tall body and eighty years of life, other than to live and enjoy every moment, and engage yourself in positive deeds? Even if you worry endlessly, what can you do ultimately, and after worrying so much, even if you gain something, what will it be? Just think, if you do not carry the burden of all these worries, at the most what will you lose?

I hope, you must have understood the facts I have put before you. You also need to understand that it is not only your body and time that have their constraints, but even your senses have their limitations. Every moment, so many explosions are happening around you in the Universe that if you hear them even for a second, you would die in an instant. But you are safe because your ears have a hearing limit. You cannot hear a sound beyond a specific decibel. And this limitation is applicable not only to loud sounds i.e. above 85 decibel but also to the sounds below a certain decibel i.e. sounds below 0 decibel. Do not think that when an ant crawls, it does not make any sound. It does, but it is of such a low decibel that it does not fall within the audible range of your ears.

Similarly, even your eyes have their limitations. It is not that the world and the Universe end at the point that meets your eye. It is way way way beyond...!!! Let us comprehend the infinity of the Universe with the help of a small example. When you see an aircraft flying in the air, after watching it for a while, it appears smaller and smaller to our eyes, and after some time, there comes a moment when it becomes invisible. The plane is still flying, but it has flown beyond your optical range. Similarly, if something is directly pasted onto your eyes, you will not be able to see it. Meaning, even in order to see, a certain distance is necessary. So, these are the limitations of the human eye.

If someone asks you, "What would be the temperature of the sun?" you would say, "Please spare me!" Then, if he asks you, "Tell me what would be the temperature at the base of the mountains under the ocean in Antarctica?" You would again say, "Ahh...forget it" and take to your heels. But you can at least be aware of the temperature of your own body! The highest temperature of your body can be 108^0F and the lowest, 88^0F; that is, it stays in the range of 20^0F. If either of the limits is breached, a human body would cease to function, and the person would die. In short, in every way, we are confined to function in a specific range.

Similarly, do even our mind and brain have a limitation? The good news is, there are no such limitations for the human mind and brain. They are potent with unlimited powers and infinite possibilities. But unfortunately,

Life is nothing but the 'Present'

**'' The future is absolutely uncertain
Nothing can be more foolish than pondering over it ''**

when it comes to the mind and brain, it is the human being who has thrust the limitations upon himself. Hence, know for sure, that your current state of mind and brain is definitely not its peak state. If human beings are able to undo the conditioning of the mind and brain, and weaken the Conscious, Subconscious and Unconscious states of their mind, then every human being can rise up to a level where he can attain the intelligence of the cosmos. Meaning, at the level of the mind and brain, all is not lost; you still have an opportunity. And, human history stands witness to many individuals who have successfully scaled the heights of this intelligence. Here, it is needless to state that the elevated status of human civilisation at present, is attributed to these few intellectuals who have surmounted the barriers of their mind and brain.

In this context, it is important for you to know that not only your intelligence, but your happiness, peace and bliss can also be transcended by the right treatment of your mind and brain. In fact, what you cognise as happiness, peace and bliss at present is in reality, not even one-thousandth part of the happiness, peace and bliss that you are potentially capable of experiencing. For, your current parameters of happiness are; having a happy family, abundant wealth, fame and status in society...but this is a façade in the name of happiness. Do you even have an idea, what happiness is all about? A human life can attain such a supreme crest of happiness and bliss, seeing which, even Nature would envy you. And if you peruse the history of mankind, you will find ample examples of individuals, who have successfully overcome the limitations and scaled the heights of joy and success.

In essence, man has definitely been bound by certain natural limitations like in the case of his capacity to see and hear, but when it comes to mind, brain and joy, it is the man who has confined himself to limitations. However, if he desires, he can always break these boundaries, by learning to live in the present.

As for the art of living in the present, the first thing an individual needs to do is, try to weaken his memory. What is the use of remembering the things that have already transpired? What significance do they hold

An effort to accommodate the past or the future in the Present is the root cause of all miseries

> Even the most intelligent of human beings cannot live more than a moment at a time

today? On the contrary, these memories only serve to harm. Why? It is because, every day heralds a new life. Man changes every moment. Observe for yourself; do your mind and thoughts not change with the passage of time? In that case, of what significance is who did what, when and why? Someone, who has caused you harm in the past, probably may not want to hurt you in the present. Also, someone who has done good to you in the past, has possibly turned hostile today. So rather than remembering the past deeds or keeping memories of a person, is it not advisable to deal with the person based on his or her present state of mind? And this principle is applicable to not just one, but every aspect of life. Take the example of business. The business, in which you may have faced a loss in the past, may have turned profitable today with the positive turn of events. Likewise, with a change in circumstances, a business that has been profitable for years on end, may incur losses today. This proves that the best decision can only be made by remaining true to the present. And I need not explain here that the quality, condition and direction of your life are solely dependent upon the decisions taken by you.

With this, I am sure you would have understood the futility of hanging on to the past. Furthermore, let me tell you that the same principle applies in the case of future as well. An extremely important fact that needs to be understood here is, your present has been shaped by your past, while your future will be

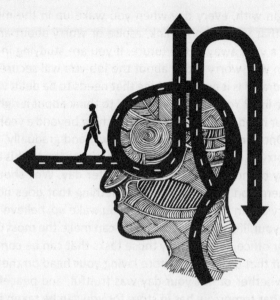

" **A human being is provided with only one option if he truly wants to live, and that is, 'the present'** "

built on the basis of your present. Hence, the more attention you pay to your present and the tasks at hand, the better will be the future effectuated by their outcomes. Worrying or dreaming about the future will not yield any worthwhile result. To grasp this point, let us look at it from another perspective - wherever you stand today is because of your past; so it means that your entire past is anyway condensed to exist in your present. Hence, the past has automatically become meaningless. And how you spend your present will determine the course of your future. It implies that your future is also very much dependent on what you are doing in your present. In short, the past and the future, both are rendered meaningless.

So, I hope you have realised the importance of living in the present... But an important question that still remains unanswered is, how does one cultivate the habit of living in the present?

To begin with, every day when you wake up in the morning, firmly resolve that you will not think, aspire or worry about anything that is at least a year away in the future. If you are studying in school right now, then why worry today about the job you will secure or the salary you will draw? Is it not something that needs to be dealt with ten years down the line? You do not even need to think about it right now. Ingrain it in your mind, that the worries stretching beyond a year's span are all futile. Once you master this, then slowly and gradually, reduce this span of worry to one month. When you have mastered this as well, then focus only on how to make today a better day. Why should you waste your energy on worrying about something that does not exist today? So every day in the morning when you wake up, believe it to be the last day of your life, and think, how you can make the most of it. Be it your home or office, take up only those tasks that can be completed in the course of that day. Then, before laying your head on the pillow, contemplate whether or not your day was fruitful, and peacefully go off to sleep. What tomorrow has in store for you can be taken care of, if you wake up the next morning. Living in this manner, all your worries and fears will get eliminated in no time. Eventually one after another, all your days will be fruitfully lived. Thus, successfully living each day as it comes, one day, the entire journey of your life will be transformed into a worthwhile experience, fully lived.

Let me explain this point to you with the example of an intelligent magician. One day, the magician, gripped by the greed for a big reward, reached the royal court to amuse the king. Pleased and intrigued, the king decided to give him a chance to display his craft. The magician thought, why perform ordinary and conventional tricks? Why not try a magic trick on the king himself? With this thought, the magician made the king's crown disappear in the blink of an eye. To his misfortune, the king construed this act as an insult. As a result, the king not only ordered the immediate imprisonment of the magician, but also sentenced him to be executed in a week's time.

The poor magician now found himself in a grave situation! He was imprisoned until he was to be hanged to death. The next day when the magician's wife heard the news, sobbing uncontrollably, she went running to him. To her utter shock, the magician showed no sign of grief. Grieving and crying, she sought to understand the reason behind his indifference. The magician said, "Six full days still remain for my execution and a lot can happen during this time. Why should I spoil today by unnecessarily thinking about tomorrow?" His wife could not comprehend the meaning behind his words. She thought, her husband had probably gone insane in the face of certain death.

Well! The time of her visit was over and still weeping, she left for home. The same routine continued for the next five days. Finally, the day of the magician's execution arrived, and before the execution, the king personally came to meet him. Seeing the king arrive, the magician hatched a plan in his mind. He immediately donned a woeful expression and began to cry, which gratified the king and assuaged his pride.

He said to the magician, "You had the temerity to make my crown vanish, then why is it that now, seeing the inevitability of your death, you have lost your wit?"

The magician said, "Oh my king! This is not the case. I am not afraid of death, but I am grieving over its timing. Actually for the last two years, I have been trying to teach my horse to fly and in a year or so, I would have definitely done so. But now, I am upset because unfortunately, I do not have that one year at hand."

Listening to these words of the magician, greed crept into the king's mind. In an imperious tone, he asked the magician, "And what if I give you that one year?"

Calmly, the magician said, "Then I will gift that flying horse to you."

The king said, "Then it is decided, you are a free man now; but remember, only for a year. If you are unable to give me the flying horse within a year, the death sentence is certain."

The magician was set free with immediate effect. Gloating gleefully, he went home, only to be shocked by the gloom that had pervaded his entire house. All the neighbours had gathered at his house. Everyone had assumed him dead, and they had arrived to offer their condolences to the family. However, seeing the magician return home alive, they were all shocked. The moment he revealed that the king had granted him freedom, their gloom instantaneously turned into gaiety, and after a while, relieved, everyone returned to their homes.

Once alone, the wife asked the magician, "How did this miracle happen?" The magician then, very proudly told her the story of the flying horse, which he had narrated to the king. Listening to the story, the wife was again dejected and began weeping as she knew that her husband had escaped by fabricating a story. At the end of the year, when the truth came to light, the death sentence would be inevitable. She went on to explain to her husband, how the entire year would now be spent in worrying because of his impending doom. The magician gently stroked her head and said, "Dear, one year is a long period of time; such a long spell holds a thousand different possibilities, and numerous things could occur during this time. For now, let us spend this guaranteed one year in joy". And this is exactly what happened. Six months later, the king passed away. Another three months later, the horse was no more. Now on what grounds could he be sentenced to death?

This is the beauty of the future. Even the smallest of events of the future is dependent upon the occurrence of thousands of other events. Therefore, why should one worry about this completely unpredictable phenomenon called future? And the past is as it is something that has already happened. So I hope, all of you will learn the art of living each day in the present and forever attain freedom from the futile sorrows and worries disrupting your life.

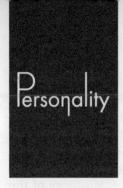

Personality

The lack of a real personality is another major reason why your life has become a living hell. It is because of this lack of personality that you tend to indulge in nonsensical acts and futile emotions such as anger, sorrow, jealousy and so on. Now, before I initiate the discussion on what exactly personality is and the role it plays in your life, I want you to take a look at your own life as well as the life of the people around you. Everyone trudges ahead in this journey of life with innumerable hopes and aspirations. Still, barely do you find one person amongst thousands, who has been able to transform these aspirations into reality. Else, mostly you will find everyone grieving over the present state of their life. Everyone is distressed, for they have digressed from the path on which they wished to lead their life. Everyone thinks life and the world around them is a pain in their neck. Ask any person, if he wants to forget his past and start his life anew and he would readily agree. Whoever you see around, just wants to get rid of his or her old relationships, old memories and old systems. People realise that they have committed a mistake, but the irony is, they are clueless as to where they have faltered; and this is certainly a matter of deep concern. Life is the one and only opportunity to live, and it is indeed a matter of worry when ninety-nine percent people fail to do so.

Now, to find a solution to this issue, let us examine how and where things have gone wrong. How did man complicate his life to such an extent that life does not feel like 'life - an experience worth living' to him anymore? So, let me tell you, the most significant and the primary reason for this is, man has always laid too much emphasis on enhancing his external personality. And the ultimate result? ...he has ended up neglecting the very important aspect of his personality i.e. his 'Inner Personality'. Man has just not paid any attention to his inner personality, whereas the reality is, to a great extent a man's life is governed by his inner personality rather than his external personality. Now, if a man chooses to neglect such a vital aspect of his life, then how will he tread the path of joy and success? Then will sorrows and worries not become his destiny?

Well, if I explain to you in brief, every individual largely has two personalities.

(1) External Personality

(2) Inner Personality

(1) External Personality

Everyone is aware of external personality because believing it to be their real personality, no one has spared any effort to groom it. Right from etiquette, manners, fashion, politeness, style to discovering innovative techniques to charm people; everything falls under the blanket of external personality. Well, I have no objection with you deriving delight from people singing your praises or being impressed by you. Undoubtedly, these are essential parts of our life... But the problem is, you have not only attached undue importance to it, but have also mistaken it to be 'your only' personality. While in reality, this is only the superficial layer of your personality. Even if it remains weak or is lacking in something, it does not really make much of a difference to your life. Being articulate, stylish or well-mannered might appeal to others, but it is not necessary that these attributes will always help you progress in life. Anyway, the topic of external personality does not require any further elucidation as there are innumerable types of teachings available in the world to help you groom it; and as it is, no one has spared any effort in enhancing it. However, despite all their efforts, their sorry state is pretty evident to all of us. Therefore, without wasting any more time, it would be better if we begin the discussion about the much more important aspect of our personality, that is, the inner personality.

> **"There are two layers to an individual's personality one is external and the other is internal"**

(2) Inner Personality

Let us begin discussing on this subject with an example, which will help you grasp what I intend to make you understand about inner personality.

Once, there was a retired managing director of a bank and since he had been an MD, he obviously had a well-groomed external personality. The marriage proposal of his only daughter was being discussed with a boy from a reputed industrialist family. A meeting was scheduled for five o'clock that day to finalise the wedding proposal. He set out from his home well in advance to reach there on time. This day could certainly turn out to be the happiest day of his life. He was very enthusiastic and joyous about it too.

Back home, the rest of the family was eagerly awaiting his return. But to everyone's surprise, he returned home early...and that too, fuming! Every member of the family was perplexed as no one could comprehend what had transpired. Could it be that they rejected the proposal? But then, what was the need to be so angry about it? Had he been sad, one could have inferred that something on these lines could have occurred. But why anger? Maybe they had insulted him! But then, why would they do that? They were cultured people. There was a possibility that they could have rejected the proposal, but they would never resort to insults. Then, what could be the matter? The question was one, but the possibilities that ran through everyone's mind were many.

The MD, on the other hand, was so enraged, that he not only threw his coat aside in anger but also refused to take even a sip of water. Finally, his wife mustered the courage to ask him, "What happened?" Hearing the question, the already enraged MD turned livid, and screamed, "That fellow, Nitesh Sanghvi! You might remember I was the one to pass his first loan. Not only the first, but I had passed so many of his loans. But today he thinks he is a big man; he bumped into me at the confectionary shop and the rogue did not even bother to respond to my greeting!"

After patiently listening to the entire story, the anxious wife asked, "All that is fine, but you had gone to fix our daughter's wedding, right? What about that?"

Realising his folly, in a sad tone, he replied, "By then, I was so put off, that I did not feel like going there." So that was it! Just because Nitesh Sanghvi did not acknowledge his greeting, he missed out on such a big opportunity and failed to fulfil such an important responsibility of his life. This is the outcome of a weak inner personality. Irrespective of how powerful your external personality is, in the absence of a strong inner personality, everything boils down to zilch, within a fraction of a second.

For example, take a close look at your own life and the way you live. Due to the lack of understanding of your own inner personality and not paying attention to it, you now have no control over yourself. Your happiness and sorrows are no longer dependent on yourself, but on the will of others. And the will of others can never be, to let you be happy. This is not the question of one Nitesh Sanghvi or one act; many people are out in the world with numerous 'tricks' up their sleeve. An abusive word is hurled at you and you immediately flare up! Let someone sing your praises and you are more than willing to do their bidding. The moment someone points out your shortcomings, you immediately distance yourself from that person. You have almost forgotten what it means to live for yourself, by yourself.

Now the situation has become so grave, that your mood or your planning has no role to play in how your day will pan out, but it depends on how others choose to interact with you during the day. And that too, to such an extent, that even joyous occasions do not permit you to rejoice wholeheartedly. Even on such occasions, there is always someone who sours the moment. Let us assume that you are celebrating your success over a family dinner at a restaurant and needless to say, everyone is in a jovial mood. But as soon as the party begins, someone rubs you the wrong way. That is it! The party is over! Leaving your dinner midway, in an irate mood, you march back home.

Just think, if you get affronted at the slightest instance, how will you ever be able to live? If you are unable to celebrate even your success, how will you remain joyous in life? If everyone around possesses the power to unsettle you or affront you, then of what use is all your hard work and determination? If truth be told, when you lack an inner personality, there is very little left in you that makes you a human. In that case, you are reduced to an object; like a fan; the moment you press the button, it begins to move. Now you have also become an object; the moment someone presses a button, you start getting jitters.

You step out attired in your finery and as soon as someone passes an unflattering comment about your clothing, all your enthusiasm and confidence fizzles out in a second. Now your confidence is shaken to such an extent that you no longer trust your own choices or dressing

The One who does not possess a strong Inner Personality is exploited by the entire world like a mere object

style. Moreover, you have conditioned yourself in such a manner that the moment someone progresses, you become jealous. Just think, how many kinds of buttons you have handed out in the market; a button for love, a button for flattery, a button for good conduct, a button for insult, a button for misbehaviour, buttons for comparison and competition, and numerous other kinds of buttons! Let someone just press the button and you are ready to react. Now, there is no button left that is controlled by you. Now, neither do you possess your own personality nor your individuality. If you observe carefully, this is the reason why you have now started living in a world of mere reactions.

The moment there is an act or action on someone's part, or any instance or an event, your reaction inevitably follows. When someone progresses, your jealousy follows. When someone comments, your anger follows. Similarly, flattery is a must for you to do someone's work. You have simply forgotten what it is to be the one to initiate an action. And this is the very reason why you are being exploited like an object by everyone day in and day out. But bear in mind that it is only human beings who are privileged to get happiness, peace and success in life, not objects.

Moreover, is your habit of reacting just limited to others' behaviour with you? No sooner do the religious heads dangle a bait for your greed, you immediately fall for their trickery. The moment you see someone prospering in a particular business, you jump into that business without assessing its pros and cons. The moment someone buys something new, you too become anxious to purchase the same. What sort of madness is this?

Whatever it is, the matter worth thinking about at this point is, how can a man be freed from living in this world of reactions? For that, it is first necessary to understand how man began to dwell in this world of reactions. How did he himself hand over the key to all his happiness to others? And what sort of 'people' are these individuals who do not let him be happy! And then, man continues to crib all his life that he is not being allowed to live in peace! Well... this is what you call foolishness personified! Why would someone else allow you to live in peace? Why would the other lead you onto the path of success? It is your life, so you have to groom your personality in such a manner that not only your life, but your joys and sorrows can also be manoeuvred the way you desire. This is such a simple and straightforward matter, but then why is everyone erring?

There are two reasons for this. Firstly, propelled by his egoistic nature, man chalks out a list of his thousand likes and dislikes; and the most ridiculous part is, he considers it as an act of great intelligence. He performs this task too under the influence of his brain; it does not have anything to do with me i.e. his mind.

In addition, man also keeps embracing several types of ideals and beliefs surrounding this long list of his personal likes-dislikes. In this entire process, he gradually develops a permanent nature and then throughout his life, he moves within the dictates of this nature. This is a very dangerous process which has badly ensnared every human being. And this is the reason why he is being used like an object today, as each and every permanent tendency of his nature can always be manipulated and taken advantage of.

Well here, it is necessary to understand the meaning of 'permanent nature' because it is the same nature that has destroyed you and reduced you, from a human being to an object. Now the choice is yours! Think, whether you wish to lead a good life or just keep preparing your list of likes-dislikes! It is quite simple - do as you please on the spur of the moment - the matter ends there. What will you gain by preparing these long lists?

This is amazing! Is it not? First, make a long list of your likes and dislikes, and then, weave principles and beliefs around it. Meaning, become obstinate about them! And then you are doomed! Because, being obstinate about anything makes it a permanent part of your nature, and then, whether you like it or not, it compels you to react. Then gradually, everyone can predict your reactions in any given situation. Anyone can take advantage of the reaction which he perceives as favourable for him, by merely pressing the button compelling you to react as per his wishes. And in the bargain, you just end up being a machine with a thousand buttons. Henceforth, look around carefully; you will see fewer humans, and more machines with these buttons.

There is no dearth of people in this world who are just waiting to take advantage of such machines. If your reputation is dear to you, then by threatening you with the button of disrepute, you are taken for a ride. If you belong to a specific religion, then you are compelled to spend money by adhering to their respective rituals. If you like listening to your praises, then you are coaxed by using the button of flattery. If someone is very dear to you, then your mood can be spoiled by passing unpleasant comments about them. What I mean to say here is, every person invariably takes an undue advantage of your every belief, principle, ideology or thought for their own selfish gains, owing to which, you eventually end up becoming a puppet whose strings are being pulled by others. Thus in the end, the principles, ethics and thoughts that you have embraced prove to be nothing but sheer nonsense, regardless of how lofty you have assumed them to be. Then, the question is, why does a man who is so proud of his intelligence, need to decide on everything beforehand? Can he not arrive at the right decision as and when the time comes or the need arises?

So, if you want to liberate yourself from these numerous buttons of yours, then there is only one solution - increase your faith in your own decision-making capabilities, and slowly but steadily begin to live in spontaneity; that is, by following your impulses and acting spontaneously. Meaning, neither should you have any permanent likes-dislikes nor any fixed ideology or principle. As and when the situation arises, the decision should be taken as per the need of the hour. Suppose, today you wish to visit the church, then for today, you are a Christian. Else, what comes tomorrow should be decided upon tomorrow. Today, if you are craving Italian food, then you are fond of Italian cuisine for today, but claim no permanent liking. Try to understand the vicious circle underlying this entire process. Once you have a thought or an inclination for something, your thoughts start making you obstinate about that particular thing. Once you become obstinate, you become emotional about it. And once you have become emotional, and if the same emotions are encouraged or your stand in that particular case is supported, it leaves you vulnerable and you are willing to go to any lengths for it. At such a time, if someone opposes you, you tend to lose your composure and rebel. Meaning, your every thought ultimately proves to be the means for your own destruction. Hence, start leading your life with spontaneous thoughts and actions, and very soon, all your buttons in circulation will automatically be rendered useless. Then you will be the master of your own joys and sorrows. And only he, who is a master of his own joys and sorrows, can progress effortlessly in life.

Let me try to explain with an example, as it may help you understand it better. Once upon a time, in a small village, there was a man who lived with his ten-year-old-son. Now, fathers, generally, are clever and intelligent, and this man too was no different. He had narrated scores of stories about obedient and dutiful sons like Rama and Shravana to his son. He was after all just a child; soon his brain was conditioned... and he became a very obedient child. He followed every command of his father and the father took undue advantage of his son, as if he were an object. From dawn to dusk, he would make his son do several petty tasks.

However, the son was not as stupid as his father had thought him to be. Very soon, he realised that his father was taking advantage

" Man is not a machine that can be switched on and off according to others' whims "

of his obedience and making him slog. He started thinking of ways to escape from this drudgery. Soon, he arrived at a conclusion – 'Do the exact opposite of father's instruction; automatically, he will stop doling out instructions. Eureka!!!' The son immediately brought his plan into action. If his father asked him to clean the room, he would do the opposite and mess it up. If his father asked him to feed grass to the cattle, he would throw the grass out. His father was baffled. He could not fathom what exactly was wrong with his son. Seeing the perplexity of the father, the son rejoiced and began to sense victory.

However, his father too was a clever man. He quickly gauged that his son was acting contrary to his commands. Well, no problem! The father now started doling out instructions contrary to what he intended. If he wished to make his son fold the clothes neatly, he would now instruct him to unfold them. And the son would fold them properly instead. If he wanted to get the shoes polished by his son, he would tell him to go and soil them; and the shoes would be polished instead! Thus, the father once again started manipulating his son according to his wishes, and things were back on track for him.

On the other hand, the son was not dim-witted either. He soon saw through his father's tricks and realised that he was again making him toil by giving him contrary instructions...and the fact was, he did not want to work or be used like a machine. So then what was the solution? Deliberating over it for a while, he surrendered to spontaneity. He decided to respond to every command of his father after due deliberation and making decisions on the spot. On the other hand, the father, unaware of this new development continued giving opposite instructions. When he asked the son to empty the vessel of water the son actually emptied the vessel. His father was shocked. Then he quickly thought that possibly, he had started following the directions as it is. So to test this, he immediately asked his son to feed the cattle. This time, the son did the opposite. He threw away the grass that his father had given him. The father was really puzzled. He was unable to understand what was happening. Now how could he make his son dance to his tune? He tried for many days to make his son do various tasks, but all his attempts were in vain.

Finally, when left with no other option, he thought it wise to have a one-on-one conversation with his son. He thought, maybe

Being influenced by Others at the drop of a hat merely shows your lack of Personality a word or two with his son would bring a solution to light; because till the time the child was obeying his instructions, he had faced no difficulty in exploiting him. When the child began to do exactly the opposite, then too, he faced no hindrance. But as soon as the child had decided to act as per his wish, on the spur of the moment, trouble began to brew. So, defeated, the father made his son sit next to him, and very lovingly asked, "Why are you troubling me? Sometimes you act contrary to my command, while at times you diligently follow it. What is the matter?" On seeing his father capitulate, the son frankly told him, "It is simple, now I have become wise enough not to be used like an object by you. Now for any task to be carried out, you will not only have to convey it explicitly, but also give me a valid reason, why I should do it. Only then, will I decide whether I will do it or not, because I have now developed my own personality." The father finally bowed down to his son's wishes...and very humorously said, "As you say, my father!"

Perhaps, now I need not explain to you the price you have to pay for every thought or belief that you have. By now you must have grasped how beautifully the habit of taking spontaneous decisions can enhance your personality. So now, I will address the second aspect of this problem and in order to comprehend this, first you must understand that your brain and I, both are totally independent entities. No authority, God or even the Universe has any control over us. For example, you can verbally abuse anyone, and as much as you desire; no authority can stop you from doing so. As a punishment, even the greatest of tyrants such as Adolf Hitler can at the most imprison your body; but no Hitler in this world has control over the fact that abuses would not be hurled at him at my level i.e. in your mind. Likewise, the body owing to its malfunctions and disorders, is free to contract illnesses, but again, it is in the hands of the individual whether he should grieve or not, due to that illness.

In the same manner, controlling the external situations may not be in your hands, but to be or not to be distracted or intimidated by them, is entirely your choice. Likewise, in spite of someone narrating innumerable stories of obedient children such as Rama and Shravana, whether to become blindly obedient or not, is again completely in your hands. For that, you must realise your supreme independence and once it is realised, shoulder the responsibility of bettering your life.

If you are still not able to clearly understand it, then please skim through the history of mankind. You will find the mentions of several such courageous individuals who have been the sole masters of their minds and have successfully lived their lives. Take the example of Jesus; crucifying him was in the hands of people, which they did. However, compelling Jesus to change his thoughts or grieve by hammering nails through his body was not in their hands, and they just could not do it. ... And what happened in the end? The man they crucified and whose thoughts they tried to crush, that very same Jesus and his thoughts became eternal.

Let me iterate this point with a beautiful anecdote from the life of Gautama Buddha. Often, Buddha used to hold discourses for his disciples and monks. In that era, Hinduism was the only religion prevalent in India, and in his discourses, let alone Hinduism, Buddha even denied the existence of God. Over and above that, he strongly opposed all kinds of superstitions and hypocrisy. So naturally, his teachings and views irked many people; some were just upset, whereas some spared no effort to harass him. However, this was their problem, not Buddha's. Whatever Buddha intended to say or do, he inevitably said and did.

Once you are in awe of Someone you stop learning from him

Only the one Who is capable of standing alone in a crowd attains great success

Once, like any other day, Buddha was delivering a discourse. His disciples, and nearby villagers were fondly listening to him. Suddenly, from a distance, a man came running towards Buddha, hurling abuses at him. Everyone was stunned, but Buddha did not pay attention to him and continued with his discourse. The man was very enraged, and the fact that Buddha did not pay any heed to him, only fuelled his anger. Now angry and unable to decide what to do next, he ran towards Buddha and spat on him. Seeing this, reflexively, many of his disciples stood up in anger. Buddha laughed, and gesturing them to sit down, he continued with his discourse. He remained unperturbed; meaning, there was no difference in his joy and engrossment. On the other hand, the person, having expressed his anger, quietly went away. And the incident was soon a thing of the past.

However, the next day, another startling incident took place. Just like the previous day, Buddha was delivering a discourse. Everyone was absorbed in fondly listening to their master's words, when the person who had spat on Buddha the previous day, came crying and howling towards him, "Please forgive me! Please forgive me!" Unlike the previous day, today he fell at Buddha's feet. However, Buddha's concentration was unwavering; even today he did not pay any attention to him. On the other hand, this man was still persistently pleading. In the end, when he saw that Buddha was not moved by his tears, he started begging for forgiveness, by banging his head at Buddha's feet. Sobbing uncontrollably, he said, "I am ashamed of my behaviour yesterday, please forgive me. Till the time you do not forgive me, I will not move away from your feet".

Now, Buddha had no option but to respond. Helping the man lift himself up, he said, "When I did not feel hurt by your act of spitting yesterday, what shall I forgive you for today? Yesterday, when you had expressed your anger by spitting on me, that very moment, I had understood that you were so upset with me that you did not have words to express it; so, you expressed it by spitting...the matter ends there. And today, seeing the way you are begging for forgiveness, I gather that you are repenting for yesterday's behaviour. But both were your problems; what do I have to do with them?" ...this is called the inner personality. Who can perturb such a person and how? Like Buddha, you too, should learn the art of holding the reins of your life in your own hands. Till the time you do not lay the foundation of a strong inner personality; your sorrows and pains will not be eliminated.

To sum it up, there are two important points I have mentioned for building your personality. Firstly, steer away from unproductive and futile thoughts, because, it is these very thoughts which slowly get converted into principles and beliefs and then you tend to become stubborn about them. As a consequence, you become enamoured by these thoughts which get firmly implanted in you. The gravest consequence of this process is, it leads to the formation of your permanent nature. And it is from here on that your exploitation as an object begins. As a result, your joys and sorrows, instead of being controlled by you, end up being dependent on another's conduct and behaviour towards you. And as for others, whenever they want to get any work done from you, all they need to do is, use the appropriate words that will either trigger your happiness, or incite anger or make you sad.

Moreover, what is the value of your thoughts, beliefs and principles? Even minor crisis blows it to smithereens. Suppose, you are a staunch Christian by faith, and God forbid, terrorists kidnap your child. The only condition they put forth to release your child is, you convert to their religion. You would immediately agree to it, and you should! But then the question is, why muddle your mind with these worthless thoughts and beliefs? Because no matter how lofty your principles are, ultimately you have to pay a very hefty price for it. Such principles have never been able to withstand the test of time anyway.

Think, then why do you need all these thoughts, principles, beliefs and resolves in the first place? Why do you not develop the ability to act the best you can, as per the need of the hour and circumstances? By doing this, firstly, your brain will never get conditioned and secondly, your Conscious, Subconscious and Unconscious minds will also never get strengthened...which means, mentally you will always stay fresh and energetic, and even I will not get an opportunity to resort to mischief-mongering. For example, you believe Michael Jackson is the best dancer. Now, there is nothing wrong with this thought; the problem is, the matter does not end here. Gradually, you a reach a point where you lose your ability to hear anything against him. As a result, anything said contrary to your liking not only makes you unhappy but also leaves you fuming. And you have to go through all this, for what? For no reason! Instead, it is better that you watch Michael Jackson dance and enjoy it to your heart's content, but refrain from harbouring any fixed ideas about him. Then, there will be no question of you being unhappy or getting angry about anything related to Michael Jackson ever. If there is a discussion about him, then you will be able to logically engage yourself in the debate, argue in his favour and enjoy it. At the same time, for any genuine criticism about him, you will be mature enough to accept it and let your understanding of him grow deeper. This means that another great advantage of leaving your thoughts open is, your ability to learn, grasp and improve yourself also increases day by day. As a result, you will inexorably head towards achieving perfection in life.

So, after such an in-depth discussion, I hope, by developing and enhancing your inner personality, you would not only try to quickly get rid of all the sorrows and unreasonable bouts of anger that are an everyday ritual for you right now, but you will also take a concrete step towards achieving perfection in life. And to this effect, if you are unable to do anything really substantial, then, at least make a firm resolution that in future, you will take all your decisions on the spot. Just by doing this, you will be able to rid yourself from your self-limiting thoughts, principles and beliefs.

———————◆———————

Complex

The third significant reason behind the ruination of human beings is their affliction with thousands of complexes. Owing to these complexes, every human being suffers a constant internal vexation day in and day out. To tell you the truth, it is due to the affliction of these complexes that he is never able to live his life to the fullest. Day and night, he dances to the tune of these futile complexes, like a puppet. And all these complexes of a man are nothing, but the creations of his own brain. The single reason for a man to be plagued by such complexes at present, is the thinking of his own brain. Here, you must also understand that I, the 'Mind', never contract any complex.

Well, before elaborating on this further, it is essential to know what exactly a complex is. Complex essentially means that you do not accept yourself as you are, or are in denial of the situation and state you are in. It is this non-acceptance of your state that is called Complex. And in future, a complex alone proves to be the means to make your life a living hell.

Now pragmatically speaking, you were certainly not born in this state of non-acceptance. A child is always pleased with the state he is in, irrespective of what it is. He does not have the remotest inkling about the differences in his nature or skin colour or status. When he does not even distinguish himself as fair or dark, mischievous or quiet, rich or poor, then where does the question of him accepting or not accepting himself arise? On the other hand, if you look at the wider canvas of Nature, you will notice that here, no entity, element or no one is discontent with their way of being; neither are the moon, the stars or the earth dissatisfied with their way of being, nor does the air or water have any complaints about their existence. Likewise, neither does any flower or thorn, nor any bird, animal or fish have any problem with their way of being. Then, the matter worth contemplating about is, when nothing in the entire Universe disagrees with its way of being; when even a child does not have any such feeling, then from where does this non-acceptance creep into an individual as he grows up?

Definitely, it is the brain which instils this discontent in man. And surprisingly, this discontent is passed on to him by none other than his own well-wishers. The innocent child, who is moving ahead in life basking in his joy and passion, on growing up a little, faces an upheaval akin to an earthquake. His parents and the elders in the family begin to nag him. They start inculcating the comparative perspective in the child by way of their tall tales. Their diktats create divisions in the mind of the child about what he should be doing and what he should not be, what is good and what is bad, what is right, and what is wrong... and then, falling into the clutches of school teachers, his condition is made to deteriorate further. Because it is from here on that his life is bombarded with teachings that encourage the tendency to compare. They say, "See this child is so quiet and you are so naughty! See! How sharp this child is and look, how dull you are. See! How this child obeys his parents and teachers and look at you!! ...you do not listen to anyone!"

Now the issue is, on one hand, the teachers do not have the faintest idea about the impact these comparisons have on the minds of children. On the other, the parents or elders in the family are also unaware of the disastrously negative imprints it leaves on the mind of the child. Without the faintest idea of the dire consequences, they just keep bombarding the children with their endless and futile comparisons. The poor child is badly shaken; the innocent child is happy the way he is...but, who listens to the poor child? Eventually, the repeated comparisons drawn by several individuals begin to take root in the mind of the child. Thereupon, willingly or unwillingly, the poor child finds himself compelled to pay heed to them. And no sooner does he start acknowledging and accepting the division of good and bad, than his entire life changes. The foremost adverse effect it has is, the child stops accepting himself the way he is. As he begins to deny or be dissatisfied with his way of being, he consequently starts contracting complexes, for not just few, but numerous matters. And this is how complex invades the happy and peaceful life of a child. Meaning, it is due to teachings that lead to comparison that 'Complex' enters the lives of human beings.

Given this, it is obvious for the question to arise - are such teachings really essential? Are these teachings really desirable? No... definitely not! To understand this, take a look at Nature; here, things just exist. Nothing is good or bad, nothing is inferior or superior. In the entire Universe, apart from human beings, no one compares themselves with others. And since no one compares, no one prides themselves on being superior or great either. For the very same reason, no one in this entire existence thinks less of themselves for being small or insignificant. Here, neither does any stone take pride in being a precious diamond nor does a piece of gravel feel inferior for being just an ordinary stone. Here, no diamond tells the gravel, "Stay out of my way, I am a sparkling diamond and you are just an ordinary, inferior stone lying on the path!" No, both are satisfied with their way of being. And because they are both satisfied with their way of being, none is trying to change itself.

However, the same is not the case with human beings. The constant comparisons drawn by family and teachers give rise to discontentment in children with their way of being. Hence from a tender age itself, they engage themselves in the effort to change. It is from here on that the downfall of the child begins. It is from this point that the children who were earlier living in utter bliss begin to get caught in the web of complexes. And as soon as the child contracts the complex, the quiet child tries to become naughty and the naughty child, quiet.

Now the question is, in order to enhance his life, does the human being really need to change his basic nature? And the bigger question is, can he really change his basic nature? And even if he can, the crucial question is, from where is he drawing this inspiration to change himself?

In the flurry of these questions, if the answer to the first one is to be sought, then there is no need for a human being to change his basic nature, because man can progress in life only by remaining true to himself. Just as there are thousands of colourful flowers in Nature and all are marvellous and unique in their own way, there exist millions of different kinds of individuals, and they all are important in their respective fields. Whether you understand this or not, but even the smallest thing in Nature is well aware of its importance of being in existence. Though you human beings have glorified the rose and lotus, see for yourself, do the rest of the flowers shrivel on being compared or contract any complexes? No, they do not! Even the flowers are well aware of the 'comparative tendencies' of human beings. They know that such idiocies hold no significance. And this is the reason why you never see any flower trying to become a lotus or a rose. Irrespective of the kind of flower, every bud has just one purpose and that is, to attain contentment by flowering in full bloom. Similarly, irrespective of the kind and the capabilities of a human being, there should be only one goal of his life and that is – live his life to the fullest.

However, this does not happen. Only one in a million is able to do this. Why? Because his family members, teachers and the self-professed caretakers of society give him various kinds of complexes and then the individual, under this stressful influence of complexes begins to make desperate attempts to change himself. The irony is, the people on whose advice he tries to change himself, are themselves afflicted with thousands of complexes. Parents expect their children to emulate them and follow in their footsteps. Suppose there are two children in a family, one who is quiet and the other naughty; then know for sure that one of the two will definitely be under constant fire. If the parents were naughty in their childhood, then the quiet child would be subjected to constant comparisons and if the parents were quiet by nature, then they would bombard the naughty child with admonishments. In both the cases, ultimately the life of the child is made miserable. It is beyond my comprehension, why these people do not realise that one child is quiet and the other is mischievous; both are equally important. But no! Since you are extra-intelligent, you ought to draw a comparison! No matter how our life is, we want the children to become our replicas.

Similarly, even teachers have their own complexes. Teaching is a noble passion for only one amongst thousands. Most people have selected the profession of teaching only as a last resort. Without even understanding the far-reaching implications, from the first day itself they start bombarding children with teachings that inculcate the habit of comparison. The truth is, neither the parents nor teachers have any idea about what and how children should be taught or what kind of upbringing they should be provided!

The primary question here is, why make such comparisons in the first place? Just so that the child grows up to achieve something in life? But then, who will decide what the child should aspire for in life, or in which field he will be successful? There are thousands of fields to excel in, millions of ways to live, and a billion types of human beings! In that case, would it not be better that instead of differentiating between good and bad, the child carves out a path for himself by making choices according to his liking, at every juncture of his life? There are thousands of fields for him to choose from, such as science, arts, painting, singing, music, poetry, writing, religion, sports, politics, social service and so on. Now, regardless of the beliefs or the perceptions of your brain, let me tell you that for me, i.e. the mind, religion is also one among these fields. You never know which field matches with his nature and talent. Therefore, one cannot choose the path of his life by way of advice, influence, guidance or compulsion. He must recognise his own talents and nature, and decide on the right course for his life.

However, before he even exercises his choice, you (family, society, religion, etc.) invariably kindle in him the ambition to excel in a specific field of your choice. But then, how does it help? Use your imagination and think, what would have happened if Edison had decided to be a painter or Shakespeare had engaged himself in scientific experiments? It would have been a disaster, right? Then, why do these parents compel their children to become doctors or engineers? There is a possibility that a child is born with the calibre akin to that of Pele and Muhammad Ali. So do him a favour, and please do not lead him onto the wrong path by drawing unnecessary comparisons. Otherwise, let alone cultivating talent in the field of your choice, he will also lose out on his innate talent, that is, talent in the field meant for him. And needless to mention, such a person remains a failure all his life. Not only this, such a person remains plagued by thousands of complexes throughout his life. And this is the answer to my second question i.e. can he really change his basic nature? In spite of making enormous efforts, a man can neither forget his original nature, nor can he change it in its entirety. In short, all his efforts to change himself prove to be nothing more than a futile endeavour.

Now, let me answer the third and most important question: From where does the child derive the inspiration to change himself? Well, the answer is, every child gets the initial inspiration to change himself from the persistent comparisons and teachings imparted by his own parents and teachers. Now this gives rise to yet another predicament and that is, from where do 'these people', i.e. family and friends draw all this inspiration? The answer is plain and simple - from society, of which each and every one of us is a part. And what is this society? It is the system which is engaged in casting each and every person's thinking in its uniform mould as society believes it to be the facilitating factor in an individual's growth and progress, and a great help in achieving one's potential. And this is the very reason why every society and culture has framed its own rules and regulations and they insist on them being followed and acted upon, by one and all. But then, the question here is, in spite of thousands of years of efforts put in by society, which is collectively made up of millions of people, why are barely one or two successful among thousands? And this fact, in itself, is proof that the insistence of the society to cast an individual in its mould is wrong. In short, what I mean to say is, society

What we know as a person's Superiority Complex is nothing but the effort the person puts in to conceal his inferiority

that insists for an individual to change is not only itself unsuccessful and unhappy itself, but is also riddled with thousands of complexes. It is a universal truth that the tree with weak roots will never be able to bloom with beautiful and fragrant flowers. Meaning, the very foundation of all such teachings that lead to comparisons is faulty.

Now it has been proven that teachings that promote comparison and competition are wrong. Here a point to note is, these are not the teachings coveted by children. Children just want to progress and move ahead in life, the way they are. The teachings that encourage comparison are thrust upon them first by their parents. So, it is the family members of the child, who need to develop the understanding that they should not compare their children with other children time and again, or even encourage them to become like some other child. Instead, I would request you to accept them the way they are and reassuringly hold their hand, give them the confidence and encourage them to carve out their own unique path in life. Then see, how this child, who is now growing up without any complex, scales the peaks of happiness and success.

However, children also must guard themselves against being unnecessarily inspired by others and desiring to change themselves accordingly. For, the path of their life will open to them only by remaining true to themselves. Even if there is a need to change somewhere, they should change themselves on the basis

"Paying attention to external factors strengthens your complex"

of their experiences alone, and not under someone's pressure or insistence...and definitely not under other people's influence.

Frankly speaking, I have never been able to understand how two individuals can be compared in the first place. Ingrain it in your mind forever that every individual is unique in this world. Neither has there been someone like him before nor would there ever be. Then, why all these comparisons?! When two faces amongst billions are not identical, then do you think two people can have the same mind or life? If there is any similarity amongst human beings, then it is their desire to attain success and lead happy lives. And these teachings that encourage comparison have proved to be the biggest hindrance in their quest to achieve this.

Just observe the growing children and at the same time reflect upon your own actions too. Children do not discriminate on the grounds of economic or social status of the ones they play with; all that they are concerned about is, playing. But the so-called intelligent adults not only restrain the happily playing child and summon him home, but also ingrain into his mind that the child he was playing with was 'inferior' to him; and thus they sow the seeds of comparison in the child's mind. And then there are the schools!! They teach nothing but comparisons, which make the child's complexes, grow even deeper and stronger.

Then making comparisons gradually becomes the very nature of the human being, which is even more dangerous. Now whether it is the prevalent society or religion, education or ideologies, ultimately they too, are nothing but the creations of human beings. Here too, he has not been able to desist from indulging in his habit of comparison. The height is, he has even drawn comparisons among rivers – the Ganges is holy and the others are ordinary. Our country, our religion is great, everything else is nonsensical. Thus the child, who is already burdened by thousands of complexes, is further weighed down with comparisons by religion and society. Alas! What a destiny children have! They inherit the property of their parents much later in life, but very early in life they inherit the complexes acquired by their parents from the society and the religion adopted by them.

Well! I hope that by now, you must have grasped how complexes are developed in an individual in his childhood. And you must have also understood how the teachings that promote or lead to comparison lie at the root of all these complexes. Now try to understand what precisely a complex is. It is a feeling which comes from the belief that you have a privation or a shortcoming or you are weak or inferior to others on any account, whereas, in reality, that is not the case; neither do you lack anything nor are you inferior to anyone. The truth is YOU ARE WHO YOU ARE. This implies that you are unique and the only one of your kind in this world. And when you are distinct, unique and one of a kind, there cannot be any comparison whatsoever!

If you have grasped this well, then let me share a peculiar aspect of Complex with you. You may be surprised to know that there is only one kind of Complex and that is, Inferiority Complex. Nothing called Superiority Complex exists. Shocking, is it not?! You must have seen many people plagued by Superiority Complex. The reason why I have initiated a discussion on this topic is to clear the air around this notion. For further elucidation, let us revisit the point of how an individual acquires a Complex. I have brought to your notice umpteen times that a Complex is born out of drawing comparisons. And these comparisons are usually made only to prove that you are inferior to others. As a consequence, gradually even you begin to find shortcomings in yourself, and it is from here on that the vicious cycle begins. During the initial stages, you try to overcome these shortcomings, but when you are unable to overcome them, you don the garb of Superiority in order to hide it from the world. In other words, the Superiority Complex that you know is nothing but certain acts and behaviour you use as a shield to hide your inner pains, weaknesses or shortcomings from others. Meaning, the numerous Superiority Complexes evident in humans are the reflections of the inferiorities hidden in them. Hence, in reality, there is no such thing as Superiority Complex! Thus, if you are able to grasp this, then in no time, you will easily be able to gauge what is going on within a person or how his life is being spent. Then it will not be difficult for you to recognise the inferiority lurking in his inner being. And you will also be able to accurately identify the pain behind his every inferiority.

Come, let us get a clear understanding of complex through some examples and see how, the inferiority hidden in a person manifests

A Complex is a gift given by others

in the disguise of superiority. For example, an elderly couple is visiting you at your house. Their sons are married and they all live together as one big joint family. Now, if the couple is unhappy with their sons and daughters-in-law or they feel deprived of care, you will find them harping about how their sons and daughters-in-law are taking good care of them! This irrelevant, ad nauseam repetition of the statement which appears to be their superiority is actually nothing, but an indication of the deep anguish they feel within. And for a sensible person, a mere indication is enough. Understand clearly that a person rambles on and repeats irrelevant things again and again only when he is feeling something exactly contrary to it within himself.

The above-mentioned point can also be understood thus; during the course of a conversation, when someone abruptly says, "What are you saying! I am still young." It clearly indicates that this person is not young anymore. The person making such statements would at least be nearing his fifties, if not more. As no youngster will ever say, "I am still young"; would that not sound absurd? The gist of my discussion is, a smug reiteration of something over and over again is indicative of the lack of that particular thing within. Therefore, rather than construing it as his Superiority Complex, please recognise this as an indication of the inferiority hidden within him. And see, how quickly this will enable you to recognise the real sorrows of other people.

And the amusing part is, no one pays attention to the funny acts that this cloak of Superiority makes an individual indulge in. However, from now onwards if you closely observe, you will be able to see at least a couple of such instances daily around you. The truth is, this superiority that a human being has cloaked himself with, has reduced him to being a mere puppet and an object of ridicule, but still, he lives in a fool's paradise. As often observed, many wives are conceited enough to think that their husbands dance to their tunes; even their children listen to them obediently. However, this may not necessarily be the case in reality. Let us understand this fact with an example...

One day a child asked his father, "Papa, may I go out to play?"

The father said, "I would not stop you from going out to play. Playing is anyway good for a child's health. But your mama may not let you go."

The son got upset. He began to think of ways to convince his mother... Even his father was racking his brains over it. Just then, the father recalled the inferiority complex his wife suffered from. Happily, he told the child, "Go tell mama that I want to go out to play, but Papa is not allowing me to go, and your work will be done!"

The son quickly ran to his mother crying, and repeated the lines his father had tutored him. Hearing this, the mother's ego flared up. In retaliation, she haughtily said, "Go...go and play! Let me see how your father stops you?" Now, did you see how the father-son duo together swung the situation to their advantage? No sooner did the mother's inferiority manifest itself externally as superiority, than she turned into nothing but a mere puppet in the hands of the father and son.

Let me recount another beautiful tale as an example. One day, unbelievably, following in the footsteps of human beings, even a lion's cub caught an inferiority complex! Actually what happened was, this meek cub was being repeatedly compared to the other ferocious cubs of his age. Due to these constant comparisons, he started feeling that he was extremely weak at hunting and other activities befitting the king of the jungle. One day, this repressed inferiority, assumed the form of superiority...and to what effect? He began to walk deep into the jungle. He was hell-bent on proving to the world that he had all the qualities of the king of the jungle. He had barely walked a few steps, when he caught sight of a deer. He roared from afar and asked, "Do you know who I am?"

The deer was stunned and scared! However, the deer quickly regained his composure. And in a timid and meek voice, replied, "You are a lion, the king of this jungle."

On hearing the deer utter the words 'lion' and 'king', the cub was elated. His hidden inferiority had now turned into the pride of

Every human being in this world is exceptional

being a king. He signalled the deer to leave, and after this exchange, puffed with vanity he began to strut along. He had walked just a few steps, when he saw a vixen coming his way. Roaring aloud, he made the vixen stop in her tracks. Already elated, he posed a straight question to the vixen, "Tell me, who is the king of the jungle?"

The vixen, being a cunning animal by nature, knew in a jiffy that the lion's cub was suffering from an inferiority complex. Very cleverly, assuaging the inferiority of the cub, reverentially she replied, "You are the future king of the jungle. And to tell you the truth, even at present, I see all the qualities of a great king in you." Now the lion's cub, who was already bloated with conceit, became ecstatic with pride. His complex had peaked. Now as he was moving further, his swagger had a new rhythm altogether. Just then, he noticed an elephant approaching from a distance. Completely intoxicated with superiority, the cub walked towards the elephant. As he reached the elephant, he asked him in the same arrogant manner, "Hey, you Elephant, tell me, who is the king of the jungle?"

Now an elephant is who he is. He did not pay any heed to the cub. The cub repeated the question a couple of times, but the elephant did not respond. By now, the earth beneath the cub's feet was shaken, but to maintain his newly acquired stance, the cub sprang up to the elephant's ear and asked, "Tell me, who is the king of the jungle?"

The elephant, who till now was ignoring the cub, did not approve of his behaviour. He did not bother about what was right or wrong, and just twirled his trunk around the cub, spun him in the air, and flung him far away. The poor lion's cub was badly bruised. Still, the cub somehow mustered courage, and limping, he went near the elephant. Trying to make himself stand on his hind feet, he then said in a meek voice, "Brother Elephant, if you did not know the answer, you could have said so, but what was the need to be so angry?"

Similarly, every individual afflicted by complex is always looking for ways to show off his superiority. And in the end, even they meet the same fate as that of the lion's cub. Therefore, if you want to stop yourself from becoming an object of ridicule time and again, please do not compare yourself with anyone, else very soon, you too will find yourself afflicted by innumerable complexes. And then, in order to hide those complexes, you will don the garb of various kinds of superiorities. But what you do not have in you, you simply do not have! Hence, you will face the music time and again for every complex of yours. Understand, drawing comparisons is the way of the world, let them do it; you please keep yourself away from all these idiocies.

Let me also make it clear that the list of losses incurred on account of complexes does not end here. On the contrary, this is just the tip of the iceberg. As soon as a man plagued by numerous inferiorities begins to don the garb of superiority, it starts having an adverse impact on his mind. And in this regard, one of the biggest undoing of man is, he begins to become 'a hypocrite'. Hypocrisy too, is a very strange and dangerous illness. When the importance of a particular thing is reiterated on numerous occasions with or without a reason, a human being is bound to get attracted towards it. Initially man tries to mould himself accordingly, but in spite of numerous attempts, when he is unable to do so, he embraces it superficially. And this is how hypocrisy enters his life. Man uses hypocrisy as a tool not only to don the virtues superficially, but also to skilfully conceal his weaknesses.

But this, in turn, gives rise to another question; how does one classify what virtues or vices are? Is it not true that if certain beliefs and

" Comparison is the progenitor of all the
complexes of a human being "

perceptions which are labelled as good or virtues by society in general,
he too considers them virtues and those which people perceive as bad
in general, are perceived as bad by him too? Yes, but in reality these
are not the criteria on which things can be judged as good or bad. But
poor man! In order to portray himself as a good human being, and
shield himself from others' criticism, he begins to externally adopt the
behaviour that others want him to. But then, what is not there within is
simply not there. Merely by embracing things superficially, he not only
troubles himself, but also makes a fool of himself. And then slowly and
gradually, even the tasks that are most natural to human beings, cause
him great distress.

Let me cite an example to explain the same. Once, a carefree
boy suddenly began to remain depressed. Had it been for a couple of
days, it would have been fine, but when it persisted for a longer spell,
it became a matter of concern for the family. However, despite being

asked numerous times, the boy did not open up. Perplexed, his parents decided to seek the help of a religious guru. At the meeting, the religious guru wanted to understand the reason for the boy's gloom by talking to him in private. The boy disclosed to him his fantasies about girls. The moment the religious guru heard this, he raised his brow and exclaimed, "What?" He lost his cool and reprimanded the young boy. He also prescribed him several religious practices to abstain from falling prey to fantasies.

But how could that have helped? On the contrary, the boy was now even more ridden with guilt. The incident had further aggravated his problem and fuelled his melancholy. Just think, can religious practices ever vanquish carnal thoughts? Never...so, these thoughts still persisted in him. But the religious head had deeply ingrained in the boy's mind the idea that such thoughts are forbidden acts, which made it all the more bothersome for him. Finally exasperated with his deteriorating condition, his parents consulted a psychiatrist. As soon as the psychiatrist heard of his predicament, he began to laugh. Between peals of laughter, he said, "This is a very natural instinct. If he had not desired such things at this age, then I would have definitely treated him." Listening to these words from the psychiatrist, the young boy was immediately relieved, the sheath of imposed conditioning was dropped and he became happy once again.

The point that I wish to highlight here is, societal distinctions of virtues or vices are

In reality there is no such thing as a Superiority Complex

obviously not the criteria to judge what is right or wrong. A human being should not give importance to such matters. Moreover, paying heed to such societal distinctions or being swayed by other's influence, a person should not even think of changing himself superficially, otherwise it brings in numerous serious ill-effects in its wake. The biggest consequence of such hypocrisy is, from this one 'ME', innumerable 'MEs' are born. Then, man goes on to masquerade himself with many faces, and every mask he wears becomes a hindrance to him in living his life wholeheartedly. Thus, the crux of my discussion is, the more the number of 'MEs' a person has, the more distressed he is. And the worst part is, as he goes through this process, the individual slowly forgets his real 'ME', out of all the innumerable egoistic 'MEs' that he has enveloped himself with.

The end result of this entire process is, the attribute of firmness gradually begins to erode from a human being. And I need not explain to anyone how important this quality of firmness is. Try to understand my statement by drawing parallels to some instances from your day-to-day life and you will find this fact proven right at every instance of your life. Well, for now, let me try to explain it to you with the help of an example. Once, at seven o'clock in the evening, a boy told his father, "Wake me up at five in the morning, I wish to go for a walk." The moment he uttered these words, his second 'ME' said, *"Why did you ask dad to wake you up at five? Do you not know, you have a practical test in college tomorrow? If you wake up so early, would you not be sleepy during the exams?"* Right then, a third 'me' surfaced, *"What are you saying, you must wake up. If you rejuvenate yourself with a morning walk, you will fare much better in the practical exams."*

But the moment he had his dinner at nine in the night, laziness crept in and a fourth thought struck him, *"No no! I do not want to get up so early in the morning."* And the boy asked his father not to wake him up in the morning. But how can the trail of indecisiveness of a person who has lost his firmness, end here? After his meal, watching television till eleven, his lethargy had subsided to a large extent. And just before he was about to sleep, a fifth 'ME' sprung into action, *"What a waste of a bright and sunny morning it would be, if I do not wake up and go for a walk."* Immediately, he again requested his father to wake him up early.

His father agreed, but when his father woke him up at five in the morning, half asleep, a sixth 'ME' mumbled angrily, "Is this the time to wake someone up? Do you want me to wake up now and sleep during the practical exams?"

The father was surprised. "He had asked to be woken up and now, he is getting angry at me!" Well! The boy once again fell back into deep sleep and his father left the room. But then the funniest part was, after waking up and finishing his morning chores, when he sat for breakfast, he regretted not being able to wake up and go for the morning walk. He even told his father, "Even if I refused to go because I was sleepy, you should have forcibly woken me up."

Hearing this, his father who was surprised earlier was now flummoxed. For a moment, he was even forced to think whether his son had completely lost his sanity. If you ask me, I have no doubts that he had; however, you are free to draw your own conclusion. Maybe he had or he hadn't, but the real issue for most people is, such incidents are a routine occurrence in their life. Being enveloped in hypocrisy, their one 'ME' has multiplied into a thousand 'MEs'. And then, the rest of their life is spent battling their very own innumerable 'MEs'. And as for the masquerading...It indeed mutates into so many 'MEs', that finding your true self amongst those 'MEs' becomes almost impossible. Then even if the individual tries to find his true self, he is not able to, as he has one face in front of his friends and another in front of his social acquaintances. He is different with his wife and different while interacting with other family members. He has a different face at home, and a different one at office, different while interacting with the peon, and different in front of the boss. The situation becomes so complicated that it becomes difficult for him to face the boss and the peon at the same time. He knows what image he must project to his friends and which one in front of his family; but his state becomes ludicrous if he has to face friends and family together as he is completely

You will never be able to rid yourself of Complex without accepting yourself as you are

clueless about which 'ME' to portray then. If you notice, you will realise, most of you often try to avoid such meetings, and this is nothing but the result of the many faces that you have put on. Now think for yourself, what kind of a life is this? You are what you are, then why so many 'MEs' and masks? Let people see you for who you are. Why hide anything from anyone? In these futile efforts, unnecessarily you end up losing your precious firmness. And without firmness, how do you expect any fruitful result to follow in life? Your life is bound to be a failure.

And then, when it comes to inflicting human beings with complexes, there is no match for our religious heads as, the complexes that they ingrain in human beings are extremely dangerous. Even the most basic and the most natural acts of human beings are deemed as sins by them... Now how can a man do away with what is very basic and natural? As all this sinks in over a period of time, it gives rise to a feeling of sinfulness in him. The feeling of self-condemnation pervades his very being, and nothing can be more destructive for a person than self-condemnation.

But neither do these religious gurus understand me i.e. the mind, nor do they posses knowledge about life. Well, they do not need it either. All that they are concerned with is furthering their fame and multiplying their wealth. Why would they care about how it impacts human beings? So, they hand out a list of 'sins' to you such as eating, roaming around, wealth, enjoying life, anger, not visiting religious shrines and so on. If you do not wake up early in the morning, that too is a sin and if you eat late at night that too is a sin; now I ask you, what is all this?

Obviously, you cannot always follow their preaching in life; hence you begin to embrace them superficially. But, what is the use of embracing something superficially for 'appearances' sake' if you do not believe in it and it is not there in you? You are unnecessarily turning into a hypocrite. A majority of your so-called religious heads are hypocrites anyway, and that too, to such an extent, that behind closed doors, they themselves freely indulge in whatever they forbid you to do.

Let me tell you an interesting story relevant to the above point. You may remember what Jesus had said, "If someone slaps you on one cheek, turn to them the other one also." Now what the statement implies or what Jesus intended to convey, need not be explained to anyone.

But, who is going to explain this to the priests and pastors? So, one day, this verse of Jesus created an amazing scene. A priest was going to deliver a sermon about the same verse. The event was extensively publicised as well. But one mischief monger could not accept the fact that if he was slapped on one cheek, how could he offer the other cheek? *"Let me go and see"*, he thought, and reached the church on time.

The priest started his sermon at the scheduled time. The delivery of the sermon was persuasive enough to bring out the true essence of Jesus' preaching. He expounded upon the verse in a manner as if the verse were his own. Listening to his splendid sermon, for once, even the mischief monger was taken aback. But then he thought, why not satiate my curiosity once and for all?

Thus, as soon as the sermon was over, he immediately went up to the priest and in front of everyone, slapped him on his cheek. The priest was beside himself with anger. Even the crowd was stunned. However, the priest was clever; he knew that he had just delivered the sermon; hence he had to practise what he had just preached. Laughing, he immediately held out his other cheek to the mischief monger.

Seeing this, momentarily even the mischief monger was baffled, but then he immediately regained his composure. He was also a very determined person. He thought when the curiosity has to be satisfied, why not in its entirety? It is not good to leave a task halfway. So he landed an even tighter slap on his other cheek. Now the priest could not contain his anger and bashed him. The mischief monger kept on shouting, "Just now, you were preaching the verse of Jesus; you must practise what you preached. And look at you! You yourself are indulging in such violence!"

The priest while still thrashing him, said, "I have followed the word of God. I even held my second cheek out to you. Well, Jesus has not mentioned a third cheek. And anyways, there is no third cheek."

The question is who is forcing you? There are innumerable things that are good and worthy of learning. But you will learn them as per the dictates of your nature. However, the habit of listening to something and embracing it superficially - is what I fail to understand. And then, why do you not understand that even if the priest had not thrashed him, what would it have proven? The priest had already become angry when he was slapped! Then what was the use of hiding it in behaviour?

No...This hypocrisy cannot bring about any improvement in you. Moreover, it is not in the interest of your present, as it will only lead you to stoop further. Over and above that, hypocrisy blocks the roads to your improvement. Since you wear the garb of goodness in appearance, in reality you do not feel the need to actually improve yourself. But improvement is an internal necessity not an external cosmetic.

Why do you not realise that the exalted personages such as Buddha, Jesus and Krishna are born once in several centuries. Well, you must learn from them, idolise them or even try to become like them, but your goal is very high and your journey, very long. How can you forsake your present for these far-fetched goals? Yes, you must focus on your inner growth but live in the present and enjoy your journey towards your aim to become like them. But do you think superficially embracing their clothes and conduct will help you in any way? If your present is not taken care of, or if it is in tatters, leave alone becoming like them, would you not slip from your existent position and your condition deteriorate further?

Take a look at children. They do not have any complex in them. And in absence of complex, they neither have a thousand 'masks' nor a million 'MEs'. This is the reason why, children possess amazing firmness. You must have noticed that once children become obstinate about something, they will not budge until they have got their wish fulfilled.

In short, what I mean to say is, the various teachings adopted by the human brain that induce comparison are largely responsible for their lives being full of sorrows and failures. Because, these teachings corrupt the human mind; slowly and gradually, man begins to lose his self-confidence which results in him contracting several complexes. And then, to hide this inferiority, he dons the garb of superiority. He becomes a hypocrite, owing to which, his thousand 'MEs' and numerous faces are developed. And these thousand 'MEs' rob him of his firmness. And it is a law that the one, who does not have firmness in him, can never do anything worthwhile in life.

Therefore, I humbly request you to accept yourself the way you are. Never lose the confidence you have placed in yourself. Because wherever and whatever you are, it is only from that point, that you will discover the path to prosper in life. For that, all you need to do is, refrain from making any effort to change yourself forcefully by paying heed to the comparisons made by others. Whether you are good or bad, clever or naive, rich or poor, beautiful or ordinary...accept yourself! Accept not only yourself, but also your shortcomings. Because a majority of them have been thrust upon you by others. Believe me, in reality, all of these are not necessarily your weaknesses. Therefore, ingrain it in your mind that you are absolutely perfect just as you are in the present. And see how a majority of your complexes will get eliminated by themselves.

Similarly, accept others also the way they are. Now, if someone is earning more, so what? Let him earn! Adopting such a line of thought will further lead to the elimination of a few more complexes. And when you have freed yourself from a majority of complexes, carefully introspect. Make a list of the areas where you actually feel the need to change yourself. And then, try to change by communicating with yourself everyday in solitude for half an hour. Then whenever and how much ever you change, it is fine. If you are not able to change yourself in some of them, drop the desire for that particular change, but never develop a complex. Steer clear of the feelings of 'sin' and 'self-condemnation' because all this will go on forever, but ultimately, you have to live the life that you have got. So, at least do not waste your life being trapped in these futile things.

It is your life, and it is only you, who has to change or improve. Therefore, you ought to decide, when and how much you must change in life. Then whatever change you are able to bring about, be content with it. Accept yourself the way you are at all times and move ahead in life. Very soon, you will become a person brimming with abundant firmness and energy. Then sorrows and grievances will not even dare to rear their ugly heads in your life.

Involvement

If you wish that your sorrows should abate, reduce your involvement* in people, objects, thoughts or ideologies. It is your involvement which is the root cause of your innumerable futile sorrows. Henceforth, whenever you are sad or worried, try to find out the reason behind that particular sorrow or worry. You will be stunned to discover that your nature of getting involved is the reason behind a majority of your miseries and worries. Let me explain this in a manner that will shock you out of your complacency. You think that you love your family, but to tell you the truth, it is not love, it is involvement.

Shocked? Do not be! In order to make you understand this, let me enlighten you about the fine difference between love and involvement which is definitely worth understanding, and once grasped, also worth imbibing in life. Love means that you surely wish the best for a person, but claim no ownership. Whereas in the case of involvement you feel a sense of ownership - a sense of possession over the individual. And it is this sense of possession that is called involvement. As a result, even a scratch suffered by that person bothers you, because knowingly or unknowingly, you have believed him to be a part of you, whereas in reality, no one can ever become a part of your existence.

Understand this and do not try to interpret my complicated mechanism with wrong definitions. Indeed the very act of defining my mechanism with the help of the brain, has led you to lose your bearing. Therefore, it is imperative for you to realise the difference between the brain and the mind, otherwise, deluded, you will end up committing the same mistakes over and over again. Hence, regardless

* Involvement - In this book, involvement denotes a deep affinity and attachment towards people and things.

of the extent to which your brain convinces you, the truth is, you do not love anyone. Oh! Love is a profound word. But you have undermined its definition, and have construed your weakness - the habit of getting involved - as love. Love is the name of an 'all-encompassing emotion', that desires the best for every individual or thing in the world, including oneself, without any bias. In short, love aspires for universal betterment, whereas, you want it for a selected few, in bits and pieces. Your desire for happiness is limited to only your near and dear ones, with no regard to the betterment of the world or well-being of fellow human beings. Then, what kind of love is this? This is nothing but your involvement with a few individuals. Now, if you are partial, indulge in erroneous deeds, and act against my laws and that of Nature's, you will have to face the repercussions in the form of sorrows and worries.

Now take a look at your own nature. You are walking on the street and someone meets with an accident. He is bleeding profusely. For a moment, it definitely upsets you, but then, you soon return to your current activity. However, if the same tragedy occurs with any of your family member or your loved one, then? Till the time he or she does not recover, you remain engulfed in a whirlpool of grief and worries. Why? Both are human beings! Both have bled! The difference is, you are involved with one, and not with the other. Had your nature been of love, you would have either been equally sad in both cases, or remained unperturbed in both. But you are paying the price for considering someone other than yourself, as 'your own'. I hope, now you must have understood the difference between love and involvement. Love is a mighty quality; whereas involvement is its perverse form.

So now, let us cast a glance at the other ill-effects of involvement as well. Ironically, it is due to involvement that you are unable to protect or act in the best interests of even those, who you truly consider your 'own'.

Funnily enough, you end up making life miserable for the very person who you consider your own, because in the wake of your involvement, you sometimes harrow or trouble each other by exercising your right over one another, or at times, become unhappy seeing each other in a troubled condition. This is not the case with one or two, but everyone who you are involved with. This is the reason why everyone becomes so tense and troubled at the slightest instance. Now think, when managing your own self has become an uphill task for you, does worrying about a dozen other people spare you with enough energy to actually take care of anyone? No…if the extent of your worry is limited to yourself alone, there are chances that you may be left with some energy to do something for someone. But, due to this nature of involvement your problems multiply exponentially. This is the reason why you find every other person stressed, lethargic and lifeless. After all, your capacity to absorb shock too has a threshold, does it not? Agreed that insanity can be treated with shock treatment, but there is a limit to the frequency of those shocks as well. Therefore, understand well that the more people you are involved with, the greater will be the magnitude of problems in your life.

However, it is beyond my comprehension how multiplying your own problems can be considered an act of intelligence! Also, it is difficult to understand how such a weak individual will be able to take care of himself or others. Why do you not understand that in order to bring about an effective change or positive result for yourself as well as others, you need energy. And what more can be said about the energy of the one who is gripped by grief and worry at the slightest instance? Also, think over how you ended up terming this sorrow-causing insanity as love, when it is actually involvement.

What is even more ridiculous is, the ones who worry for others at the slightest instance have been termed as emotional beings by you! You do not pay attention to the fact that these very emotional beings who just keep harbouring anxieties, prove to be of no use to anyone. Henceforth, cogitate on who exactly are those labelled as emotional beings. They are nothing but a total liability, who are good for nothing. Often, when you learn about a relative's sickness and someone is needed to tend to them, and if by chance, an emotional being reaches the scene, the grand show he puts up is nothing short of marvellous.

Seeing the patient's illness, his own condition deteriorates to such an extent, that he has to be admitted on the bed beside the patient! What is even more comical is, the patient recovers, but it becomes difficult for the emotional being to recover from the trauma. Many a time, it has been seen that the patient whom he has gone to see, actually has to nurse him. Therefore, from today onwards, if you carefully observe your family members and friends, you will realise that in reality, only those who seem to be less sensitive are actually the people who have proven to be useful at the need of the hour. They may not sit with you very often and share your grief, but during times of trouble, they are the ones who actually show solidarity and stand with you in support.

So overall, involvement is not only the root of all your sorrows and worries, but is also the catalyst that rapidly increases your sorrows and worries. Therefore, you will first need to stop glorifying this involvement of yours. Segregate it and separate it from words such as love and other emotions; at least do not confuse involvement with other positive emotions. If you really wish to get rid of it, then you will have to perceive it as a fatal affliction. I hereby promise that once you recognise involvement as an affliction, all the sorrows and worries will begin to dissipate from your life. Simultaneously, your energy levels will also shoot up and your state of mind too will become positive and joyous. Only then would you be able to share or associate yourself with the process of improving your life as well as that of others.

I hope you have grasped it well. Now proceeding further, another dangerous aspect of your nature of involvement is that it increases and spreads its web day-by-day. Once if you are gripped by involvement, then it rapidly grows and spreads its tentacles within you. After that it does not remain restricted to a few individuals or your near and dear ones. Slowly and steadily, this habit induces you to get involved and identify yourself with each and every thing. Involvement then runs so deep in your veins that you become involved even where it is not necessary. And if you observe carefully, you have not spared even religion and earth. You strut around being a Hindu, Muslim, Christian or Buddhist. However, you fail to understand how this pride is depriving you of so many joys. Identifying with one religion, in the end, only serves to add fuel to the fire of your nature of involvement. For instance, you have identified yourself with Christianity and being a Christian serves no purpose or reaps no benefit, but still you must understand that your habit of involvement definitely serves to magnify your sorrows and worries.

Then you divided the world, demarcated your countries and became involved in them as well. And as if that was not enough, you then cloaked your involvement in the garb of a beautiful word - Patriotism. I say, why not love the earth and the entire Universe? Why do you not consider the entire Universe as yours? When everything, every element in Nature has embraced all human beings equally without reservations, why can you not? Why are you accepting some and rejecting the others?

You may be able to rationalise it at the level of the brain, but at my level i.e. at the level of the mind, it makes no sense. Please do not confuse yourself with these lofty words, rather make an effort to understand the reality of my nature. I am mischievous by nature and these divisions which are the creations of your brain are beyond my comprehension. My system of functioning is simple; no sooner does your attachment or affinity for something grows, than I recognise it to be your habit and immediately fan the fire of your nature of involvement. And the moment your involvement increases, you begin to get afflicted by innumerable new types of miseries and worries.

Ironically, the game involvement is playing with you is right in front of your eyes, and gradually, it has extended the sphere of its influence beyond people, and now it has made you develop an attachment for your wealth, your house and many other things too. Certainly, it is due to your habit of getting involved that all these attachments have come to exist. In a way, there is nothing wrong with having an attachment for your house, your wealth or your business, but then, the moment there is a threat to your house or your wealth, you are besieged with stress for months at times. But what is the use? Is somebody going to snatch your house away if you do not get involved? No...It is still going to remain yours. Then enjoy it! Why do you get attached to it? Moreover, what are you gaining by involving yourself with it? Caught in this vicious trap, as it is you are unable to enjoy anything and if something goes wrong with any of them, you become grief-stricken too. Scrap this loss-making deal and enjoy what you have in the present. Who is stopping you? But then why create circumstances which compel you to be involved and lead you to mourn over its losses? Always bear in mind; be it relations or objects, only the one who is not involved can enjoy them whole-heartedly.

Let me explain the same fact with a beautiful example. The story goes back to ancient times. In the Indian epic, Ramayana, there was a King named Janaka who was the epitome of wisdom. He had overcome all my perversities; consequently, he was brimming with my powers. King Janaka was the father of Sita, the much revered consort of Lord Rama. Such was the height of his wisdom that, he was a man devoid of involvement. He was called the Videha i.e. a totally detached man. There was no person or thing that could affect him in anyway. So much so, that when his daughter, Sita had to unnecessarily spend fourteen years in the wilderness, during which she was even kidnapped; it did not bother Videha Janaka for a single moment. He believed that when it came to Life and Karma, it was each to his own!

As he was a man totally devoid of involvement, the reputation of his wisdom had to spread far and wide. Many scholarly sages and saints of the time revered him as a paragon of virtue. Now, the best part was, since Janaka was devoid of involvement in anything or anybody, he did not need to possess or dispossess anything. Hence, naturally, after he gained wisdom, he neither abdicated his throne nor did he bring about a change in his routine of enjoying life, for, there was no reason to change. He was especially fond of wine and dance. Late in the evenings, gatherings were often held at the palace which saw an evocative blend of music, dance and freely flowing wine, reflective of his royal lifestyle. As a result, like his wisdom, his passionate pursuits were also equally famous.

" No individual or thing possesses the power to make a person unhappy "

Well! In those days, there also lived a famous guru. Inquisitive students would come from far off places to acquire knowledge from him. Most students were obedient, but one obstinate student, in spite of the arduous efforts made by the guru, was unable to rid himself of his involvement even though he desired to. Though he had renounced his home and family, and had begun to live in the ashram*, he still missed them. However the guru was not the one to give up easily. He was determined to help his student get rid of attachment towards his family. His efforts were not yielding even a sliver of progress. Tired, the guru finally summoned the student and asked him to acquire wisdom from King Janaka. The student was stunned by his guru's command, as he had heard a lot about Janaka's hedonistic indulgences and passionate pursuits. He thought, *"When King Janaka himself is in need of wisdom, what wisdom could he possibly impart unto me?"* However, since the guru's command could not be disobeyed, the next morning, he left for King Janaka's palace with a

*Ashram - A hermitage, monastic community or other place of religious retreat.

143

pair of clothes and a letter from his guru. Now, although he had left to meet King Janaka, it was still difficult for him to digest the fact that an individual like Janaka could impart any wisdom unto him. His ego on the contrary made him think, "Of all the people, why Janaka? Maybe I could impart wisdom to Janaka, and thus not only break the guru's illusions about him, but also prove myself wise."

Thus, consumed by his ego, he reached the palace of King Janaka. Now, the guru, whose letter the student was carrying along was a highly revered man in Janaka's court. Therefore, the moment he handed over the letter, he was presented before the King. On seeing the student, Janaka promptly gauged the course of action to be followed. He immediately made arrangements for the student's stay in one of the grand rooms in the palace itself and asked him to rest and return to him in the evening...then, he would impart the wisdom the student was seeking.

This was as far as King Janaka was concerned. As for the student, on seeing Janaka's impressive grandeur, he swaggered even more arrogantly. He was consumed by the conceit of changing his guru's perception of King Janaka. It was not the student's fault; in the blurry mist of delusion a majority of saints and hermits in India have misunderstood renunciation, sacrifice and austerity for religion. They are strongly against women, and in general, the joy of life itself; even this student subscribed to the same school of thought. Therefore, with this definition of religion as the foundation of his knowledge, it was natural for him to be gripped by ego.

Anyway, evening was not far off. As soon as dusk set in, the student was ushered into the entertainment hall to be presented before King Janaka. Obviously, it was time for the exquisite performances of the dancers and singers. Janaka asked the student to sit next to him and enjoy the performances. But since such sensuous activities were considered a sin by the student, it was difficult for him to remain seated there. He requested Janaka to grant him an audience in the morning to which Janaka agreed, and asked the student to meet him in his chambers, early in the morning. Janaka laughed to himself at the conduct of the student and thought, *"If he really had no interest in singing and dancing, what was the need to run away from here? This meant that somewhere deep down this dancing and singing did affect him."* Understand, at my level, every action always has a two-way reaction i.e. Involvement is not necessarily about having a sense of ownership over something, but also the act of running away from something that affects you.

Since this is a very important point, I will explain it to you with yet another beautiful instance. As I said, many monks are living in imperious conceit, considering women and indulgence as sin. They seem to have forgotten that they owe their very existence to women. However, at any given time, there has never been a dearth of Gurukuls* in India. Some Gurukuls were founded and run by wise men, while others by ignorant ones. The instance that I am now about to narrate, is that of a prudent guru and his Gurukul, known for its academic excellence. This guru had a unique method of imparting knowledge to his students. In order to help his students get rid of their involvement, he would ask them to abstain from being attached to a particular thing for a month. This month, he had forbidden them from being involved in women. One more peculiarity worth a mention about these Gurukuls is that no student ever disobeyed the command of his guru.

Well, barely a few days after this command was given, four-five students who were out on a stroll, happened to reach the

A human being is unhappy because of his involvement with things & people

* Gurukuls – A residential school in India where students stay in close proximity with the teacher.

Any kind of choice or having any kind of preference fuels your involvement

banks of the river. It was the monsoons and Nature was at its playful best; the river raged as the water flowed with full gusto. A woman, having a house on the other shore was stranded at the river bank. Due to the raging torrent, she was unable to muster the courage to get across the river. At about the same time, these students also happened to reach there. The moment she sighted them, the woman saw a glimmer of hope and pleaded with them to help her cross the river. Hearing her cry for help, one of the students replied in an arrogant manner, "Impossible! This month, our guru has commanded us not to be involved in women." All the other students supported his stance, with the exception of one, who immediately lifted the woman on his shoulders, helped her cross the river and returned. *Such an act of defiance! He had disobeyed the command of his guru!* He was reprimanded by all his fellow students. All through their way back, his fellow students kept tormenting him with taunts.

However, it did not stop with only the condemnation. Upon reaching the Gurukul, the students promptly narrated the incident of his disobedience to their guru. But, to everyone's surprise, the guru was delighted to hear this; he instantly embraced the student and said, "Great! At least one person has rid himself of involvement." Upon hearing this, the other students were shocked. They thought, *"What? Did the sun rise from the west? How could the guru retract his own command?"* On seeing the stunned expressions on their faces, to assuage their curiosity, the guru said, "You see, he was able to help the woman cross the river because at that time, he had actually risen above his involvement in women. Had women been affecting him even a bit at that time, he too would have declined to help her like you all did. And secondly what I can see clearly is, he helped the woman cross the river and forgot about it, but you are all still carrying that woman on your shoulders." It is true; any act performed at a physical level holds no significance! The importance lies in what transpires at my level i.e. at the level of the mind.

Hopefully, you must have grasped the double-edged effects of involvement. So now, let us return to the story of King Janaka. Even Janaka was stunned, on seeing the involvement of that student towards dance and music, since it was just because of involvement that he had fled from the hall. Well, now the night had passed and at the break of dawn, the student reached Janaka's room well in time. However, since Janaka was resting, he asked the student to sit peacefully next to him for a while. But the student had run out of patience. He pleaded with Janaka, "Look! My guru has sent me to gain wisdom from you, so please impart it unto me, so that I can take your leave. Being a sanyasi, I am not comfortable in your grand palace." Janaka peeped into his eyes and said, "Alright! First, let us have a bath. Come, there is a beautiful lake behind the palace where we shall take a bath, then I will impart wisdom unto you."

The student readily agreed, for he thought, *"Fine. What is the harm in bathing in a lake? If he had invited me to bathe in a pool, then I may have thought, what does a sanyasi have to do with splendour."* And both began to walk towards the lake. But before leaving, Janaka called his commander-in-chief and whispered something in his ears. Upon reaching the lake, both of them took a plunge. However, even while bathing, there was no exchange of words between both. While Janaka was enjoying his bath, the student had become anxious about when his bath would end. That was when all of a sudden, Janaka's palace was engulfed in flames. Seeing the inferno right in front of his eyes, the student was baffled. He said to Janaka who was enjoying his bath, "Your palace is ablaze and my clothes are in there." Janaka paid no heed to his utterance and continued enjoying his bath. Seeing Janaka still quietly enjoying his bath, the student was stunned and the realisation dawned upon him,*"Though Janaka's entire palace is up in flames, he is still relishing the moment, whereas I, who have only a pair of clothes inside, am gripped by worry"*. He had gained the wisdom his guru wanted him to. The question is definitely not about what and how much you possess; it is also not about whether a particular thing interests you or not; the question is only of whether you are involved in it or not. If you are involved, neither can you enjoy it, nor can you bear the grief when it is separated from you. The same was the case with the student as well. Not only was he unable to enjoy his bath, but due to his involvement, he also had to endure the stress of his clothes getting burnt. Well, the student could get rid of his involvement because he had found a sagacious wise man such as King Janaka. However, you will have to get rid of this menace called 'involvement' only by reading this parable.

Nevertheless, in the end, I am giving you two tips to weaken your nature of involvement. Involvement gets strengthened by two habits; one, partiality and the other, choice. If you want to get rid of the sorrows that involvement brings in its wake, then firstly, keep yourself away from being partial. For example, even if you believe in a particular religion, do not confine yourself to that religion alone, but embrace all the other religions existing on this earth. Do not fall in the trap of 'mine' and 'yours'. If the sorrows of one individual affect you, then you will have to learn to be affected by the sorrows of everyone. Without rising above this differentiation and discrimination between 'mine' and 'yours', you will never be able to relieve yourself of involvement.

Similarly, you will also have to stop making unnecessary choices, because once the choice is made, one day you will surely develop a sense of possession for that particular thing. The moment you consider something as your own, involvement will be kindled in you. It would be better, if you enjoy what you like and what is available, but by making a choice, do not tag it as your own. Under the influence of fascination and attachment, do not develop an obsession for it. If you are able to do this, you will find yourself enjoying every relationship and thing; and in absence of involvement, you will be free of all the unnecessary sorrows arising out of it.

I have revealed a secret to you and if you want, with this one magical technique you can fill your life with utter bliss. And with the hope that you will surely walk that extra mile to usher this bliss into your lives, I hereby end the discussion on this matter.

———————■—————————

Expectation

Expectations are such an integral part of human beings that as long as human life exists, it is natural to harbour expectations. However, not understanding its meaning and magnitude, the human being has made his life a living hell. 'Expectation' has emerged to be such a vicious element in human life, that it has made him forget what the joy of living is all about. Therefore, first let me explain to you, what expectation exactly is. It is not necessary that whatever transpires in and around an individual's life happens as per his wishes; and that is not possible either. Consequently, the individual desires to bring about a few changes, and this is where he begins to have expectations. He thinks, "How can a lone brick build a castle?" This thought first leads him to build expectations from his family and friends, and then gradually from his education, business and even religion. And that too the expectations of a kind, wherein he believes that with the help of all this, everything would fall in place as he desires it to. But this is where he falls into a trap, as his expectations intensify his involvement, and each instance of his involvement further fuels his expectations. Then for the rest of his life, he is unable to break free from this vicious cycle.

So far, this was about the psychology of expectations and its correlation with involvement. I have already explained to you the consequences of involvement, and have also provided you the solutions to safeguard yourself from it. So now, I will discuss expectation in detail. The root cause, that gives rise to expectation in a human being, is his desire for change. Propelled by the same desire, he forms relationships in the hope that with these relationships, everything will fall into place just as he desires; meaning, he has also expanded his circle of relationships with certain expectations. Now, the person with whom he has forged a relationship on the basis of his expectations fails to live up to his expectation. Ironically, the other person, too, has allowed the relationship to foster with certain expectations in mind, which too are not met. As a result, bitterness begins to brew between the two. But because involvement, which has been nurtured under the shadow of expectations, has also entered the relationship by now, a person is neither able to vent out his bitterness in its entirety, nor is he able to put an end to the relationship. Hence, throughout his life, he is compelled to walk the dead mile of this relationship. If I were to state explicitly, he is burdened with the baggage of such relationships throughout his life.

From this day onwards, closely observe your interpersonal relationships; you will find that the higher the expectations, the deeper would be your involvement in them. This is because both expectations and involvement inevitably strengthen each other. Therefore, wherever there is an expectation, bitterness would have already crept into the relationship. Even when two people cannot stand the sight of each other, their mutual involvement does not allow them to find a solution to it either. Whether it is the relationship between a husband and wife, parent and child, lovers or friends; each has its own joy when there is no expectation. But, ordinarily this is not possible for a human being. Therefore in the end, all his relationships become the scourge of his life, in such a manner that gradually he even stops realising it. Often, he finds that he either has to compromise or find a midway solution to drag on with the relationship.

So should a person stop forming relationships altogether? Because he does not know how to forge a relationship without any expectation, and as soon as his expectations fail to fructify, he is inundated with sorrows and agony. With the expanding horizons of today's age of communication, an individual's relationships are not limited to just a few people. And when he has forged so many relationships, everyday some or the other person is bound to fall short of his expectations. Meaning, the person has made elaborate

Expectation inevitably brings miseries in its wake

arrangements for himself to get perturbed or distressed on a daily basis. So think, what is the solution for this?

In this context it is easy to say, not to have expectations at all. The sentence must have resounded in your ears several times from all around. But, when I am around, can it be as easy as it sounds? And anyway, how much does one really know about me? Do you think my complexity is a joke? Do you think, things would work, just by saying,"Do not have any expectations?" We ought to understand the reasons that give rise to expectations and discuss the remedies to control them. And who else can do this for you, if not me? These so-called great saints and psychologists can only preach. If there is pain, you will be advised to take some medicine...but the question is, which one? So now, let me tell you, what is the root cause of all these expectations?

I have already explained to you that the root cause giving rise to expectations is the desire for change. Now, there is nothing wrong with the desire for change, if it is limited only to yourself. Meaning, if you are unhappy with the life you lead at present and desire a change, then bring about a change in yourself; it is your life! But, in order to improve it, if you desire to bring about a change in the other person or circumstance, then that approach in itself is wrong. Actually, you are being troubled by your habit of expectation, but instead of bringing about a change in yourself, you go about changing the designs and aesthetics of

" **Whether it is religion or society, a person or a thing,
nothing can fulfil your expectations** "

the house in the name of vastu, fengshui or wearing different rings in the name of astrology. Where did you get this amazing intellect from?

If you want to change something, change yourself, and your right to change anything is limited to yourself alone. In just a few attempts, you will realise how difficult it is. In spite of persistent efforts, have you been able to get rid of your anger, worries and fear? Think, when you are unable to bring about a change in your own self, then how unreasonable it is to expect a change in other individuals or situations!

If you have realised this, then firstly decide, until you do not transform yourself into who you really want to be, you will not attempt

Anytime **Anything** can that **happen** with **Anyone** can **happen** with **you** too

to change any other person or situation, and neither will you expect a change in their conduct. This will immediately provide you with two benefits. One, all your expectations from others will dissipate, because you will primarily be engaged in changing yourself according to your expectations. Meaning, you will be engaged in self-improvement. And now it is absolutely clear, that it is only the improvement that you have brought in your own self that will reap you any benefit. Secondly, lowered expectations from people around will make your relationships all the more amiable. Thus, you will not only be of better help to them, but will also be able to derive happiness from your interpersonal relationships.

In summation, the process of breaking the habit of having expectations must begin with bringing about the desired changes in yourself. And this realisation of, 'how difficult it is to bring about a change in yourself' will in itself diminish your expectations from others.

When you undergo this procedure and reach a stage in which you are satisfied with yourself to a large extent, then do not push yourself to the edge for change. After that, whatever mental state you find yourself in, accept that as who you really are. Because, any attempt to change beyond a certain limit will lead to self-loathing. And this is no less dangerous, as self-loathing mostly leads to a person becoming criminal-minded. So, after a few attempts at self-improvement, accept yourself the way you are. And just accepting yourself the way you are will work not one, but a thousand wonders. The greatest benefit of all will be, your complexes will weaken drastically. Because when you do not have any complaint or are not discontent with yourself, then how will you contract any complex?

To hand you the key to happiness, the power of acceptance is magic. It begins to work the moment you start accepting yourself the way you are, and further, it provides you relief from your three major problems which are involvement, expectation and complex. So all you have to do is, strengthen your power of acceptance. Now that you have accepted yourself for who you are, accept others also for who they are. As soon as you begin to accept others for who they are, not only your involvement, but your expectations from them will also wither away. As a result, more than half of your sorrows and worries will be eliminated by themselves.

Once you have effectively dealt with this, and are brimming with energy after the reduction of your sorrows and worries, take this a couple of steps further and start accepting the circumstances the way they are. The outcome will be nothing short of a miracle. Thereafter, even if the circumstances do not change, you will not be perturbed. Because with the magic of acceptance, you will become proficient at quickly adapting yourself to situations. As a result, not only will your sorrows and miseries abate further, but consequently, your energy will also get a further boost. And then, with the

All the Expectations that one has begin with the notion that someone or something is 'one's own' help of this invigorated energy, begin to accept the harsh realities of life too. For a clearer perspective, skim through history and glance at the circumstances unfolding around you. You will find the immutable truths manifesting all around. Even after that, if you are living with the expectation of changing those immutable truths, or are sad at your inability to do so, what are you if not a fool? Why are you living in grief with the expectation of wanting to change, that which cannot be changed? In that case, tell me, on what grounds can you be termed as intelligent?

Hence, I ask you to look around and reflect upon the realities; you have no other option, but to accept them, for, without accepting these realities, you can never succeed in life. If you have not understood...let me explain in detail. Have you ever seen anyone being able to stretch their life span beyond eternity, including even those whom you call Gods? No, right? Then why do you not simply live in acceptance of the fact that you, too, shall die. The first wonder that it will work is, more than half of your fears will dissipate by themselves. Bear it in mind that at the root of all fears of a human being lies only one fear - the fear of death. The one who has accepted the inevitability of death cannot be made to feel afraid time and again.

Proceeding further, have you ever seen a human body immune to diseases? Even if it is someone who is disciplined and a diligent follower of his exercise regimen, or a person dwelling at the supreme heights of his mind, his body too can contract illness and so can your relatives and friends. Only if you live with the acceptance of all this, will you be able to rid yourself from unnecessary grief, when any of these situations arise. If someone else's car can meet with an accident, why not yours? Thus, there is not one, but thousands of such truths; and intelligence lies in living in the acceptance of these truths. Understand well that without the conscious acceptance of all these immutable truths, you will never experience the high of feeling lighter than air and gently flowing through life.

I am sure you must have grasped all that I have explained so far. Now let me draw your attention towards the other kinds of expectations that you have harboured...and bring to your attention, the expectations that have made life difficult for every individual. Even you may have probably noticed every second individual aggrieved by the 'no one understands me' syndrome, which leads them to say, "I do good unto people, but receive no good in return". Now, it would have been understandable, if this was the grievance of a few people, but speaking from my experience, ninety percent of the people seem to be plagued by the same feeling, which eventually leads them to becoming disillusioned and disheartened with the entire world. And then, they begin to make absurd statements such as, "There is no place left in this world for the noble-minded. What is the use of living here?" and so on and so forth...!

However, at its root lies the misunder-standing and misjudgment that an individual has harnessed about himself. Everyone scrutinises the other's actions and also carries out a detailed analysis of it, but they hide their own actions behind such virtuous thoughts that it never allows them to realise the dark side of their own nature. Well, if you really want to get rid of these, then take a look at history. Who understood Jesus? Had he been understood, would he have been crucified? Who understood Socrates? Had he been understood, why would he have been poisoned to death? Had they been understood, neither Buddha or Kabir would have been harassed, nor would a virtuous woman like Sita have had to undergo the test by fire. Do you consider yourself even greater

Your acceptance or non-acceptance does not change the reality at all than these great personages that you have been lamenting about no one understanding you? All you need to do is understand yourself, that is enough. Till date, never has it happened in history that one man has understood another. So, at the least get rid of the sorrows arising out of the delusion that you are an exception to the rule.

As I mentioned earlier, there is not one, but thousands of such truths that an intelligent person must accept and move on. But if I discuss them, there would be no end to this discussion. Hence, I would request you to recognise these truths resounding through the annals of history and ensure that you live in total acceptance of them. With this exercise, a majority of your expectations will wither by themselves, and simultaneously, you will also be freed from the sorrows brought about by these expectations.

In summation, expectations are the root cause of a majority of sorrows in life. Chanting, "Expectations are evil" over and over again, is not going to eliminate them from your life. You will be able to get rid of them only by showing a keen interest in bringing about a change in yourself and abandoning the desire to bring a change in others. Once you have put in reasonable efforts to change yourself and when your desire to change has substantially waned, you will have to first accept yourself the way you are. Once you have learnt to accept yourself, you will understand that there is no greater magic in human life, than self-acceptance. Taking self-acceptance a notch ahead, begin accepting others also the way they are. Once you attain significant success on these two levels, learn to accept the circumstances and all the immutable truths of life. It will simultaneously weaken both, your involvement as well as your expectation. As a result, your life will definitely be filled with happiness and success.

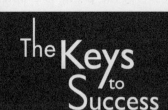

The Keys to Success

Indubitably, as imperative as it is to shield oneself from sorrows and miseries in human life, it is equally important to reach the pinnacle of success. Because, this precious human life cannot be squandered at any cost, by leading an ordinary life. Every human aspires to become successful, and it is his birthright too. Yet, it is only because of a few of their mistakes and ignorance about my functioning that a majority of human beings are unsuccessful today.

So now, I will straight away begin the discussion about the solutions, understanding and implementing which, you can surely reach the heights of success.

Intelligence

In the previous chapters, we have sufficiently discussed the reasons leading to the formation of the Conscious, Subconscious and Unconscious mind, along with the solutions to weaken them. I have also discussed at length the reasons which give rise to sorrows and the solutions to get rid of them. Now, let us move on to the keys to success, as every individual has a dream of becoming successful; moreover to aspire for success is human. So let us begin with the discussion on the essential qualities that a man should develop or must imbibe in order to attain stupendous success in life.

Prior to commencing this discussion, I would like to draw your attention towards the difference between a human being and Nature. The biggest difference between the two pertains to time and energy. Nature has a history of over a billion years, whereas a man hardly has a life span of eighty to hundred years, during which he faces innumerable woes at each stage of life, i.e, childhood, adolescence and old age. Over and above that, eight hours a day are spent sleeping. So if you calculate, you hardly have any time. Speaking of Nature's energy, the sun has been shining, the earth has been revolving and the wind has been blowing for aeons. Meaning, Nature has an inexhaustible reserve of energy. On the other hand, as far as your energy is concerned, not much can be said about it, as you all are well aware of your energy levels.

Yet surprisingly, it is only humans who seem to be performing, all that is effective and important; be it arts, literature or science, all are creations of human beings, this is the truth. However, the fact that needs to be emphasised here is, all these wonders are not being performed by the entire human race, but is the culmination of the feats of barely a few. Then it is obvious for the question to arise that, why a few people are performing feats that can take even Nature by surprise, while the rest are compelled to endure a life, which is akin to dying every moment? Why is it that some people are touching newer, unprecedented heights of success, while the mundanity of the lives of the rest has blurred the difference between life and death?

Well, this is largely due to the varied methodology of utilising time and energy by each human being. I have stated before and even you are well aware that, there are two resources at the disposal of human beings, which are scarce - time and energy. Even then, if an individual is hell-bent on whiling away his time and energy, you tell me what would be the condition of his life? Unfortunately, this is the case with ninety-nine percent of the people today. In other words, the inability of man to utilise his time and energy in an effective manner is the very reason behind his failure.

Now the question is, how can a man learn to utilise his time and energy effectively? To know the answer, first tell me, what is it that differentiates a human being from the other elements in Nature? Struggling to find the answer? Well, one is me, i.e. the mind and the second is the brain. And thanks to these two, a human being is different, unique and more important than all the other elements in Nature. Additionally, in the same vein, if I were to recap the difference between the mind and brain, then the 'brain', despite being immensely useful in certain areas, makes you waste your time and energy in most of the cases, whereas there exists intelligence at my level which is solely focussed on saving time and energy. But unfortunately, very few individuals are able to rightly utilise this intelligence. And you must understand, only if you are left with enough time and energy, will you be able to achieve anything remarkable in life.

This directly implies that in order to achieve success in human life, it is imperative for an individual to activate his intelligence. And, intelligence lies hidden in all individuals in equal measure, at my level i.e. the level of the mind. Meaning, as far as intelligence is concerned, I have not been partial to anyone. The only difference amongst human beings is, the ones who are able to activate this intelligence, progress ahead in life by saving their time and energy, while for the rest, who are not able to activate their intelligence, are compelled to lead an ordinary distressed life, full of hardships.

Now, before I begin with the discussion about the ways individuals can activate the intelligence lying dormant in their mind, and its influences, I will explain to you the difference between intelligence and brilliance. Intelligence is an innate quality that you are born with but in most human beings, it remains latent. On the other hand, brilliance is intelligence acquired by the brain through various sources, especially through education or skill training. The difference is very subtle but highly significant. Moreover, understanding this difference will tremendously help you recognise your intelligence and activate the same.

Intelligence pertains to the mind, whereas brilliance pertains to the brain; and to be brilliant is necessary as well as useful. However, brilliance is not the end all and be all of everything. Brilliance by itself cannot help you progress or sail through life. More importantly, most people are ruining their lives by using their brilliance where it is not needed. Therefore, first let us understand the domain of the brain's influence as well as how, where, and to what extent, it needs to be used. Simultaneously, let us also clearly understand and identify the areas of life where one must avoid using the brain.

To begin with, the most significant attribute of the human brain is its vast memory reserve. Meaning, whatever memory base a person uses to grow and progress in life is exclusively bestowed by his brain. This encompasses all his learnings; right from his education to all the good and bad he sees, listens to or perceives in life. Memory certainly plays a very important role in life. Right from his name to all other important facts of life; from the basic alphabet to several other teachings, whatever a man remembers, can only be ascribed to his memory function. It is also true that it is solely on the basis of his various kinds of learning, that he is able to progress in life. However, an important fact worth understanding here is, you do not need to remember everything in life. If you remember what is essential, it is understandable, but remembering unnecessary things is not only an unwanted burden, but invites great risks as well. As memories not only disturb you time and again, but in remembering them, a lot of your precious energy is frittered away too.

With the losses listed above, I hope you would have surely grasped the consequences you suffer on account of the unrequired use of your memory. If I talk about the other qualities of your brain then thinking, scheming, decision-making, analysing, all fall within the domain of the brain. All these qualities of the brain are essential to progress ahead in life, but here too, the unrequired use of these qualities by the brain, proves to be dangerous for a person. But without understanding these serious implications, most people keep contemplating over the smallest of things and soon analysing them, whether it is necessary or not. This is the reason why most people have become enervated. Now you tell me, how can an enervated and exhausted person achieve anything in life even if he wants to?

Thus, all I wish to imply is, the brain is useful for a variety of purposes; but it is absolutely ignorant as far as time and energy are concerned. Therefore, it makes you waste these two precious resources on numerous unnecessary things on various occasions. In explicit terms, the problem with the brain is, it deems everything necessary. Hence, it immediately engages itself in understanding, remembering and analysing whatever it comes across. Now obviously, nothing can be gained by knowing or remembering futile things; on the contrary, it results in unnecessary wastage of time and energy. And this is where intelligence proves to be of great help because it is very well aware of the difference between what is 'necessary' and what is 'unnecessary'. Thus, it stops the brain from engaging in unnecessary tasks. But, the problem with intelligence is, it gets activated on its own as per its law. The plain and simple requisite for intelligence to get activated is, your Conscious, Subconscious and Unconscious minds should be weak. Why intelligence alone? This is applicable to all my energy centres. They will get activated only when you have vanquished my weaker forms.

Sharp memory or the ability of reasoning are certainly not the signs of intelligence

And how does one weaken them...well, I have already discussed the solutions for that.

So for now, I will directly come to the point and explain what exactly the role of intelligence is. Firstly, it very well recognises the difference between the essential and the non-essential. It does not allow the brain to get attracted towards the inessential, due to which, both your time and energy get saved. Well, I have already elaborated on this point earlier. So proceeding with the power of intelligence, you must note that the greatest power of your intelligence is, using experience as a tool, it is capable of nullifying the 'inessentials' gathered by your brain. Simply put, the crux of the matter is, it is your intelligence which not only restricts your brain from being attracted to all that is inessential in the present day, but it also has the capacity to eliminate the accumulated inessentials of your past. This, in turn, saves both your time and energy. Now it seems superfluous to explain to you how useful this saved time and energy can prove to be in your life.

I hope you must have understood how important intelligence is, and as I have stated earlier, intelligence cannot be sourced externally. It exists in everyone in equal measure at my level. Educational qualifications, worldly knowledge and religion cannot be the means to acquire intelligence, as you already posses intelligence. It implies, that to become brilliant enormous effort is required, but when it comes to intelligence, you already possess it! It is only a matter of it getting activated. The activation of your intelligence will automatically result in the weakening of your brilliance, because the main function of intelligence is to prohibit all the activities of the brain, which drains you of your time and energy. Simply stated, you can either be brilliant or intelligent. The choice is yours! Most people are exceedingly brilliant, due to which they neither have time nor energy at their disposal.

In order to explain to you the difference between brilliance and intelligence, let me cite a few anecdotes. It is an age-old story. There were three friends who were masters of sorcery. One day, they, along with a charioteer, embarked on a trip. While passing through a forest, they stumbled upon a lion's skeleton. Upon sighting the carcass, one of the sorcerers said, "I can put flesh and muscles on the skeleton." The second sorcerer responded in sheer excitement, "If you can put flesh and muscles on the skeleton, I can make blood flow through his veins." Hearing these words, the third sorcerer could not contain himself and blurted, "If you two actually translate your words into actions then, I can certainly breathe life into the dead lion."

On listening to these haughty claims, the charioteer was unnerved. Fearfully, he pleaded with the three sorcerers, "Even though you are capable of performing this feat, you must refrain from going against the laws of Nature. You will get ample opportunities to prove your prowess in sorcery, why would you want to experiment with the lion?"

But they were in no mood to listen to him. They not only reprimanded him, but also insulted him by calling him a coward. What could the poor charioteer do? He became a silent spectator. Meanwhile, the first sorcerer covered the skeleton with flesh and muscles just as he had claimed. Seeing this, the apprehensive charioteer was alarmed. Now, it was the second sorcerer's turn and he made blood flow through the lion's veins. Watching the sorcerer's tall claims turn into reality, the charioteer was now on his guard. Though illiterate, he was intelligent enough to safeguard his own life; hence before the third sorcerer showcased his skill, he mounted the chariot and escaped. Paying no heed to all this, the third sorcerer brought the lion back to life. Well,

" The one who recognises how and when to use water is far more intelligent than the one who knows its formula "

who knows, how many years ago the lion had died! Hence, as soon as he came to life, it ripped all three of them apart and ate them up.

Now it is for you to see and evaluate, what is greater; brilliance or intelligence? That is why I reiterate, irrespective of the level of your brilliance, without intelligence, it does not prove to be of much use. For example, if someone possesses an understanding of when and how thirsty he feels, but is ignorant of the chemical formula for water, it is alright; at least he will not die of thirst. However on the other hand, if a brilliant person knows the formula of water, but is completely ignorant of his body's need for water, then according to you who is more intelligent between the two?

Acquiring knowledge about everything, thinking extensively and harbouring lofty aspirations are the key functions of the brain. But, of what use would that be? These functions are useful, provided, they are utilised in moderation, as and when the need arises, in accordance with the demand of the situation. In fact, in order to progress in life, knowing one's little needs is far more important than possessing vast knowledge on scores of subjects. Using your common sense, you must think and question, is all the information, education and subjects that you are gathering knowledge about, really necessary for progressing in life? Because, every such effort comes at a price. For this purpose, you not only have to toil, but also have to devote your precious time. And how much time do you actually have?

Let me illustrate the above fact with an episode from the life of the great saint Shri Ramakrishna Paramahansa. During those days, Ramakrishna's ashram was located on a river bank. Like any other day, one morning, he was sitting with his disciples outside the ashram when a haughty sanyasi who lived in the same village reached there. He always criticised Ramakrishna for reasons best known to him. For many years, he had been learning the art of walking on water, and on that day, he had actually succeeded in doing so. Filled with pride, he had come with an aim of belittling Ramakrishna. Needless to say, the sanyasi had come prepared with his plan of action. Upon entering, he addressed Ramakrishna in an

If a person wishes to grow he must know the difference between brilliance & intelligence audacious tone and asked, "You are proclaimed to be a wise man, but do you know how to walk on water?"

Ramakrishna answered him in a humble tone, "No, brother. I do not know, but it does not hinder my life in any way. Yes, I know how to walk on land and that is useful to me in my daily life."

The sanyasi retorted arrogantly, "Do not try to hide your weakness with polite words. I have mastered the art of walking on water, have you?"

All the disciples present there were stunned. But, Ramakrishna began to look at him in bewilderment. Exhibiting his curiosity, he simply said, "If you really know how to walk on water, then show us. Even we would like to amuse ourselves with your art."

Hearing this, the haughty monk took everyone to the river bank. There he not only walked to the other side of the bank, but returned as well. Everyone was filled with surprise, but Ramakrishna. With a sombre smile, he looked into the sanyasi's eyes which left the sanyasi puzzled. The sanyasi could not make head or tail out of it. He thought to himself, "No praise, nothing... he is just standing and smiling!" Anxious, he even tried to decipher the meaning of Ramakrishna's smile. But he could not. Ramakrishna simply stepped on the bank and asked the boatman to row him across in the boat to the other shore and bring him back. Since it was a business opportunity for the boatman, he quickly ferried Ramakrishna across. The sanyasi and the disciples were startled at this act of Ramakrishna. On coming ashore, Ramakrishna quietly alighted from the boat and asked the boatman the fare for the boat ride. The boatman asked for two paise which Ramakrishna paid him. Then, turning to the sanyasi, putting his hand around his shoulder, he asked, "How many years did you spend learning this art?"

He said, "Twenty years." Listening to this, Ramakrishna let out a hearty laugh. And laughing aloud, he said, "After twenty years of rigorous effort, you mastered an art, and that too, worth only two paise!"

Every individual repeatedly commits the same mistake. He does not realise the value of time in his short span of life. He does not understand the fact that what is essential to others, may not necessarily be essential for him. Stuck in the same trap, millions of hermits are learning the Vedas, Quran and Bible by rote without understanding and assessing its necessity in their respective lives. No matter how great or precious the thing is, if it is not aiding your progress in life, then for you, it is worthless. Similarly, billions of youngsters waste twenty valuable years of their life in an effort to complete their graduation and secure a degree. They never even bother to question the usefulness of these educational qualifications in their life. They tend to forget that nothing in life comes for free. Therefore before investing your precious time and energy in achieving anything, firstly, you must thoroughly evaluate its importance in your life. What if all your efforts go in vain? The one who, before initiating any kind of effort, evaluates the usefulness of the results that his efforts would bear, against the extent of time and energy required for the task, is an intelligent individual. As for others who do not follow this process, they are extra-intelligent!

Understand once again that time and energy, both are required in order to progress in life, and these are the only two things that you do not have in abundance. Truly speaking, the very term 'intelligent individual' signifies a person, who knows how to apply his time and energy effectively, that is, at the right places. Whereas, a brilliant person is the one who fritters away his precious time and energy even on trivial matters. And then, just when it is most needed, these brilliant people neither have the time nor energy left in them. The reason why I am reiterating this is because, those who are phenomenally successful have achieved it by utilising every moment of their life to the optimum; they have achieved it by saving their energy from being squandered on inessentials. Hence, if you too wish to taste success in life, then you must learn to clearly differentiate between what is essential and what is inessential.

In the same context, one more thing that you need to understand is, your brain plays a very crucial role in this entire process. In fact it is curious by nature; always eager to know more and more. However, the evaluation of the necessity for knowledge does not fall under its

" A human being lacks only two things - time and energy "

purview. Similarly, the brain has a keen interest in impressing others, which is often the reason behind it accumulating all possible generic information. Contrary to this, intelligence focuses only on what is most essential...and that is how it should be. But unfortunately, in case of most people, the brain is quite successful in ignoring intelligence. As a result, majority of the people spend their lives accumulating useless information and indulging in futile tasks. Even you are no exception! Upon close observation, you will find that you too are in the league of the 'exceedingly brilliant'. You will also realise, how you are squandering your precious time and energy on futile matters.

Over and above this, consider the numerous other dire consequences you have to face. Let me cite a few examples which will help you grasp the brain's tendency of building castles in the air. You must have definitely observed many people who begin to search for information about expensive luxury cars the moment they secure a high-paying job. Now, whether it will yield any result or not is a mystery, whether they would be able to buy a big car is a matter of the future; yet, this foolishness on their part afflicts them with unhappiness from that very moment. Now think! Did they not sow the seed of grief for themselves by collecting these futile pieces of information?

This is where intelligence is of great help. It always believes in collecting information that is relevant, and dreaming about things that are practically within one's reach at present. If allowed to function effectively, it will not make an effort to gather information about the expensive cars, until it does not have sufficient funds to buy. This is the difference between brilliant and intelligent human beings; an intelligent person is always on the lookout for the path of happiness, and a brilliant person, the path of grief. And you all know that an aggrieved person's sense of judgement gets impaired. This is the reason why the ones who excessively apply their brain are unsuccessful in life.

But, what can be done about it? This fact does not sink into the mindset of a majority of the people. According to them, if one gathers or possesses only the most essential knowledge, then how can he be called intelligent? If he is unable to showcase his skilfully acquired futile knowledge on numerous subjects to others, then how can he be termed intelligent? But the reality is, the extent of positive influence exerted by it is not as enormous as the magnitude of negative impressions it leaves on me i.e. the mind. To give you a few examples of this; many people, despite being healthy, keep themselves abreast about the effects and ill-effects of various kinds of foods. They go about accumulating tonnes of information on the cause of illnesses and the preventive measures for the same. Now its benefits are best known to them, but it surely leaves an imprint at my level. Thus affected, I, being who I am, get up to my tricks. Then, gradually the information they have compiled on illnesses, food and preventive measures begin to affect them. If you observe closely, this is one of the prime reasons for such widespread obesity in the world at present. Since the brain has assumed various foods to be fattening, the information is imprinted at my level, and then I invariably affect the body. When this vast reservoir of information was not available, an individual's appetite was double than that of an individual today, but obesity could not afflict him in the manner that it has at present.

The more a person reads about a particular illness, the stronger imprint it leaves at my level. Then sooner or later, he starts getting plagued by the same illness, or an illness similar to it. Remember, for a majority of your diseases, physical reasons are not as responsible as much as their imprint formed at my level.

In short, what I mean to say is, before utilising the scholastic aptitude or brilliance of your brain, first understand how it affects your mind and life. At the same time, remember that without awakening your intelligence, the happiness quotient in your life cannot exceed beyond a certain limit. And the intelligence will be awakened only when the brain stops imposing unnecessary knowledge on it.

Moreover, while we are discussing the difference between intelligence and brilliance, it is essential to know one more fact, that even in case of things that are necessary, in order to utilise them to the fullest, it is important that along with your brilliance, your intelligence should also be active. Agreed that memorising and analysing things is the greatest quality of the brain; I also agree that utilising it to the fullest is in the best interest of your life, however, intelligence is necessary here too. Because which piece of information should penetrate to what level, or when and to what extent it must be utilised, is an art solely possessed by intelligence, which is lying dormant at my level. Else, one day, this accumulated information ruins the life of an individual, for attaching undue importance to anything robs you of your precious time and energy.

Most importantly, irrespective of the volume of information accumulated and processed by the brain, until it is not embraced by intelligence...all these efforts of the brain do not yield any significant results. That is because the information collected by the brain only gives rise to thoughts, and thoughts do not carry much weight. An individual's brain has one more peculiarity; it has a natural tendency to get attracted towards lofty thoughts and principles. Here, it needs to be clearly understood that there is no place for idealism i.e. lofty principles and thoughts in practical life. Even if a thought is useful, the question is, what will an individual do with that thought? How much control do his thoughts have over him? Were I to state it explicitly, then the reach of the brain is peripheral as well as marginal, whereas, my influence is deep and absolute. The decisions taken by the brain can be negated a thousand times, but in my case, an individual does not have that option. To state it simply, any decision made by the brain does not yield effective results till the time I do not accept it. This is the reason why my intelligence outweighs the brilliance of the brain as far as decision-making is concerned.

Allow me to elaborate further, because without understanding the point that I am expounding upon, even the finest of your learning or teachings will not yield any results in your life. For instance, you are taught that getting angry is bad, that it is only we who are at the losing end, and it is only we who have to bear the repercussions of our anger; so you decide that in future, you will not get angry. However, these are nothing but the thoughts instituted by the brain. Every human being has reiterated these thoughts to himself not just once, but numerous times. However when anger actually arises, how many are able to control it? What is the bearing of an individual's thoughts that he

Recognising what is necessary or inevitable is not as important as eradicating all that is unnecessary from life

can keep me in control? All of you know and are also of the belief that negativities such as jealousy, partiality, complexes and so on are bad and most people wish to be rid of them. To this effect, they even go to the extent of visiting temples, mosques and churches. However, these are nothing but an extension of their thoughts. Tell me, how many have been able to get rid of their anger with prayers and rituals? Take a peek into your own life's experiences; irrespective of the lofty thoughts your brain has created on the basis of the curiosity or the information it has accumulated, irrespective of the ideals, principles or manners you have cloaked yourself with, does it prove to be of any use until a transformation takes place at my level?

How did Buddha walk? How did he sit and stand? What did he wear? How did he behave? Millions of people can imitate him and are actually imitating him better than he actually was. But the question is, how many of them have actually become Buddha? Not even one! Therefore understand well, that reading, understanding and contemplating over good things or forming beliefs regarding them is not a big thing. These are the functions of the brain, and for ages, it has been pulling the strings and making human beings dance to its tune. Whereas, intelligence brings about change, a transformation. If there is no change, then what is the use of these lofty thoughts? Instead, is it not better to be the way one is?

However, it is not going to do you any good even if you remain the way you are, as all of you are aware that certain changes are a must. Meaning, certain changes will have to be brought about! But the predicament is, you try to bring about these changes with the help of your brain, that is, with the help of your thoughts and ideals. And, I have already explained to you the extent of control your thoughts have over you. Hence, this point onwards, the trouble begins to brew. Your brain proves to be ineffective in bringing about the change in you. Thus, distressed and nervous, you embrace the change at a superficial level, even though it has not occurred within. And as soon as you embrace it superficially, you lose whatever little scope was left for you to change from within. So, all I am trying to convey is, change has to be propelled by the intelligence hidden at my level i.e. at the level of the mind.

Well, after having reiterated the same thing in various ways, I am sure you must have understood that although it is absolutely necessary for certain changes to be brought about in you, it is imperative that those changes stem from my depths. Only then would they be effective and yield results. So now, let us discuss how to transmit the instruction to my depths and thereby bring about the requisite changes in you, meaning, let us understand how to communicate these transformational messages to your intelligence. In the same context, one more point that needs to be grasped is, every individual is the way he is, and there is no possibility of any change in him until he experiences something new. However, mere experience will not necessarily bring about a change in him. Because to change with experiences is the function of intelligence, but if you experience something at the level of your brain, meaning, only at the peripheral level, there will not be any change in you at all. Moreover, intelligence will be able to experience only when the brain does not interfere. And as long as the brain is strong, it will continue to intrude. That calls for the reiteration of the fact that a person cannot be brilliant and intelligent at the same time. The statement that I am making is of utmost importance, so make sure, you grasp it well. In order to make sure that you have really understood this well, I will spell out the significant differences between brilliance and intelligence, so that if you are excessively brilliant, you can veer yourself in the direction of becoming intelligent. Because, without being intelligent, happiness, peace and success will elude you forever.

Brilliant	Intelligent
1) A brilliant person is persistently engaged in an effort to know and grasp something new in order to impress others.	1) An intelligent person is inclined to know only that which is most essential at that particular point of time.

2) A brilliant person is always interested in having all the information, including minor details.	2) An intelligent person is only concerned with the gist of the matter.
3) A brilliant person can commit the same mistake repeatedly in numerous ways.	3) For an intelligent person, one or two experiences are enough to realise his mistake.
4) A brilliant person assumes everything as essential.	4) For an intelligent person, anything that does not serve the immediate purpose, is worthless.
5) A brilliant person perceives life as an endless journey of constant struggle and hard work.	5) An intelligent person only believes in grabbing and exploiting the big opportunity.

Now, if I were to summarise all the facts explained so far, then the human intelligence has two significant attributes. The first is, to recognise the difference between the necessary and the unnecessary. In this context, you must correctly understand the definition of the word 'necessary' and imbibe it in your mind that in order to achieve anything in life, you have to expend two vital elements i.e. 'time' and 'energy'. This proves that in life everything comes at a price. Hence for an intelligent person, something is essential only when its significance and worth outweighs the time and energy spent on it.

The second most important attribute of an intelligent person is his ability to bring about self-transformation. In this context, let me clarify that the present condition of man's existence does not repose confidence that he will achieve any notable success in life. Hence, most people have no option, but to bring certain changes in themselves in order to taste success in life. With regard to this, let me spell it out in black and white that without experience, it is impossible for an individual to change. In simple words, the very art of experiencing is the criteria for judging your intelligence, that is, the depth of your experience reveals the level of your intelligence.

On the basis of this art of experiencing, human beings can be classified into four distinct categories. Buddha often elucidated this differentiation with the metaphor of four types of horses. The first and the best type of horses are those, who begin to run, merely upon seeing the shadow of the whip. For the second category, the shadow of the whip alone is not enough; for them to run, the sight of the whip is a must. For the third category, just showing the whip does not suffice; for them to run, they need to be whipped once. The fourth and the last category of horses are those who refuse to budge, irrespective of the extent of whipping they are subjected to. And, please do not be startled to find that most individuals fall in the fourth category! Irrespective of the number of thoughts or decisions taken, they are not able to translate their thoughts into actions; they inevitably fail at the last moment. Not being able to learn from experience and being repeatedly fooled in the same manner, is the peculiar quality they possess. And if the responsibility for this were to be ascribed to a single factor, then it is the habit of human beings to superficially adhere to lofty thoughts and ideals. And they provide a human being with an illusion of being great; so why would anyone feel the need to change?

Let me explain this with an example. If you are getting gripped by jealousy, ego, anger, partiality and so on, and if disconcerting thoughts and dishonesty are clamouring your mind; then tell me how can you be termed religious? But look at the marvel of your thinking! Most people are plagued by these negative emotions, but still they are living in the smug belief that they are religious...How? Because their crafty brain, with the help of their thoughts and ideals, has created the concept of God, rites and rituals. Now, in order to be religious, an individual need not curb his ego or jealousy; all he needs to do is, visit religious shrines day and night. To be religious, a man need not rid himself of dishonesty, but merely perform rites and rituals once a week. Such short cuts have been devised by the brain with its thinking and that too, not in one, but in all areas of life! However, when put to test with practical parameters of life, the solutions devised by the brain prove to be ineffective and futile.

This hypocrisy and dishonesty does not work at my level and the actual reins of your life are in my hands. At my level, irrespective of your praying and charity to religious shrines, if you do get gripped by jealousy or ego then you are inevitably irreligious. In short, to me, you are intelligent only if you can truly transform. And transformation is possible, only when an individual stops resorting to these lofty thoughts that are thrust upon him from all around. In order to understand this more clearly, observe children carefully. As they do not mask themselves with lofty thoughts, the resultant transformation is quick. The elders on the other hand, think till they are blue in the face, but do not transform even a sliver's worth.

If you have grasped the points mentioned above, then you must also understand that all kinds of success in human life are solely dependent on the capability, the flexibility and the pace at which an individual continues to change himself, on the basis of his experiences. No matter who and where you are, you will not reap any significant success, as, thanks to your brain, at present you are inundated with inessentials. Therefore, you will first have to dispel these clouds of inessentials that have over-shadowed your existence. And they can only be dispelled with the help of experiences. The moment you experience a particular inessentiality, that cloud will disappear. And, without initiating this process of change, it is not possible for your time and energy to be channelised into an effective task.

Therefore, if you seriously wish to take a decisive step towards being successful in life then at least now, desist from getting entrapped by the brain. Do not even think, what is necessary for you to know or learn. First, chalk out those thousands of 'inessentials' that you have treasured in life, assuming them to be essential, and then think, how to get rid of them.

In order to do away with these inessentials, it is imperative that you live within yourself, that is, live your life in a compact manner. It is your compactness alone which will provide you with 'The Third

Eye' that will start identifying the inessentials that cast a pall of gloom over your life. Obviously, it identifies these inessentials on the basis of experiences, but once this third eye is awakened, just one or two experiences are enough.

Meaning, you have to first bring yourself into the mode, in which, you stop seeking any more inessentials. Then becoming compact in what you are, you have to awaken your third eye. And once the third eye is awakened, you have to give it complete freedom to search for the inessentials in your life on the basis of your experiences and eliminate them. With this process there will come a day, when all the inessentials in your life will be eliminated, and only that which is truly essential for you will remain. Or to put it differently, that alone will serve to be effective and decisive for your life. And it is a foregone conclusion that without reaching this state, you will not be able to perform any feat that will earn you a place in the list of illustrious personalities.

Well, let me explain this entire process by citing examples of a few great people which may, perhaps, help you comprehend the functionality as well as the importance of the third eye. India has been the motherland to many great saints; one of them was Dayanand Saraswati. Since his father believed in idol-worship, one day, he took him along to a temple. At the temple, people, adhering to traditions and rituals, were offering sweets and milk to the deity. Just then, Dayanand caught sight of the rats feasting on the sweets that were offered to the diety. Seeing this, a surprised Dayanand asked a very plain and simple question to his father, "To whom are these sweets being offered?"

His father answered, "To God."

To this Dayanand said, "Then these rats are robbing him of his right. Now he will definitely get angry and kill the rats."

Father said, "No, nothing like that is going to happen."

Dayanand asked, "Why? Does he not have the power to do so?" His father was simply left dumbfounded. With this one incident, Dayanand immediately realised that this idol, too, was nothing but a stone, like other ordinary stones. From that day onwards, not only did he stop idol worship, but moving a step ahead, he spent his entire life preaching against idol worship. Moreover, he also established a distinguished institution called 'Arya Samaj', which even today is actively functional in every part of India. So, it was his third eye that had recognised the futility of idol worship in a second. And once the third eye identifies anything as 'inessential', there is no turning back. It uproots and eradicates that particular inessential from your brain forever.

Here the biggest question is, can anyone, who calls himself intelligent, tell me, how much time and how many experiences would he require to identify his inessentials? Ten years, twenty years, or many many births? It does not matter, take as much time as you want, but at least do not call yourself intelligent!

I will now explain the same fact citing another incident that transpired in the life of Steve Jobs, a highly successful businessman and the founder of Apple Inc. Once while studying, Steve came across an issue of Life magazine with the cover page featuring two African children in great distress. Steve was aghast on seeing the plight of those children. A curious Steve, with the magazine still in his hand, ran to the church. He showed the cover page to the priest and asked him a simple question, "If I raise my finger, will God know which one I'm going to raise even before I do it?" The pastor answered, "Yes, God knows everything." Steve then pulled out the magazine and showing the cover page to the pastor, he asked, "Well, does God know about this, and what's going to happen to those children?" The pastor replied, "Steve, I know you do not understand, but yes, God knows about that."

Listening to the answer of the priest, Steve was so infuriated that from that day onwards, he stopped visiting church altogether. Think, one experience and the decision was made; the matter was laid to rest permanently.

Now take a look at the great Edison. A couple of years after being enrolled in school, owing to the persistent humiliation of being called a 'dull' student by his teachers, he and his mother together decided to put an end to his formal schooling forever. Meaning, after a few bad experiences, he and his great mother, Nancy, gauged schooling to be inessential. From that day onwards, Edison never attended school. And the end result is there for the world to see - he went on to become the scientist with the maximum number of inventions to his credit of his time.

Take the example of Buddha. He saw one ill person, one poor man and one death, and realised the darker side of life. Renouncing the royal lifestyle, he became an ascetic, embarking upon a journey to seek supreme bliss, and he successfully found it too. History is replete with thousands of such examples. As for the people who have been successful and great, their third eye had identified and eradicated the inessentials of life in an instant. When all the inessentials were eliminated, all that remained were essentials, which made them great and successful eventually.

In essence, the success of life lies in identifying the 'inessentials' and getting rid of them. Because, as soon as you get rid of the 'inessentials', you are left with a reservoir of time and energy. And only then can you effectively utilise this storehouse of time and energy for what is necessary and achieve the desired success in life. The art of being able to do this is intelligence; everything else is the naivety of the brain which does nothing but ruins your life. Therefore, kindly assess the necessity of an act before indulging in it, and if found unnecessary, let the act be forsaken from your life forever, but under any circumstances, save this valuable time of yours. Because, your brain will inevitably find every information worth grasping, every act necessary, and every discussion worth indulging in. Definitely, everything will seem enticing, but you must safeguard and preserve your valuable time, and utilise it only where it is essential. Remember, it is this saved time and energy which will ultimately put you onto the path of success.

Just think, what will happen, if you quell these inessentials from your life? You will have ample time and abundant energy! Now with ample time and energy at your disposal, you will definitely not sit idle. But, at that time whatever you do, would be both essential as well as effective, as you have preserved this time and energy by refraining from indulging in the inessential. So, I am sure, you will definitely not squander them in inessentials again. Thus, in short, awaken the third eye of intelligence, and burn out all the inessentials from your life. Thereafter with the help of the essentials that will remain, you will continue climbing newer heights of success.

Creativity

The 'Power of Creation' i.e. the ability to create, is the ultimate art of Nature and the entire energy of the cosmos flows through it. If you look around, everywhere you will see the abundance of Nature's creations. The rivers, the mountains, the sky, the moon, the stars, the vegetation, the water, the rain and the gusts of the wind...are all nothing but the creations of Nature. Well, you all are aware of the Power of Creation of Nature, however, you may not have paid attention to the infiniteness of this power. Truly! Creativity is the only power that has no beginning, no end. For proof, we have the sun, the moon, the countless stars and the never-ending space in front of us. Why only this, if an individual carefully observes himself; how many creations are there in his less than one foot long and barely six inch wide face! There is so much creativity in such a small face!? Like this one face, billions of faces have been created for nearly millions of years, but barring a few exceptions, has it ever happened that any two faces are identical? Is this single facet of Nature not enough to ignite your curiosity about the power of creation?

You may well say, my curiosity has been aroused now! I have also understood the unlimited power of creation of Nature; but what can I do about this? Well, it is precisely to explain this to you that I have touched upon the subject of the power of creation of Nature. So now, to begin with, every human being is endowed with the same ability to create as that of Nature. Moreover, if you look at the history of mankind, you will find, all the names etched in history as legends have one thing in common, and that is, they all have effectively utilised their power of creation. If you also aspire to climb the summit of success

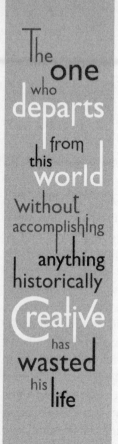

The one who departs from this world without accomplishing anything historically creative has wasted his life

and leave a mark in history, you too ought to utilise your power of creation.

Let us try to understand the above-mentioned fact with the help of a few examples. These will make it clear that regardless of the field of interest, success is achieved only by those who are creative. Speaking of science, Edison, Einstein, Newton or Galileo, are all great because they invented something new or discovered a new formula. Edison secured his place in history by inventing the first light bulb. Thereafter, so many variations and improvements have been made which were even better; yet, we do not even give their names a mention. Why? Because it is the first bulb that is important. Similarly, in the field of painting, be it Picasso or Van Gogh, the artist who first painted something new, in an innovative style, became immortalised in history. Then, no matter how much one tries to replicate these masterpieces, nothing can be achieved.

Likewise, in the plays of Shakespeare or the works of Mark Twain, it is their creativity that holds significance. The same applies to Charlie Chaplin, Laurel and Hardy or even Michael Jackson; the importance is of their creative style. Imitating them has not helped anyone achieve anything. Even in the field of religion, we remember only those who imparted a new thought or philosophy, who showed mankind a new path. For example, Jesus, who despite being born in a Jewish family, defied Jewish traditions and inculcated a new thinking, which is now spread across the world in the form of

Christianity. Likewise, Buddha, who despite being born in a Hindu family defied Hindu traditions and today millions of people are walking the path shown by him, as Buddhists.

Take note that in every human being, there invariably lies a point - a fount of creativity which is eager to explode and spring forth and manifest itself. Then no matter which field you are in, without creativity flowing from within, you can never prosper. Even if you take the case of business, whether it is Bill Gates or Steve Jobs, their success can only be ascribed to the innovations they offered to the world. Even in politics, a leader cannot survive for long unless he comes up with new slogans, speeches and ideas.

One must bear in mind that just as no two faces are absolutely identical, no two human being's natures can be identical either. With faces there may be a few exceptions, like in the case of twins. However, when it comes to human nature, there is no scope for any exception whatsoever. It means, every individual in himself, is a unique creation of Nature. This is the reason why creativity flowing through each individual will inevitably be different. It implies that the harmonious melodies that flowed from Mozart or Beethoven will never flow from any other individual. By plagiarising or altering notes, one may adapt them, but one can never become a 'Mozart'. Likewise, be it poetry or dance, or a novel thought, once it flows out from one person, the same will never flow from another. With this, you can frame a better picture of not only the vastness of Nature's creativity, but also the magnitude of human creativity.

Now if you have grasped it well that without any kind of creativity flowing from within, you cannot achieve great success in life, then I shall go on to discuss the ways to be creative. At the outset, first understand, what is the biggest obstacle faced by man on the path to become creative? It is his habit of imitating. One Siddhartha became Buddha and thousands of Buddhist monks emerged who dress like Buddha, and repeat his verses. But how would it help? Are they going to attain the wisdom of Buddha? They will waste their entire life and ultimately die as 'Buddhus'*. The same applies to the followers

* Buddhus – foolish (in Hindi)

" Creation is priceless. Nothing can be greater than it "

of Christ, Krishna, and Muhammad or for that matter, any great saint. And this is how a man digs the grave for his creative capabilities.

Therefore, he, who desires to be creative, should neither have blind faith in anyone, nor should he imitate anyone. Buddha and Jesus are a part of history; you can draw inspiration from their life and teachings, but can never become Buddha or Jesus and that is not the purpose of your life either. The purpose of your life is not to become someone's replica. They are the past, now you have to pave a new path for yourself in the present and become something different. Remember the last words uttered by Buddha, when his disciple Ananda asked him about what path he should tread, to which Buddha replied, *"Appa Deepo Bhava" (Become a lamp unto yourself).* How can

Buddha enlighten someone about the path and the purpose of his life? All that he could do was to prod you to find your path, but ultimately it is you, who has to discover your own path and tread the same. And if you do so, it is you who will achieve the purpose of your life.

Similarly, you can be inspired by the poems of Rabindranath Tagore or the couplets of Kabir, the plays by Shakespeare or the philosophy of Socrates; but can never become one like them, nor can the same creativity ever flow from your depths. Anytime, anything that flows from within will inevitably be a new, unique and unprecedented creation of yours. If you wish to rise to their level, you will have to do something uniquely creative. Most often, the reason why academic toppers prove to be losers in the race of life is, their process of learning poems, plays and other works by rote is so intense, that their own creative capacity dies out in the bargain. Similarly, these monks, sanyasis, mullahs, pundits and priests learn the Vedas, Quran, Bible and other scriptures by rote to such an extent, that their connection with true religion gets severed.

On the other hand, the one who wants to be successful will think out-of-the-box or put in efforts to do something creative. Just think, will you become Aristotle by memorising Aristotle's treatise word for word? No...at the most, you will score good grades, but then what about life? Therefore, if you want to kindle your creativity, firstly stop memorising the teachings and thoughts of others, or imitating

In nature no one other than a human being is endowed with the power of Creativity

Blindly believing anything without due verification is the greatest enemy of human Creativity

them. Instead, utilise the same time and energy to think or do something new and that too, in the field where your creativity supports you.

Likewise, if you really want to be creative, bear one thing in mind; take inspiration from everyone, but do not get influenced by anyone. Drawing inspiration aids your progress, whereas getting influenced by any person, thought or an object leaves you standing where you are. Let me explain this with Galileo's example. It was stated in the Bible that the sun revolves around the earth. Ordinarily, no Christian would show distrust in the Bible or question it. However, Galileo did not let his mind be influenced by conventional thinking. He applied his mind and intelligence and found that it is, in fact, the earth that revolves around the sun, and not vice versa. However, it is a different story that the court and the religious heads strongly rebuked him for this conclusion; he was also threatened and compelled to take his words back; but that did not change the truth that it is the earth which revolves around the sun. Since this is an established scientific fact now, the Bible does not act as a hindrance to it; and, Galileo has finally become immortal in history.

In brief, in order to progress in life, drawing inspiration from a great person or a great thought is understandable, and even positive; but, setting your own thinking or style aside under their influence, always proves disastrous. It is the world that should be influenced by you; you should not be influenced by anyone to such an extent that your own thought process ceases to function. If Science would have relented in their efforts thinking, 'If people like Krishna, Buddha and Jesus could not invent a car, plane or bulb, it must not be possible to invent them', what would have been the scenario today? That is precisely why I am saying, if you want to become creative, do not constrict your thinking, but believe that if it can be imagined, it can be created. There invariably lies a world beyond the point that our eyes can see. You should be inspired by every shining star; but at the same time, remember that you have to transcend them too.

If you have assimilated the points stated above, then, the last and most important point to be grasped is, without doing something highly creative, it is not possible to achieve phenomenal success in life. That being the case, the question that now arises is, how can an individual awaken his point of creativity and identify the field in which his creativity abounds? Remember, there invariably is, some kind of creativity latent in every individual, which is keen to manifest. Just as no flower can be without a fragrance, no human being can be devoid of any creative potential. Just as there are millions of types of flowers with different fragrances, human creativity also has millions of facets. There are numerous fields such as science, arts, religion, music, sports, literature, painting, management and business, in which a person can be creative, and subsequently, each of these fields has thousands of respective branches too. Just as there are numerous kinds of sports in which a person can explore his potential, science too, offers millions of specialised disciplines to an individual to spread his wings.

The obvious question that now follows is, how should one identify in which field one's creative potential lies?

It lies in the field which interests him, pursuing which, he never feels exhausted. If he always enjoys, or is always in the mood to do that particular work, then that is the field he should pursue. Or in other words, the area of work which invariably triggers enthusiasm in a person, is the field of his creativity. Just think, if an individual identifies and pursues his field of interest from childhood itself, then, would he not find himself at the top in that field one day?

Well, it is not as easy as it seems. Here, he faces hindrances on two fronts. Many a time, the individual desists from pursuing the field of his interest, while very often, his near and dear ones prove to be a hindrance. Now if a child is brimming with potential in the field of sports and wants to play day and night, his parents act as a hindrance in his path. They advise him to study, become a graduate first and then play. But how would he play then? Upon reaching the age of twenty five, it would be surprising, if he can even enjoy watching a game! This is where the parents and near and dear ones of the children need to adopt a sensible approach, and instead of posing obstacles, they must encourage the child. They need to understand that the world is filled with graduates, but what have they achieved? They must realise that it is between the age of eight and twenty five, that a person's energy flows at its peak. If a child wishes to pursue a particular field and devote himself to it during those formative years, then what more could one ask for?

Suppose, a child shows a penchant for music from an early age, and can play different instruments well, will you still snatch his music away from him and force him into academics? If you do, do you not think you are robbing a flower of its fragrance? Then, that child, upon becoming an adult, will assume an artificial persona for sure and move about in formal clothes as a mere puppet in the hands of the world. Whether it was Mozart or Beethoven, they had grown up with music. In fact, Mozart had composed his first tune around the age of six, while Beethoven had composed his first tune by the time he was twelve years old. And look at the outcome; today, both their names are indelibly inked in history as being synonymous with music.

What I mean to say is, if you really want your children to become great and iconic, then rather than becoming a hindrance, please provide them with a conducive environment and nurture the creativity flowing in them. Consider it a blessing bestowed by Nature that your child is not meant to lead a mundane life. Be happy that he is born with the potential to accomplish something great. In the same vein, think if a child has an interest in literature, and if he reads and writes extensively from childhood, would he not become another 'Shakespeare' one day? Therefore, it is my request that please do not crush the natural fragrance of these budding flowers and turn them into artificial flowers. Similarly, even children should make sure that their dedication towards honing their art should remain unwavering. Endure the pressures and disappointments, but do not give up on your field of interest. One day, you will surely reach the zenith in the field of your interest.

The last, but the most important fact worth understanding is, creativity is the gift bestowed to every child by Nature, but to enhance this creativity, unwavering determination and incredible courage are a must. And an inability to harness these two, is the reason why barely one among millions is creative and successful. Let me explain this fact with the help of the example of Thomas Alva Edison. He had received formal education for barely a few years. But he was a very inquisitive child and his inclination towards science was evident right from early childhood. It did not take long for Edison or his mother Nancy to realise where his interest lay. Hence, his mother, who herself was a teacher, began to tutor him at home and encouraged him to read books on science.

However, the family's financial condition was not stable. Therefore purchasing expensive books or accessing them was extremely difficult. Despite all the odds, neither did Edison stop reading books on science, nor did his mother stop teaching him. By the time Edison turned

If you wish to be Creative then abstain from Imitating

You cannot 'do' anything creative Creativity simply flows

eleven, he had started selling fresh fruits, candies and newspapers. Undoubtedly, Edison's sole intention was to be able to purchase new books on science. This may have been a small feat, but imagine, at such a young age, he had even set up a small laboratory in the basement of his house with the money he earned. However, it was a different story that his laboratory was forcibly shut down, when he tried to make his friend Michael fly in the air, after luring him to drink one of the chemical concoctions prepared by him.

However, if someone were to lose their determination and give up so easily, how would he grow to become Edison? By the age of twelve, he had started selling newspapers in the trains in order to earn money. He used to board the train daily from Port Huron to Detroit, and sell newspapers to the commuters en route. Upon reaching his destination, he used to spend his day reading books on science in the Detroit library, and in the evening, he would board the same train to return home in Port Huron. Now determination tends to fuel itself; thus, very soon, he managed to set up a small laboratory in the train as well. But then things went awry again. One day, his laboratory accidentally caught fire and an enraged conductor, not only gave him a sound thrashing, but also threw him out with his equipments.

But, was Edison the one to accept defeat so easily? Certainly not! Whenever he found an opportunity, he invariably took a purposeful step towards furthering his passion. And this

" **Every human being invariably possesses talent in at least one field and persistent honing of this talent is the only way to achieve great success** "

is the point where we must applaud his courage. Why? Because he was fortunate to have over a thousand inventions to his credit and ensure a place for himself in the league of the greatest scientists in the world; but think, what if he would not have succeeded? Due to his dire financial condition, the probability of his death due to starvation always hung precariously over his head like the sword of Damocles. However, he was fine with living under the sword, but was not ready to give up on his passion. Clearly understand that great achievements do not await you with open arms. For that, you need to have the courage to put your life at stake.

Simply put, in order to foster your passion, exemplary courage is highly essential. You must withstand the pressures of the people around, and yet remain dedicated to your passion. Suppose, your interest is in the field of sports and you sincerely wish to pursue it, then your academic studies may get neglected. But later, what if you do not become a renowned player? What will your future be? This sword dangles over your head all the time. However, ignoring this, even if you decide to pursue it, then the people around, not only repeatedly remind you of the risks, but insistently mount pressure to avert you from taking such risk. But at that point of time, if you show courage and stand resolute on your choice, without vacillating, success will inevitably follow.

And then, what is business? Nothing but a venture that requires courage; and that too of a kind in which one cannot achieve success without taking a big risk. What is this 'big risk'? The risk is of doing something new, or the determination to create something. Now in an attempt to do this, you can even draw a blank. But then, can one prosper in business without taking the risk? No; which means that even a business does not flourish without taking a risk.

So, if you wish to achieve success in life, you will definitely have to be creative. And, in order to hone this creativity, you will have to take risks as well. But here, it is important that you do not have any misconception about your talent and potential. At the same time, ingrain it in your mind that to be successful is your birthright and you must become successful. But without being creative, you cannot achieve great success in life. Therefore, not only should you keep your interests and talents alive, but also, develop and hone them with utmost dedication and extraordinary courage. If you have not erred in identifying your passion or interest or judging your capability, I promise that one day, you will surely scale the peak of success.

Furthermore, the positive fallout of working in your field of passion is, even if you are unable to achieve great success in the field of your interest, you will definitely experience lifelong peace and contentment within. And experiencing peace and contentment is also one of the important objectives of human life. On the same lines, be aware of the fact that even if you achieve great success in a field other than your field of creativity, you will always feel restless within and in that case too, your life will become a living hell. In truth, ninety nine percent of people are living in this turmoil, because they have not been able to muster the courage and firmness to follow their passion. If you observe closely, you will find very few people working in the field of their interest. And now, when the work in hand is not of your interest or that which you truly enjoy, does life remain worth living? No... In that case, life becomes so mechanical! Nevertheless, it is in the best interest of your life, that you pursue your field of creativity.

———◼———

Concentration

Concentration is sheer magic. If a person cultivates this one quality in life, then no one can stop him from reaching the zenith of joy and success. Surprisingly, everyone is well aware of this word, and it is also extensively used in schools and colleges. Yet, ironically, this quality is rarely found in a few amongst millions. And, its consequences are right in front of our eyes, as only these few amongst millions, are found to be happy and successful.

But then, why is this the case? This is because man's brain has formulated its own definition of concentration which has nothing to do with concentration in reality. Concentration, as commonly defined by a human being is to focus on one particular thing. One can see that in schools, colleges, homes or offices, the words commonly uttered by everyone are, "Your efforts do not yield results because you are unable to concentrate on one particular task; have focus in life." And in order to reap the desired results, everyone repeatedly attempts to concentrate, yet, the end result is nil; no one is able to concentrate and no one can either. Because nothing can be more foolish than asking someone to concentrate on a particular task and even more foolish is to expect them to follow the advice, make an effort to concentrate and succeed in that attempt!

The crux of the matter is, man has never been serious about my profundity, i.e. the profundity of his mind and the surmountable heights of life he can achieve with it. Even when men of wisdom attempted to explain it, they have always been ignored. Human beings have been so enamoured with their own ludicrous ideologies that right from education to religion, they perceive everything with the same jaundiced eyes. Neither do they perceive the reality with open eyes, nor do they correctly analyse the perceived facts. As a result, they have made grief and failure their destiny.

Well! The world will understand and accept it at its own pace. But if you really want to make your life worthwhile, it is possible only if your actions bear extraordinary results. And, that is not possible without concentration on the task at hand. So now, the question that arises is, how does one increase concentration? Well, this question in itself is wrong. It is nothing but a reflection of the old, imprudent definitions. If you have understood this, you will be able to grasp the magic of concentration in its entirety. Concentration, in fact, is an intrinsic attribute of every human being. It is invariably present in him. It can neither be produced nor increased, nor can it be applied anywhere. For instance, you are solving mathematical calculations and you direct your concentration to be applied to the task; do you think it is possible? No! The entire Nature works on automation, and since concentration is a natural quality of a human being, it too works in complete automation. Neither is it bound by your orders, nor can it be applied to anything in particular at your direction. It just exists; neither does it function as per your need, nor does it have an inclination or affinity towards anything in particular.

I agree that owing to age-old conditioning, it is not easy for you to digest the facts stated above. Therefore, let me elaborate upon it in simple words. As I said, concentration is your natural attribute; it explicitly means that it is always present in you in its totality. Also understand that a human being is bound by physical limitations, because of which he can perform only one task at a time. But the fact that spells trouble for you is, the same is not the case with your brain and me i.e. your mind. We, your mind and brain, can assimilate thousands of things and have already done so. Like concentration, we too are an integral part of your existence. The grave consequence of this is, most of your concentration remains divided amongst those thousands of assimilated things. Then even if you desire, you are unable to concentrate on one task in particular; because, concentration does not function as per your desire, but according to its own principle. And the principle is that it gets divided into your numerous thoughts, various worries and desires, friends and foes, near and dear ones and your acquaintances, according to the emphasis you have laid on each one of them. Well, you are still able to concentrate better on subjects or matters that interest you, but not sufficient enough to yield fruitful results. So, I hope, you must have now grasped what I intended to explain.

For those who have still not, let me elucidate with a simple example. Suppose, lured by a tempting advertisement, you went shopping to the supermarket with a big bag, in the hope that you may find something useful, or get an attractive discount, even though you did not need anything in particular. Now, in order to understand the point I am trying to explain to you, imagine that the bag that you are carrying, is 'concentration'. The fact is, you did not need to shop for anything in particular, but you were dragged there by your greed. However, on reaching there, you gave in to the temptation of discounts so much so, that you even purchased numerous things and returned home with the bag full. Like your concentration, the bag is still with you, but the difference now is, it is filled with scores of items that you did not really need.

Upon reaching home, you felt an urge to have apple juice that you have just brought from the supermarket. If you deal with the bag in a manner similar to the way you deal with concentration, and instruct it, "I am holding you up-side down...carefully throw only the apple juice out." Is that really possible? No! Obviously, all the goods stuffed in the bag will fall out too. Yes, if the bag had contained only packets of apple juice, then only apple juice would have fallen out.

I hope you have understood the point I am explaining. In life, you too deal with your concentration in a manner similar to that of the bag. Every child is born with supreme concentration, but unfortunately, as they grow up, they get enticed by everything attractive that comes their way. Whatever you like, you just keep adding to your bag, which in this example signifies concentration. Taking advantage of this, the clever people who are aware of this habit of yours, have devised numerous tempting offers to lure you. They lure you towards all these inessentials either in the name of school and career or religion, society and culture. And by the time you reach twenty five to thirty years of age, what all have you not collected! You have an educational qualification; you have your own religion and numerous aspirations from your career, family, and so on. Why only this? ...You have countless assimilated theories, principles, knowledge and beliefs too. If you observe carefully, actually you do not spare anything. However, as you reach the age of thirty five to forty, you realise that your life has miserably failed. You could not accomplish anything; on the contrary, you have gathered piles of grievances and worries. And, as if this was not enough, you have burdened yourself with thousands of additional responsibilities. Now, why did this happen? Because you could not perform anything fruitful and effective in life. Being divided among a thousand futile things, you could not concentrate on any one thing. And now bearing the brunt of your failures and the burden of your responsibilities, you are simply awaiting death.

If you actually want to make your life fruitful, then do not give into the temptations and enticements floating around you. Wholeheartedly follow the field which interested you since childhood, where even your talent and capability supports you; enhance it with each passing day. Thereafter, when you find some leisure time, indulge in all the worldly pleasures of life. Enjoy every colour of life to the fullest. Meaning, embrace as many things as you desire that bring you happiness, fun and blissfulness; but not more than two, when it comes to purpose and pursuit in life. Generally you do exactly the opposite; you allow thousands of tasks to become a part of your existence, but gripped by the fear of religion and society, you keep foregoing on your hobbies and passions. As a result, having numerous aims, neither are you able to achieve success in life, nor does life remain an interesting journey after relinquishing your hobbies and passions. And, you are so intelligent that you cannot comprehend or realise such a simple fact of life!

Concentration is the very nature of a human being. It can not be applied at will

I can assure you that your life will become a beautiful journey; for once, just walk the path I have shown, and then see how success follows you at every step. Let me try to explain the same with the example of the great Edison and his remarkable invention. You are all aware that Edison invented the light bulb. As stated earlier, Edison had received formal education for barely a few years. But as he was deeply interested in scientific experiments and was spared formal schooling, he had ample time and opportunities to conduct experiments without any constraints, right from his childhood. Consequently, as he grew up, not just his age but the list of his inventions also continued to grow and he went on to become one of the most acclaimed scientists of the century. The incident I am referring to dates back to the late 1870s, when he decided to discover a filament which would aid his invention of the light bulb.

For Edison, once he made up his mind, there was no turning back. He wasn't the kind to let his focus shift and be divided by the tempting 'offers and advertisements'. He entered the laboratory with his team of fellow scientists with a singular aim, and began work on a war footing. Now, the trait peculiar to Edison was, neither did he carry worries about his wife or children to the laboratory nor did he keep a track of time while working. He did not feel the need to keep himself abreast with the current affairs of the world by reading the newspaper daily. In other words, his bag of concentration always remained empty, and as his focus was

" For a human being,
there is no magic greater than concentration "

solely on experiments, he immediately became absorbed in the search for the filament. And he was engrossed to such an extent that one day, even when it was quite late in the afternoon, he did not have his lunch. Concerned about his health, the house-help brought his lunch to the laboratory. But, since Edison was absorbed in his experiments, he asked the help to place the plate on the table and leave.

After a while, one of his colleagues entered his laboratory. Seeing Edison engrossed in the experiment, he did not wish to disturb him; hence, he sat down on the chair facing him. For a while, he watched Edison's total absorption in his work, but after some time, he ran out of patience. Since, he too had not had his lunch, he polished off the meal that was kept for Edison. As soon as Edison took a break from his experiment, he turned around and found his associate sitting at the table, and immediately began talking to him. While speaking, as his eyes fell on the empty plate, he mentioned to his colleague, "I believe I ate too much today. Look! I have left nothing in the plate." Now tell me, other than his passion for experiments, what did this man carry with him to the laboratory? Success was inevitable. If such is the concentration, success is bound to follow as closely as one's shadow.

However, success is not something awaiting you with open arms. It invariably tests your patience, concentration and determination, and then knocks at your door. Even Edison took more than a year's time, and more than 6000 fibres before he could finally discover a filament that could light the bulb. Think, 6000 failures, and he did not get tired. Why? Because, his concentration was absolute and undivided. Even those who believe in the popular definitions of concentration, commonly cite this episode of Edison's exemplary concentration; how his concentration neither broke nor dwindled even after the 6000 failures he faced during a year. Truly, this is what you call concentration! It is only by applying this kind of concentration that you can create wonders.

However, you will not be able to apply such concentration by following someone's advice. It is simply not possible. You must understand clearly that Edison had not 'applied' concentration, but had stepped inside the laboratory, after giving up all the other futile matters. And, if he had not carried anything in his mind when he entered the laboratory, what was left for him to do, apart from experimenting? Even if it would have taken him ten years to accomplish his goal, you tell me, how could his concentration have deviated? Concentration cannot be achieved by attempting to focus on one thing in particular, or by deciding to do so; for that, the rest of the things have to be relinquished. And once everything else is dropped, your concentration will automatically be channelised into that which remains. This is the one and only law of concentration.

Now, you may say, "We have grasped this point as well as the fact that we must increase our concentration by saving ourselves from giving into temptations and enticements. However, this is a matter pertaining to the future. For now, the concern is, how do we get rid of the divisions we have created within ourselves because of attaching undue importance to a thousand different things? What should we do, to have concentration like that of Edison?"

If these are the questions arising in your mind, then you have grasped what I have stated. I shall now provide the solutions in order to facilitate a better understanding for those who have grasped what has been explained so far.

However, you will first have to comprehend the principle of energy. You must be aware that the more concentrated the energy in a source is, the more powerful it will be. You all know that the smallest part of any element is an atom, yet the most powerful is also an atom. Similarly when it comes to mind, concentration is the most condensed form of the mind. The word 'concentration' has stemmed from the fact that it is the concentrated energy of your mind. In Hindi, it is termed as *'Ekaagrataa'** because it is the most condensed form of energy which has worked many wonders. Once in Russia, a girl had made the hands of a clock move with the concentration of her mind. Moreover, with persistent concentration, she had also stopped the moving hands of the clock.

History has not one, but a thousand such examples. Science has also undertaken extensive research in this regard and has gathered ample evidence. One significant observation made by them is, according to one's level of energy, an 'aura', meaning, an energy field is formed all around a human being's body...and it inevitably does. You too, may have experienced it in your daily life. In case you have not, then I will make you experience it right away. You all must have experienced that some people are quite magnetic, or in a matter of a few minutes of meeting someone, you feel energised. Do you know why this happens? This is the magic of the aura that emanates from the concentrated energy of that individual. The more powerful the aura, the more magnetic he will be. In general, an individual's beauty is defined by his skin colour and facial features; the more beautiful a person is, the more attractive he or she is perceived to be; likewise in the case of the mind, the more powerful the mind, the more powerful

* Ekaagrataa – Concentration

" Concentration is possible only in one's field of interest "

his aura would be. And the more powerful the aura, the more magnetic a person would be. In other words, an aura reflects the beauty of an individual's mind or the intensity of his inner energy.

In order to make it easy for you to understand, let me explain this to you the other way round. Have you come across a person with a powerful aura? Perhaps, you may not have as, very few individuals exist in this world with a powerful aura. Hence, in all likelihood, you may have never encountered a person having a powerful aura. Chances are, you may not have come across a person whose company you long for, or being with whom, you instantly feel renewed with hope and energy, or seeing whom all your sorrows vanish. Well, it does not matter. You must have definitely encountered numerous individuals with a weak aura. If you look around, you will find many of them. The people with weak aura are characterised by their ability to make you feel instantly uncomfortable; you desire to run away from them, avoid them, and when you spend time with them, you are plagued by thousands of anxieties. And because the world is full of people with a weak aura, there is so much of chaos and turmoil amongst human beings. Everyone is always on the edge, waiting to cross swords with each other. It has become a norm for everyone to rant about how they are sick and tired of others.

Now, I am sure, you must have understood the role one's aura plays. Moreover, I have already explained that the more concentrated the mind is, the more powerful will the aura be. And to be more explicit, just as people yearn the companionship of beautiful people, everyone's mind longs to be in the company of a person with a powerful aura. And just as no one would be willing to marry a girl who is not pretty, no one likes to be in the company of people with a weak aura.

Well, why should you be bothered if someone is happy with you or not? Does it even matter if someone desires your company or not? And because you are exceedingly brilliant, you may say, "Forget it, how does it matter to us if our aura is weak?" Then I would say, "Have you not you spoken like an extra-intelligent person?"

Allow me to open your eyes to the importance of a powerful aura. Your weak aura signifies that your energy is not concentrated, and since your energy is not concentrated, you will never be able to taste happiness and success in life. You will find yourself incapable of performing any task effectively. Successful people, irrespective of the place and field, invariably have powerful auras, though their intensity may vary.

Now, you will say, "Oh! Is that the way it is! We also wish to make our aura powerful... we also need to condense our energy and concentrate it."

See? When I spoke in the language that piqued your interest, how quickly you grasped what I have been saying all along!

No problem, better late than never, because the only way to make your life successful is by concentrating your energy. Other than concentrating your energy, even if you try numerous other ways, you will never be able to taste success or happiness. No human being is successful because of his academic qualification or religion; but only because of his concentrated energy. Look at it from a different perspective; can a car fly in the air? No; not with its present energy and technological constraints. So then, will it never fly? It definitely will; only when the necessary technical barriers have been surmounted and the requisite energy is sourced. It does not matter, whether the car is manufactured in a Hindu country or a Christian country, but it is not possible for a car to fly in its present condition. If the car has to fly, there is no alternative other than supplying it with the requisite energy.

Yes, planes can surely fly, because they are supplied with the requisite energy to fly. However, at present, they too cannot overcome the earth's gravitational pull and fly to the Moon and Mars. If they also have to travel beyond the pull of the earth's gravity, then they too need to be provided with the adequate energy. Similarly, if you want to elevate your life from the level of a bullock cart to that of a car, you will have to provide yourself with the requisite energy. And if you want to further elevate your life, from the level of the car to flying high in the sky, you will need to provide even more energy. Furthermore, if you wish to radically change your life and make it synonymous with success, you will need to break past the gravitational pull exerted on you by the world. And you do not need to be told about the amount of energy you would require to do that, right?

Moving on, you have now understood that mankind cannot progress without increasing the 'energy concentration' in their lives, meaning, if a human being wants to grow and drastically transform his life, there is no other option but to increase his energy levels. But then the question is, where to source that energy from? There are no gas stations available to fuel energy into the minds of human beings.... Wait!...I will explain that too. In human life, energy can be acquired from two sources. There are certain acts which when indulged in, can give you extra energy and on the other hand, there are acts, which if avoided, can help you conserve your energy. In both the cases, for a human being, the ultimate result is a rise in his energy level.

So, first let us discuss the available sources from where one can garner this energy. As stated earlier, a human being's mind, brain and body have a deep connection. Though energy is solely my subject, an individual's brain and body too have a deep impact on it. Therefore, I will begin with the human body. In order to energise mind, a high level of physical energy proves to be of great help. But if you wish to be physically energetic, it demands some time and consistent dedication from your end. To attain energy at a physical level, you need to undertake the following measures:

1) **Exercise:** It is extremely important for every individual to exercise daily for an hour. For human life, exercise is a great natural source of energy. Exercise helps in restoring the impaired acid-alkaline balance thus keeping the *Pitta*[*1], *Vayu*[*2] and *Kapha*[*3] (called *Tridoshas*[*4]) well-balanced, which leaves you physically energetic.

2) **Sleep:** Sound sleep, in itself, is an amazing source of energy. But the sleep needs to be scheduled in a manner that you can wake up at sunrise. Waking up late, even if you complete your sleep, it will not reap you any benefit in terms of energy.

3) **Regular Meals:** Depriving the body of food or binging, both are equally dangerous for the body. A small regular meal of your liking, every three hours, is a tried and tested formula for energy. An empty or excessively full stomach disrupts the acid-alkaline levels, which gradually drains you of energy.

You must have had several experiences of the ill-effects of being physically weak. If your body is bereft of energy, even a trip to Switzerland cannot bring you happiness. Without physical energy, increasing the energy of the mind becomes merely a pipe dream.

[*1] Pitta – Qualities reflecting the element of fire and water
[*2] Vayu- Qualities reflecting the elements of space and air
[*3] Kapha- Qualities reflecting the elements of water and earth
[*4] Tridoshas - The Tridoshas are the primary and essential factors of the human body
    that govern our entire physical structure and function.

Inability to focus denotes a dislike for that field of work or a lack of energy

Therefore, if you have understood how to gain physical energy, then we shall discuss the energy at the level of the brain. The brain is an integral part of the body. Hence, the brain also feels energised by the same things that energise the body. The same diet that strengthens the body, more or less fuels your brain too.

Now, if I begin to talk about myself i.e. your mind, then what can I say? ...I am altogether different. As far as raising the level of my energy is concerned, there is just one formula for it; if things happen in accordance with me, then energy is gained and if one acts contrary to my wish, energy is drained. Hence, this matter does not need further elaboration. You must have had thousands of such experiences. If you have not observed it earlier, pay attention to it now. After just a day's experience, you will realise that you feel energetic, when things happen as per your desire...otherwise, you invariably feel enervated.

Now, as far as loss of energy is concerned, human greed has made sufficient arrangements for it in many ways. The greatest undoing of man is, owing to his greed, one human being has become the enemy of another. For the fulfilment of their selfish interests, they have placed thousands of magnetic 'siphons' all around to suck the energy out of people. Understand this matter from a scientific perspective; in a human being, the source of concentrated energy is situated in my deeper recesses, i.e. at the depths of his mind near the navel, whereas, a human being functions as per his brain. Just as energy is required to lift something up, an individual also requires energy to advance, from the level of the brain to the concentration point located in the depths of his mind. Just as the gravitational force of the earth exerts a pull and does not allow an object to rise, greed and fear, bred all around by human beings, do not allow human beings to progress to the depths of their mind.

So open your eyes, and first recognise these various forces that pull you back in the name of career, religion, caste, creed and society. The more one is able to safeguard himself from these traps, the more easily he would be able to save himself from the futile waste of his energy. And the higher his energy level rises, the deeper would he be able to delve into his mind. And, the deeper he delves into the depths of his mind, the more intense his level of concentration would be. This is the only formula to increase one's concentration.

Then, this rise in the level of concentration has one more interesting facet, and that is, if your mind is focussed on a certain task, your energy moves in a circular motion. When energy moves in a circular motion, no loss of energy occurs. Here, you must note that the energy of the entire Universe also moves in a circular motion. And that is why, as you can see, so many complex functions are being performed by various elements of Nature, yet, their energy never gets depleted. In the same manner, whenever an individual carries out any task with full concentration, his energy never gets drained.

Additionally, if you require proof of this fact, then skim through the lives of the energetic people born so far, and read their life story. See, how they safeguarded themselves from the web of various forces, spun out of greed and fear by fellow human beings. You will be surprised to know that a majority of these people did not receive great formal education or have even a semblance of religion in their lives. Most of them had stayed free from numerous unnecessary responsibilities too. Meaning, they simply did not waste their energy in learning, knowing, reading or doing futile things. They just went about making their minds more and more condensed. And then, one day, with their concentrated energy, they accomplished great feats.

At this juncture, what you need to understand is, the maximum amount of energy of a human being is consumed in using his brain. Ordinarily, an individual keeps applying his brain to every trivial task or even matters irrelevant to him. He keeps thinking for no rhyme or reason, which ultimately results in him being unable to use his brain at the critical moment, when it is genuinely required. And this in turn leads him to complain that his brain does not function properly.

How will it work? All your energy was spent in knowing and understanding futile things. Therefore, on careful observation you will find that the people who think a lot may appear brilliant to you, but in reality, at the level of the mind, they are indeed foolish. The one who possesses knowledge about numerous subjects may seem talented to you but in reality, such a person is substantially lacking in energy. This is because he has wasted all his energy in thinking and accumulating futile information. And, when energy is required to accomplish a certain task, he does not have any left in him. You must have often seen people cribbing, "Despite having immense potential, I am unable to accomplish anything; my destiny is not in my favour." It is not that their destiny is unfavourable, but their actions are wrong! They have wasted all their 'life energy' in vain.

Therefore, please do not give unnecessary importance to any subject, apart from the field in which you wish to excel and achieve phenomenal success. If you are really interested in becoming a doctor, engineer or scientist, then it is alright to take studies so seriously, otherwise, be ready to face the dire consequences of your action. For example, if Mozart did not have knowledge of any other subject apart from music...would that have changed the melody of his mellifluous compositions? No, but if this music had not flowed from the depths of his mind, he would never have become a Mozart. He is Mozart because his concentrated energy was applied to music.

Perhaps, now you must have grasped the importance of the concentrated energy of the mind, the ways to achieve this concentration, and the obstacles you could encounter in doing so. I shall now reveal the most amazing quality of this point of concentrated energy lying in the depths of your mind. This is such a powerful centre of energy that it will not be wrong if I say, it is the 'only' source of the qualities required for progressing in life. Because concentration is the magic which encompasses all the qualities necessary for progress, right from confidence to enthusiasm. This is the reason why concentration is the king of all qualities. In other words, if concentration is attained, then all the qualities required for progressing in life will invariably follow. Let me explain this to you with the example of Edison that I have used earlier.

I had already elaborated upon Edison's experiment, entailing the search of the filament used for illuminating the bulb. Now think, what would his absorption in a single experiment for an entire year be called? Indeed, it was the height of Edison's concentration. However, what I wish to iterate here is, at such a high level of concentration, all the qualities required for progress in life automatically manifest. For example, if Edison thought that to illuminate a bulb, a filament could be discovered, would you not call it a marvel of Edison's vision and foresight? In spite of 6000 failed attempts, if he still remained unperturbed and persisted his search of a filament to light up the bulb, what else could it be termed, if not his self-confidence? Was it not his faith in his vision that gave him the conviction that there must be a filament which could light the bulb? Even after 6000 failures, neither did he accept defeat nor did he get exhausted, or abandon his experiments; would you not call this the height of Edison's enthusiasm? All in all, what I mean to say is, concentration is that magical quality, which, if achieved once, automatically leads to the manifestation of all the other qualities required to progress in life.

So, I am sure, you have now comprehended the fact that concentration is a magic wand, without which, one cannot taste success in life. As the current topic is about concentration, let me recount a story. Years ago, there lived a hermit in Turkey. As he possessed profound knowledge of all facets of human life, his reputation soon spread far and wide. People came from great distances to learn and gain knowledge from him. However, his ways of imparting knowledge were somewhat strange, which some could comprehend, while others could not. Regardless of this, his fame was spreading far and wide. Finally, the news of his wisdom reached the ears of the king as well. The king thought, "Such a sagacious hermit is in my kingdom and all my subjects are benefitting from his wisdom; then why should I not use this opportunity?"

Thus one day, along with his retinue, he reached the doorstep of the hermit. The hermit was digging a pit in his garden. The king instantly commanded his soldiers to inform the hermit of his arrival. The king thought that on hearing the news of his arrival, the hermit's joy will know no bounds. However, to his disappointment nothing of that sort happened. The soldiers gave the news and returned, but the hermit continued with his digging. The king was taken aback for a moment; he felt insulted in front of his retinue of servants and soldiers. But he retained his composure and began to stroll in the backyard where the hermit was digging the pit. However, the hermit was still engrossed in digging the pit. After some time, the king lost his patience. He wondered, *"Is he a hermit or a madman? Had he been involved in something important or offering prayers, it was understandable, but he is just digging a pit...and he still has the audacity to make me wait!"* For a moment he thought to himself, *"Instead of being humiliated, I should leave."* But then he thought, *"Now that I've come so far, let me at least meet him and leave."* Hence in restlessness, he began to stroll even faster.

True to his nature, the hermit was still completely engrossed in digging the pit. On the other hand, with every passing minute, the king's restlessness was turning into anger. He wanted to return, but now, curiosity had gripped him. Irritated by the act of the hermit, he did not wish to leave without knowing the reason. Essentially, he had come to gain wisdom, but since the hermit seemed to be a madman to him, there was no question of his acquiring knowledge from him. Now, he was anxiously waiting only to know the reason why the hermit was behaving in such a strange manner. While the king was mulling over these questions, the hermit finished his task and walked towards the

212

king. He immediately welcomed the king, asked for his forgiveness for making him wait and offered him a comfortable seat.

However, as the king was furious, he did not pay any heed to the hermit's warm greetings. On the contrary, he vented out his anger on the hermit and said, "I had come to gain wisdom from you, but now I do not care. Tell me, why did you make me wait for so long while you were doing such a menial task?"

Listening to the question, the hermit looked straight into the eyes of the king, and then, letting out a hearty laugh, he said, "As far as the triviality of a task is concerned, no task is ordinary or great. When it comes to knowledge, I have already imparted it to you. Now whether you wish to grasp it or not, is your choice."

"Given it...?" Now, the king was startled. "We did not even begin a conversation. I have not asked a single question, yet he says, he has already imparted knowledge to me! Undoubtedly, this hermit is a madman." Now the hermit's answer had piqued the king's curiosity. He was compelled to think whether the hermit was actually mad or was pretending to be so? He thought, "If the entire village believes him to be a wise man, then the entire village cannot be mad...or maybe they are!" Still to clear the air, he pointedly asked the hermit, "Please tell me, what knowledge did you impart? Since the time I have arrived, you have just been digging the pit."

The hermit replied in a compassionate manner, "This is where you are mistaken Your Majesty. You did not observe carefully; in fact, I was not digging the pit, but had become one with the process of digging. Had you carefully observed my concentration in digging, you would have learnt all that you needed; because, apart from such concentration and passion, there is nothing worth learning in life."

Now what lesson did the king learn from his interaction with the hermit is not our subject at present. But the lesson that you need to take away from this story is, if you wish to reach the zenith of success in life, then remember, without delving into the point of concentration lying in the deep recesses of your mind, you cannot progress or do any good unto yourself. You can surely look for thousands of other

In Concentration your energy mOves in a circular motion

solutions or seek support from numerous other avenues, but it will all be in vain. Everyone is seeking thousands of such solutions, but then what is happening to others, will happen to you as well. You will never find yourself in the league of Newton, Beethoven or Shakespeare. Forget that, without concentration, even ordinary success will elude you forever.

So, if you have understood this, and if you really want to reach the highest levels of concentration, then you not only need to amass energy, but also need to conserve the energy that is being consumed on numerous other futile things. You first need to forestall your concentration from being divided under any circumstance, and then channelise it into a unified direction. If you are currently living with divided energy, you will have to retract. After that, you will have to erase the information and the thoughts you have gathered and relinquish the responsibilities you have assumed so far, one by one on a daily basis. And I promise, as you go about shedding and undoing one thing after another, your concentration will keep increasing. The great philosopher Vivekananda also brought the same fact to light. When he gained worldwide fame, a journalist asked him, "You seem to be a supremely wise man. Does there still remain anything for you to learn?" Do you know what Vivekananda's reply was? He said, "As such, learning is not much needed in life, which, unfortunately, I have realised now. Today I'm only being troubled by whatever I have learnt in the past. Now all that I am engaged in is forgetting and unlearning them; there is nothing left to learn."

You, too, observe your life carefully. See what all things and information you have learnt and accumulated in your life considering it necessary. On close scrutiny, you will realise that these are the very things that have become the root cause of your problems, and this is applicable to almost everything you know. Be it your acquired knowledge, adopted religion, accumulated things or cultivated relationships. If you observe closely, you will find, it is only these factors that are sucking the life energy out of you. It is futile to talk about increasing concentration at this juncture, when you are bereft of the very life-energy. What can I say about reaching the zenith of success and prosperity, when living a normal life has become a task for you? But you still have a chance, if you immediately start following what Vivekananda said and give up one thing every day, then even today, you may become re-energised. No doubt it is late, but not so late that you cannot set things right.

In short, life is nothing but the play of energy. The higher the level of energy, the higher will be the level of concentration. The higher the level of concentration in your work, the more effective will your actions be. And even if your energy has already been divided owing to learning, knowing and indulging in futile things, by understanding the methodology I have outlined, you can always start afresh. Then, why wait? From today onwards, relinquish whatever seems inessential and henceforth, refrain from accumulating anything that is not required, and then see, how soon you begin to feel energised again.

And once you have restored your energy levels, sit peacefully in solitude and introspect upon the acts that interest you or bring you joy, and then stay in tune with them. In fact, take the decision to quit your present job, if it does not interest you and it is only due to high salary that you are dragging along. Instead, find a job in the field of your interest. Even if the salary is less, bear with it, because you will be able to concentrate better on the work of your interest. If you are focused, you will be able to work more efficiently. And if you work efficiently, your work will speak for itself, and you will definitely be noticed by the new management. It may take some time and some painstaking efforts, but your growth in this new company will be faster. Because of your sustained focus on your work, your energy will begin to flow in a circular motion, which in turn, will energise you further. Thus, you will progress much faster and attain a good position at the new job. Also remember, the only way to discover the field in which your potential lies is by rightly identifying the task on which you can easily concentrate, and work which you truly enjoy doing. And know for sure that you cannot leave a lasting impression in any field apart from the one, in which, you are able to easily concentrate on your tasks, and also feel joyous while doing them.

The previous discussion culminated on the subject of joy; well, joy is also one of the major sources of energy. As I have said before, whenever you are engaged in a task in the field of your interest, your energy is not expended. On the contrary, it gets accumulated and rises exponentially. However, you cannot do the same repetitive work all the time. There is a limit to working, even if the work is to your liking, and once you have reached the limit, then even that work begins to drain your energy. This is the time when you need to take a break from your routine tasks, meaning, you need to indulge in a hobby or some recreational activity; be it listening to music, sports, relaxation or travel. Definitely, this break helps you regain your lost energy and such activities should be an integral part of your life. Doing a task of your choice has its own joy, so is the joy of taking a break from that task.

Therefore, if you do not want your energy to be drained ever, then it is important to take a break every day from the humdrum of life. This break from work will replenish you with the energy to work again next day. To enjoy this break, it is necessary for an individual to have a zest for life, that is, be a lover of arts, fond of sports or have some hobbies. These are the only ways that can help an individual regain the energy that has been consumed while doing his tasks. If you do not take the breaks, the amount of energy you have harnessed will surely get exhausted one day. And this has been the case with not one, but thousands of intellectuals. You must have seen that many artists, businessmen and people from various fields display avid enthusiasm till a certain age, and achieve phenomenal success, but then suddenly, they hit a wall. Why? Because they fail to understand that the secret source of regaining the energy lost in the monotony of the tasks is, maintaining the right balance between work and recreation. If you have a love for fine arts…Wonderful! There cannot be a greater source of energy than the love for art. When I say 'love for art', I mean, you need not be a great painter, but you can just paint something for yourself, or watch a good play or a movie, or listen to the nice, melodious music of your choice for an hour or two a day. Just as it is necessary to exercise daily for an hour to keep yourself fit and energetic, it is equally imperative to let yourself be absorbed in arts or music for an hour or two.

Moreover, for a blissful and brighter life, it is equally necessary for an individual to indulge in self-gratification, whether it is through dancing, eating, dressing or travelling; in case of hobbies, it is always the more the merrier, because that leaves you permanently high on life. Also the exhilaration you experience while indulging in these activities always re-energises you. Indulging thus, you will never feel enervated. If you observe closely, you will find that those who do not indulge in self-gratification invariably lack energy. Similarly, having a fun-loving, naughty or humorous nature will always keep you light-hearted. Hence, do not ever be serious in life. Do not stop being 'childlike' because, seriousness is a disease that drains all your life-energy.

You, too, must have surely experienced the facts that I have stated. In case you have not, try doing what I have stated above and experience it now. This is the beauty of all matters pertaining to the mind; true psychology always proves what it states. Science, on the other hand, has to conduct innumerable experiments to prove its point; well, at least it gets proven! In case of these so-called religions, the points made by them, are never proven. Leaving that aside, let us discuss psychology, which is self-sufficient when it comes to proving itself. You must have experienced that when you take a break and go for a vacation for five-six days a year, upon returning, you feel re-energised for the next six months. However, I would like to address a common problem here; most people do not even know how to take a break. Even in times of relaxation and enjoyment, their phone keeps ringing. Even while travelling, they carry the burden of their office work on their mind. No! You will not gain energy in this manner. The very meaning of taking a break is, every day in life for an hour or two you relax and have fun, and for five-six days, twice a year, enjoy leisure time and take complete rest. If you learn the art of resting, I assure you that you will never feel drained of energy. But here, let me clarify that this is applicable only if you are working in your chosen field of interest.

Well, I hope by now you have understood the secret of concentration and the calculations of energy that I have revealed to you, and also grasped the ways to acquire them, and the means to increase them. So, I hope, after understanding this secret of concentration and energy, you will leave no stone unturned to make your lives successful.

———————

Curtail your Ambitions

If you really wish to succeed in life, keep your ambitions weak and low. You will say that I am making a statement contrary to what the world preaches. No! In fact, I stand in stark contrast to your brain's definition ...hence you perceive me as a contradictory entity. Since 'success' is my subject, that is, the subject of the mind, and not of the brain, the brain is unable to grasp the formula of success. It consistently convinces you, "If you wish to grow and prosper, then aim high, harbour great ambitions." But this is absolutely wrong!

And remember, I do not talk through my hat! My statements are backed by proof and so is my functioning, as well as its consequences. Let me clarify one more thing here; just as the entire Nature and its every element is governed by a law, I too, am governed by certain laws. And one among them is, the greater the ambitions one harbours, greater are the failures in life. History stands witness to this statement of mine. Is there anyone in this world without an ambition? Is there any child from whom one does not have great expectations? Who does not dream of becoming someone 'big' in life? However, in reality, how many are able to achieve success? Surprisingly, barely one amongst thousands and millions! Are these numbers not enough to prove my statement?

If you have understood the point I have made, then I will discuss its causes with you. Because whatever I say, I will substantiate it too. However, since I am invisible, the matters pertaining to me and their influences are not going to be proven in a scientific laboratory. My laboratory is human life; hence take a look at your life as well as that of others, and you will find ample proof of all that I have stated.

Now I will try to explain to you, how your ambitions become an obstacle in your path to achieving success. The first thing to note here is, either these ambitions are being thrust upon you, or you have embraced them under the influence of the outside world. However, I have nothing to do with these ambitions that you have embraced from external sources. Because I have my own reasons and accordingly, I function in my own unique way. The external world does not exert even a shred of influence over me.

Now the question is, how can an individual achieve success abiding by my unique system of functioning? A straight and simple formula for this is, he should become a master in one particular field. But who will decide which field it should be? Definitely, I will decide that! I am the one who instils interests in a human being, and it is only I, who has the potential to enhance those interests too. Additionally, it is only I who attracts the individuals towards those interests. This is my sovereign rule, where I do not tolerate any interference from any external force. And to tell you the truth, the external forces cannot do anything about it either. I am the one who instils business acumen in some, and scientific aptitude in others; someone possesses the art of music, while someone has an inclination towards literature. Even if the whole world unites and forces a child to transform into a poet, then too, it is not possible, unless leaning towards poetry is not instilled in him by me.

If you have understood my sovereignty then also understand that success is the birthright of every human being. But, the problem arises when there is interference in my domain. Since it is I who creates interest in an individual, it is obvious that in which field he will achieve success is also determined by me. But as soon as I try to make the child walk the path that I have chosen for him, his family members hinder his path and veer him away. The mother inculcates the ambition of becoming a doctor in him, while the father insists on making him a businessman. His uncle asks him to be a scientist, while his grandfather advises him to be a poet. And the poor child has to listen to all of them. And when he listens to them, he will aspire for those goals and have high self-expectations. And it is these expectations which lead him astray from the path meant for him. By the time he steps into his youth, he usually has nurtured ambitions in several fields, and has already tried his hands at a few of them. However, it is all in vain, because he is trying to work against my wishes. While I am prompting poems from within, he is trying his hand at business! This is where the friction between me and his brain begins. The brain does not provide an outlet for the poems to spring forth and I do not support him to succeed in business. Human beings must understand that they can become successful only in the field I have chosen for them. Therefore, the family members must closely observe the changing interests of the child rather than thrusting ambitions upon him. Encourage the child to pursue the field in which he shows great potential. One day, he will definitely attain success in that field.

Now that you have understood all that has been discussed so far, let us move on to the second point. Mood, concentration and confidence are all my subjects and not that of the brain. I ensure that mood, concentration and confidence be applied only in the field that I have chosen for him. Any attempt of the brain to engage a person in some other field would be rendered ineffective by me. Simply put, I will not let a human being concentrate on any field other than the one I have chosen for him, neither will I accord him the mood required for that work. Just think, without mood and concentration, irrespective of your hard work,

Success is achieved in an unexpected manner at an unexpected time by people least expected to

would it yield any result? Do you not know that the people who toil are called 'labourers'? And take a look at the people who have gone against me; I have reduced them to nothing, but ordinary labourers!

Now, let us take a look at another dangerous consequence of going against me. Agreed, consistently persevering in one particular field certainly makes you knowledgeable about it to a certain extent. It is also true, that due to the persistent efforts put in that task, your intelligence does get awakened and you may achieve a fraction of success in life. But after such painstaking efforts, of what significance is that little success? How many troubles do I make you endure, for choosing a field other than the field of your interest chosen by me! How many times do I make you cringe from within! Moreover, even after achieving success, I make you experience restlessness till your very last breath for not working in the field of your interest. Instead, if you traverse the path suggested by me, I will confer upon you a life in which you will enjoy your work and also achieve a thousand times greater success with minimal amount of effort.

I hope by now, you must have realised my absolute authority over making your life a success; and must have also seen how because of your ambitions prompted by external influence, you deviate from the path of success. Moreover, I have already explained a number of times, how to identify the field in which I want your talents and intelligence to grow. Even so, to make it absolutely clear, I will explain it to you once more. The field that repeatedly captures your interest; working in which, you are completely focussed and through which you derive a sense of joy; realise that to be the field, in which I am trying to awaken your intelligence and talents. Furthermore, if completion of the task gives you a feeling of satisfaction, then clearly that is the field meant for you. Just pursue it wholeheartedly, and see, how I make you scale the unprecedented peaks of success.

Now proceeding further let me acquaint you with the numerous other losses you suffer on account of your ambitions. By now, you must have understood that your life is nothing, but the reflection of all that transpires at my level, that is, your entire life is played out on my 'screen'. Be it happiness or sorrows, content or discontent, I am the medium through which you experience every emotion. Moreover, my system of functioning follows a set of laws. Since it is systematically governed, it effectuates automatic reactions at my level, based on your decisions and actions. Since you are unaware of my laws and its system of functioning, certainly, the effect of all those reactions are contrary to what you would have thought. Hence, your life can definitely change for the better, provided you establish a harmony with my laws, and act accordingly. Else, be prepared to bear the consequences as per the laws of my complex mechanism.

If all this has been understood, I will also reveal another nuance of my mechanism. Please understand this carefully, as it is imperative for you to know how I crush ambitious people who violate my law. Now, the moment you harbour an ambition, you immediately deviate from the actual task at hand. However, effective results are possible only when tasks are carried out with precision and perfection, and not ambitions. For example, a child harbours an ambition to top the class. Let him do so, but the moment he sets this goal for himself, I get down to my job. Then, whenever he sits to study, I flood him with not one, but many thoughts. No sooner he focuses on his studies, than I sow the seed of doubt, *"I am making sincere efforts...but will I top the class or not?"* Thus, at the first step itself, I reduce his faith in himself and shake the very foundation of his confidence in his capabilities.

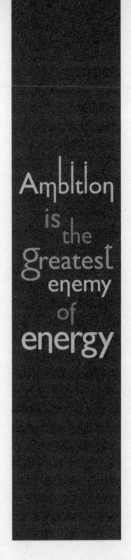

Ambition is the greatest enemy of energy

Ambition diverts your focus from the work

Well, even if he vanquishes these thoughts and tries to bring himself to focus again, how would it help? Again, I interfere and compel him to be lost in the dreams of topping the class... He thinks, *"Indeed, when I stand first, I will become the apple of my parent's eyes. When I am felicitated by the principal, the entire school will be in awe of me."* Now ask yourself, does day dreaming and studying go hand-in-hand? In that case, how do you expect him to study attentively? And even if he manages to dodge those dreams for a moment, how would that help? Mischievous that I am, I once again prod him with the thought, 'What if I do not come first in class?' and so on. In short, I will create thousands of distractions and make sure that he is not able to concentrate on his studies. Then, how will he be able to top the class?

In contrast to this stands the example of a boy who is interested in academics and enjoys studying; he just need not think about the results of his actions. The chances of him becoming the topper are definitely high. Fruits are borne out of actions, not thoughts. Why do you not simply comprehend that diligent actions are bound to bring the desired results. And of course, the results will be proportionate to the quality of the task performed. For that, you need not bear the additional burden of thinking about the results of the tasks. Then why should you unnecessarily fragment your energy by dwelling upon the results?

Remember, this rule of ambition is applicable to every task, from the smallest to the biggest, irrespective of its kind and nature. A thousand miles can easily be covered by walking a step at a time, but the person who stops to think at each step cannot reach anywhere. Even if he ultimately covers the distance, he will surely not reach in time. Therefore, the man who solely focuses on the task rather than thinking about the results inevitably succeeds in taking a thousand successful steps, one at a time. For example, if a musician thinks about creating a thousand successful tunes, what will happen? If he harbours such an ambition, at the very onset, he would distort the quality of his tunes. Now how can such an ambitious person, who remains engrossed in his dreams of awards and accolades, compose a mellifluous tune?

If we take the example of another musician who, unlike him, enjoys composing creative melodies; then because he derives pleasure in composing, one after the other, classic compositions will flow through him. And soon, accolades and fame will become his destiny. For that, why would he need to harbour ambitions separately? In other words, only the one who concentrates on the task and thoroughly enjoys it, can scale the peaks of success. This is what is called an individual's passion or devotion. For a passionate person, there is no need to harbour ambitions. Bear it in mind, that if, even a passionate person, progressing with each step becomes ambitious when he is halfway through, then he too will stagnate and will not be able to progress from that point onwards. Because, the rise of ambition automatically leads to the deterioration of the quality of his work. And as I stated earlier, it is the quality of work that begets effective results, not ambitions.

I hope you have grasped what I have explained so far, that if you focus on the work, results will inevitably follow. Being ambitious leads to the fragmentation of your concentration which in turn, makes the quality of your work suffer. In order to progress, it is not necessary to think about progress; just consecutive successful completion of tasks at hand will inevitably help you progress and succeed in life. Whether you think of it or not, whether you wish for it or not, you will find success at every step of your path.

However, the facts mentioned above are applicable to people who are active in a single field of work, meaning those who are living with one ambition. But, what about those who are living with a thousand ambitions? Neither do I need to say anything about them, nor do you need to ask! Take a look at your life as well as that of the people around, you will understand everything yourself.

If you still do not understand, then you have failed to realise the importance of your life. Life is meant to be enjoyed to the fullest, and to accomplish something great, before death knocks at your door. Just as everything in Nature is precious, so is every human being. Just as the sun, air, water and every element of Nature is so important that it is impossible for life to exist without them; your presence or your absence both must leave an impact on humanity. Life is not just about breathing, but leaving your indelible mark on the world.

In order to make it explicitly clear, let me cite a few examples. I shall explain to you how those who did not harbour any ambitions, but just enjoyed their work were conferred phenomenal success by me. You must have heard the name of the acclaimed painter, Vincent Van Gogh. Painting was his passion, which he even pursued to his heart's content. However, commercial gains, accolades, fame or money was never his goal. For him, the sheer delight he gained from painting was the only desired outcome he expected from his works. Then how can his passion for painting be paralleled by anyone in this world?

He merely created the paintings and stored them, or at the most, gifted his friends when he visited them, or hung them on their walls. Friends with no sense of appreciation for art would take them off from the wall, as soon as Vincent left. They thought, why unnecessarily spoil the beauty of the living room? But how could such acts distract Vincent's concentration? His focus remained steadfast as he was deeply passionate about painting.

One day, he was watching the sunset from a mountain. Watching the glorious beauty of the sunset, he was awestruck and decided to bring it to life on his canvas. Then, stationing himself on the mountain for months, he was absorbed in painting the sunset. Now,

> **" Results are achieved by working towards them
> not by being ambitious "**

with that kind of passion, results were bound to follow. That painting became immortal in history. However, it was only after his death that his painting received recognition. Later, this painting earned him the glory of being one of the most renowned painters of the world. Thereupon, all his works stormed the market and began to fetch very high prices. Needless to say, his friends were also greatly benefitted.

All in all, diligent execution of the task inevitably brings success. Success is proportionate to the quality of work and quality is proportionate to the concentration in that particular task. There is no other formula for success. The failures of innumerable human beings can be solely attributed to a lack of understanding of this simple formula. If they understand it, I am keen to take them to the unprecedented heights of success.

Still if the mists of doubt fog your vision, take a look at your own lives. What is ambition? It is nothing but a kind of desire. As I have already stated, the moment you desire, your focus shifts away from the task, whereas accomplishment is the result of wholehearted action, not of desire. Here, let me state it explicitly that, let alone your desires for great success, I treat even the basic human desires in the same manner. Hence, if you observe your life closely, you will notice that you never get what you desire. And what you get, is not what you have desired. You desire success, but receive failure. You desire happiness but receive sorrow. You desire harmony in relations, but receive bitterness instead. Why? That was because the very act of your very desiring diverts your focus from the efforts necessary to bring the task to fruition. And the resultant present state of your life is right before your eyes to see.

Well, if you are hell-bent on not learning from the failures of your life, the choice is yours! Perhaps your ego is acting as an obstacle, because, the acknowledgement or acceptance of one's fault or failure is not amenable to the human ego. So, I would request you to look at the history of mankind. History and the lives of successful people will stand in mute testimony to the truth I have stated. And history bears witness to not one, but many such examples. There will be no exceptions because everything is transpiring in accordance with the law.

Just think, could a child-like Edison, who received barely a few years of formal education, aim to become one of the most successful scientist of the world? No! Read about his life, it was his passion that made him successful. Similarly, could Albert Einstein, who was considered an ordinary child in school, afford to nurture an ambition of being known as the most intelligent man of the millennium? No, it was his concentration that earned him the status of a legendary personality. Just think, could Dhirubhai Ambani, the founder of the gigantic empire of the Reliance Group, who worked at a gas station, ever aim to be noted as one amongst the most affluent people in the world? No, it was his foresight and an unparalleled understanding of the changing circumstances that enabled him to accomplish such a remarkable feat. His venturing into the domain of his interest acted as fuel to the fire of his intrinsic abilities, and transformed him into the man of steel that he was. Now, take the example of Steve Jobs; could a person like him, who faced the stigma of being born out of wedlock, and had renounced the luxuries of life right at the peak of his youth to become a monk in India, ever aim for the kind of success that he got? The odds were heavily stacked against him. But, his unconventional thinking and self-reliance made him one of the most noteworthy innovators of the century.

In essence, a human being's ambition is the biggest obstacle in his path to success. As, these ambitions not only divide his concentration, but also lead him astray from the field of his interest. And it is an immutable truth that it is only in the field of an individual's interest that his intelligence develops to the fullest. When tasks are performed in the field of interest with due diligence and complete concentration, they are bound to bring about miraculous results. It is only with persistent accomplishment of the tasks in this manner that an individual can attain the peaks of success in his life. Therefore, I will end this discussion with the hope that after reflecting on the facts that I have stated, you will keep your ambitions at bay and focus on the tasks at hand, and thereby reach the pinnacle of success.

———————————————■———————————————

Self Confidence

"Self-confidence is the key to success!" This statement has been echoing in your ears for ages, "To accomplish anything without self-confidence is just not possible." However, the true meaning of self-confidence is known to barely a few. Like the other attributes of the mind, self-confidence is also an attribute intrinsic to a human being. It can neither be acquired nor augmented.

Before delving into this subject, first understand the ultimate freedom of a human being and my i.e. your mind's vehemently independent nature. All the powers of the world put together, cannot compel me to do anything against my wish, even for a second. Even the collective strength of the armed forces of the world cannot force an individual to forget a particular thing forever. He is always free to remember it. Yes, he can fool the armed forces by feigning to have forgotten, but to forget it or not in reality, is solely his own prerogative. A human being can always be subjected to physical bondage, but as far as I am concerned, I am absolutely free in all circumstances and situations.

Now, the significant point worth mulling about is, no other element or living being in Nature is endowed with this privilege of ultimate freedom. And since it is I who has the privilege of this ultimate freedom, the responsibility of your growth and progress also lies on my shoulders. Hence, I consistently boost the self-confidence of the one who entrusts this responsibility to me. And, the one who entrusts this responsibility to others, I, instantaneously shake the very foundation of the confidence that he has in himself. And, how can a person with waning self-confidence ever taste success in life?

It is your life, so how can the responsibility for it lie with your boss or family? It is you who desire success, then how can you depend upon educational qualification or a good-luck charm for it? It is you who wants to progress in life, how can you expect religious shrines or God to help you progress? How absurd is that? This is nothing but a violation of my law...complete distrust in your own self. And when you do not trust yourself, how can you even expect a result to follow? As it is, when you rely on others, you avoid or hesitate to take any effective actions yourselves, whereas the results are, in fact, the consequences of your own actions.

Having grasped this, let us advance our understanding of the subject, with the fact that confidence exists at two levels. The first level comprises routine experiences which you all would have had in ample. For example, since going to office is a routine affair, hence you remember the directions very well. On being asked, you will be confident while giving the directions to your office. Similarly be it cooking or accounting, driving or any task for that matter, a person will always be confident about any field or an area in which he has experience.

Yet, progress is not possible solely on the basis of your existent knowledge or experience. For progress, something innovative and unprecedented must be done, and this is where you fail. You are unable to build the confidence in yourself to do something new, something unconventional. First, you marry according to your traditions and abide by rituals in order to attain marital bliss. But when you get accustomed to marital life, you do not visit your respective religious places every day to make your relationship work. Similarly, people inaugurate their shops according to a *mahurat** prescribed by the almanac, but as soon as they have the requisite experience, they alter their timings to suit the need of the business and the customers' convenience. In short, when it comes to pioneering or innovating, barely one in a million has the guts to venture on the basis of his strength. And only the one who exudes such confidence is actually entitled to success.

Overall, what I am implying is, the one who bases his trust solely on his capabilities even at the time of doing something innovative is the

Tasks that are executed without Confidence never fetch the desired results

only one who can actually succeed in life. If you too wish to build such self-confidence, then the only solution is to place your trust in your own thinking, talent and intelligence for everything, from the most insignificant to the most significant of the tasks and decisions of your life. And anyway, it is just not possible to completely trust anyone apart from yourself. When trying times knock at the door of your life, the trust placed on others is bound to get shattered.

Well, let me explain self-confidence to you with the help of a few examples. Think, what does a money lender do when he has to lend money on interest? He writes a credit note, and enters into a fool-proof agreement. In contrast, take the case of money lent by an underworld don; neither does he need any credit note nor an agreement. The best part is that often, the money lent after writing credit notes and agreements, turns into bad debts; people get tired chasing the defaulters and doing the rounds of courts to recover their money, while the money lent by the don without the support of any credit note or agreement is never lost; because to recover money, he has placed trust in his abilities, rather than a credit note or an agreement.

Let me narrate a beautiful instance related to self-confidence. Once, there lived a wise and compassionate hermit, who was highly revered by the entire village. Being an adamant, austere man, he never accepted a gift from anyone and led a very simple life. He lived in a hut with just two blankets in his possession.

**'' Even all the formidable powers of Nature
put together cannot enslave man ''**

It was the winter season and the weather was extremely cold. It was midnight, and the hermit was sleeping on one blanket, using the other to cover himself. Now a hermit is essentially one who lives with complete trust in himself. So, the question of him locking the door did not arise. Around the same time, a hungry thief was out on that chilly night scouting the area. Since he had still not found a place to steal from and saw that the hermit's door was open, he immediately stepped inside to burgle the house. He searched the hut for some time, but did not find anything apart from a small pot and a broken glass. Now, of course, on such a chilly night, he had not undertaken such arduous efforts for the sake of two broken vessels. So, it was obvious for him to feel disappointed.

Confidence increases either with growing experience or by pursuing the field in which your potential lies

The hermit, who was a light sleeper, had woken up as soon as he heard the first rustle. But, as he was also a man of a different mettle altogether, he pretended to be asleep, enjoying the drama unfold before him with half-closed eyes. Finally, when the thief was unable to find anything that he could pilfer, he grabbed the blanket that the hermit had covered himself with. He thought, "There should be some satisfaction at least!" After all, his reputation as a thief was at stake. Despite taking so much trouble in the dreary, chilly night, if he fails to find anything worth fencing, then how would he be called a thief? Thus, satisfied with stealing the blanket, he was just about to step out of the door when the hermit, who was quietly watching the drama, sprung into action.

He sternly asked the thief to stop. Listening to the stern voice of the hermit, the thief felt his feet going numb. There, the hermit stood up and asked him to come inside. Perspiring profusely, even in that chilly night, the thief quietly stepped inside.

Seeing the frightened expression on the thief's face, the hermit, with utmost humility, asked for his forgiveness and said, "Forgive me, brother! You have come so far on such a chilly night and I could not help you in any manner. There is nothing in the house that I could offer you. Next time, should you wish to come, please inform me in advance. I will make sure that I have something collected from the neighbourhood so that you will not have to leave disappointed."

The thief, who was already frightened on hearing the hermit's stern voice, now dropped the vessels and the blankets on listening to the hermit's generous proposition. Fumbling, he was ready to make a quick getaway without taking anything. Seeing this, the hermit sternly said once again, "You must take all that you intended to steal. Also, on your way out, close the door so that I stay protected from the cold." The poor thief! He had become so submissive that he was bound to follow every command of the hermit. He again picked up the fallen vessel and the blanket, closed the door and left, just as the hermit had instructed.

All is well that ends well. But in this case, the thief was caught the next morning. The entire village was well aware of the fact that the blanket belonged to the hermit. Everyone was fuming with anger, "What a vile thief! He stole things from the noble hermit's house!" He was caught and produced before the village assembly. Meanwhile, the news spread like wildfire, and reached the ears of the hermit too. He immediately reached the village assembly. He stated, "The accused has not robbed the blanket and the vessels, but I, in fact, asked him to take them. He is a Good Samaritan; while leaving, he also closed the door so that I would not catch a cold."

After the testimony of the hermit, the village assembly released the thief, but the thief wept inconsolably. He just could not stop crying. He fell at the feet of the hermit, and insisted that the hermit give him an opportunity to serve him.

Depending upon others including God dwindles your Confidence

The hermit, a little hesitant at first, decided to give him a chance and brought him home. Needless to say, along with the thief, the blanket and the vessels had also returned home. To the thief's surprise, upon returning home, the hermit let out a hearty laugh. Grinning he said, "Did you see my trick! Along with my blanket and vessels, I also got myself an assistant to serve me." No deal that a hermit makes can ever result in a loss. This is what is called self-confidence. He knew that it was not easy to rob his blanket and get away. Definitely, this is the greatest illustration of the hermit's self-confidence.

This is the self-confidence I am referring to! Full faith in one's own capabilities and intentions, is what self-confidence is all about. No other kind of self-confidence exists in the world. If you do not have faith in your abilities, you will never be able to execute any task confidently. Similarly, in the absence of trust in your intentions, at the very outset, you will find numerous questions sprouting, "Is it a sin?" "Is this the right thing to do?" Meaning, for the successful accomplishment of the task, you will be heavily dependent on the scriptures and society. And, how can the one whose thinking rests on the perception of others, carry out any task confidently? But, if one has full faith in his own intentions, why will he worry or bother about what the scriptures or society have to say? He would be assured that whatever he does would be virtuous as well as right. He will surely and confidently do what he thinks is appropriate, without any expectation or being bothered about what the world will have to think or say.

In short, since the human being has been blessed with absolute freedom by Nature, it is solely his own responsibility to make his life successful. Life can become successful with the effective execution of tasks and without confidence no task can ever be executed effectively. And confidence is the by-product of experience. Now you would say, "First let us gather experience, kindle our self-confidence and then we will act." But, how is this possible? How can you gain experience at a particular task without executing it? It is akin to saying that you want to swim, but are afraid of entering the water. You think, "First let us learn swimming and then we will take a plunge in the water." Alas, the reality of life is that without taking a plunge in the water, you cannot learn to swim. Well, this is the predicament in which your entire life is spent.

The key to overcome this predicament is, as a human being, you have no option but to execute newer tasks; and when it is imperative that you do, then why not do it with full confidence? However, in order to kindle this confidence, you cannot afford to bank on experiences alone. If you are not confident of learning to swim, then irrespective of the number of attempts you make, you will not be able to learn, whereas with confidence, you will learn to swim in a couple of days. Thus, the elixir of confidence saves both, your time as well as your energy.

Of course, experience acts as a catalyst to fire up your confidence. But it is also true that experience comes over a number of years, and unfortunately, you do not have that many. So, now the question that arises is, bereft of experience, how can you execute the newer tasks with full confidence? And without confidence, success seems to be a distant reality. Then the only solution is to release yourself from the clutches of your brain and seek refuge in me. For, the brain is keen on having numerous experiences, and thousands of people incite the brain for countless reasons and lure it with numerous temptations. The funniest part is, the brain even succumbs to those temptations. However, I, on the other hand, advise you to stay true to your talent and abilities. Moreover, it is not a herculean task for you to have faith in your own talents and potential because, for that, you are not at the mercy of experience; all you need to do is, rightly identify the field in which your talent lies.

For example, business is a promising avenue of profit, but you do not possess business acumen. Then do not succumb to societal, peer or familial influences to study for a business management degree. You may secure a degree with hard work, but in the absence of business acumen, you will never be able to garner the confidence to do business. Your time and energy both would go down the drain, and ultimately, you will find yourself taking up a job. In contrast to

Man
has
absolute
freedom

this, the one who has an aptitude for business need not depend on a business management degree. By the time you secure the degree, he would have made his mark in the field of business. It is highly probable that you may even be employed by such an unqualified person. Because, often, the employees are better qualified than the proprietor!

Therefore, in order to progress in life, please do not follow the dictates of your brain to choose your field of work. Also, do not choose the field under duress or other people's advice. For, in spite of strenuous efforts, you would not be able to build up confidence in the field that you have been pushed into. Your field is, where your talent lies. And you will automatically be confident in the field of your talent. And most importantly, confidence is not something that can be borrowed from the external sources. But since you try your hand in a field against the directives of your mind, you feel the need to seek confidence from the market. There are various kinds of shops set up in this market; some offering tempting degrees and some, magic spells and religious amulets. Lured by them, you even buy confidence from those who peddle these things, but it proves to be of no use to you, because it is not in compliance with my laws. On the contrary, whatever is left of your confidence also gets shattered into smithereens.

Nevertheless, the fact of the matter is, it is not a few individuals, but the entire human race is caught up in this vicious circle. Firstly,

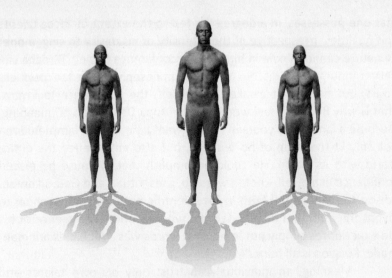

" It is impossible for man to trust and have faith in anyone other than himself "

propelled by not one, but numerous reasons, they make desperate attempts at the wrong places, and when those attempts do not fructify, they further set forth searching for newer avenues of confidence, which dwindles their confidence further. Thereafter, their life is relegated to struggling and after falling flat on their faces a few times, they look for even newer ways to get confidence. And in the end, the poor people lose confidence in themselves as well as life! And in this vicious circle, do you know who hits the jackpot? The peddlers of confidence, who make a fortune out of your desperation! Under the pretext of selling you confidence, they dupe you of your earnings. The situation comes to such a pass, that you lose on both accounts; confidence is not gained and life-savings are lost too.

Well! You may not have noticed, but this is the reason why confidence is called self-confidence. Meaning, confidence, in its true sense can only be reposed in your soul, that is, your own self. And one can have this confidence only on the basis of talents and qualities that one possesses, in a degree limited to the extent of those talents and qualities. Irrespective of the intensity of his desire to sing, a poet by nature cannot kindle in himself the confidence to sing. Buddha can deliver innumerable discourses on the philosophy of life for countless hours, but he cannot awaken in himself, the confidence to invent. That is why Buddha's last words were, "Appa Deepo Bhava" meaning, 'Become a lamp unto yourself'. If you want light, be the lamp! Buddha not only lit the lamp of his wisdom, but also enlightened the entire world with its flame. He could accomplish that, because he placed confidence in himself – not in worship, rites, rituals and God. Likewise, Edison too placed full faith in his scientific aptitude and went on to invent the bulb that illuminated the whole world. The essence of his life experiences simply put in his own words was, "All Bibles are man-made. Religion is all bunk."

Meaning, an individual can trust only his own talents and qualities. Fuelled by this trust and confidence in himself, if he enhances his talent, then very soon his life brightens up, and he prospers. He seeks borrowed confidence and ultimately departs from the world without substantiating his life with any achievement. Can the confidence placed in others ever prove to be useful? To help you understand better, let me put it in a straightforward manner. Most of the people say that the world has been created by God. You would have also heard people saying that 'without God's will, even a leaf does not move'. Then if your life is in shambles, have you reached this stage without the will of God? Then why do you not consider it as his will and accept your failures and enjoy life? Why do you keep admonishing yourself and others? That is because, to listen and believe is one thing, but to really have faith, is simply not possible. No sooner someone hurls an abuse at you than you become angry. At that point in time, you do not think that he abused you because of God's will! You believe that even a leaf does not move without the will of God, and yet, you have harboured animosity against so many of God's creations! Is your brain not really incredible?

So, I say with full conviction that if you need to superficially cloak yourself with confidence, then no matter what kind of confidence it is, you are on the wrong track. This implies that you are making desperate efforts, with wrong aspirations, in the wrong direction. Return to your true self and you will be redeemed. Search for the task that you can carry out with utmost confidence, and you will become your true self, that is, what I intended you to be. Thereafter, you will not require anyone's support, help or confidence. When you reach such a state of mind, know it for sure, that your life is all set to blossom.

Lastly, I will proceed with the hope that from today onwards, you will safeguard yourself from falling prey to fallacious confidence and reaffirmations. It is your life, so are your deeds and experiences. It is you who has to become successful, then how can you place confidence on someone else? You are talented – so why do you need support, help or confidence from others? Just understand this and see how you transform from an ordinary human being to an individual par excellence. Because, it is better to indulge in the tasks you can carry out confidently rather than seeking confidence from external sources, as your confidence is the only path that can lead you to achieve your goal and help you sit on the throne called success.

———————◼———————

Contentment

"Contentment is supreme wealth" is an age-old adage you may have heard numerous times. I, too, am saying that nothing is more precious than contentment, which eliminates all the troubles and chaos from life and takes you to the peak of success. But then, you will interject and ask, "If we become content, how will we progress?" You are not alone, there are thousands of people propagating the same thought, *"Want progress and prosperity? Jump into the ring, engage yourself, have lofty ambitions and never be content!"* Unfortunately, it is deceptively simple; its appeal cuts across all strata of society and people get caught up in the rat-race. Pause for a while and contemplate; even after so many ups and downs, and such strenuous efforts, what have you gained? Notice, how many frustrations, anxieties and grievances you are living with! And even after going through all this, let alone success, even leading a normal life has become an ordeal for you. The truth that is evident to our eyes is, everyone is caught up in this insane rat race to progress, yet, barely does anyone seem to. Then, there is no option but to accept that running from pillar to post and knocking on every door is not going to open the door of progress for you.

Well, I know that your brain will not grasp this easily. Therefore, let me enlighten you with the psychological facets of this fact. Firstly, what is the meaning of contentment? It means wherever and in whichever condition you are, whatever you have and however it is, you are satisfied with it. But your brain interprets this definition differently, and asks, 'If you become content, then how will you progress in life?' However, the brain does not understand the calculations and the mechanism of the mind, so it deludes itself as well as you.

Just ponder over this for a while; what effect would it have on me, if you were to become absolutely content with your present? Certainly, I would feel instantaneously relaxed and experience peace and bliss. All your grief, anxiety and anger will be dissipated. I will be exuding joy and exhilaration. Indeed, attaining this state of mind is no less an achievement in itself. For, in the end, man runs this rat race, only to be able to live a relaxed and peaceful life. In that case, if you get such a life right here, right now, instead of the future, then how is it a loss-making proposition?

Now, let me reveal the greatest advantage of leading a life of contentment. As stated above, with contentment you instantaneously experience joy and exhilaration. When you attain this blissful state of mind, your brain, which so far has been engaged in futile tasks due to its erratic tendencies, also sets into the right thinking mode. The decisions taken then turn out to be the right decisions. The ultimate outcome of your life depends on the right and wrong decisions you have taken. For example, you have strong aspirations to become another Bill Gates, but you take a series of wrong decisions; then how do you expect to be placed in the same league as him?

Why is it so difficult for people to understand the simple fact that being content does not mean stopping all your activities? It also does not imply that you do not keep an eye open for the things unfolding around you. No, even when you are content, all your routine activities will still continue. You will still be engaged in your day-to-day work, but now you will not be part of the mad rush and will not indulge in comparisons. You will be absorbed in your routine life and business as usual, but with a very positive state of mind.

And since you will be in positive state of mind, away from the rat race, you will be able to accurately spot the opportunities for progress. Moreover, when you sight a good opportunity, you will also be able to grab it and utilise it to the fullest.

Contrary to this, when you are making desperate attempts to progress, you tend to perceive everything and every situation in life as an opportunity. And this is where you falter. When you are not

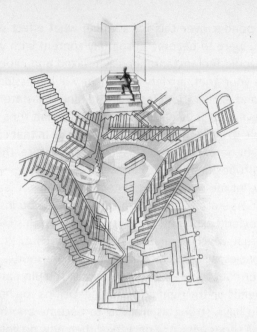

> **" When it comes to climbing the ladder of success
> there is nothing more magical than being content "**

content with life, your mind is already enmeshed in thousands of worries and anxieties which has led your decision-making ability to betray you, and the worst part is, in such a mental state you begin to hunt for thousands of options to progress in life. Consequently, nine out of your ten decisions prove to be wrong, and finally, instead of progressing, you actually begin to retrogress; whereas, if you live with contentment, then at least you will not backslide. And you are all aware of the fact that, only the one, who is steadfast wherever he is, can progress. The guarantee that there will be no backslide infuses in you an extraordinary confidence, and I have already explained to you how important this confidence is, in order to progress. I will now reveal the second advantage of contentment. A content individual has all the time in the world to thoroughly enjoy his life and pursue his hobbies, whereas a person caught up in the rat race is not able to find time for himself. And for the person who has no time for himself, life has become a waste anyway.

So, let me conclude with a beautiful incident. Once, there lived a content, well-established businessman named Nirv who was leading a happy life with all his necessities taken care of. Allotting six hours for his business provided him a lot of spare time for himself. Hence, he not only followed a well-balanced diet and fitness regime, but also had ample time to indulge in his hobby of listening to music and reading. Additionally, he could spend quality time with his family too.

He had a brother-in-law, Akin, who was a software engineer. Being highly ambitious and impatient to climb the corporate ladder, he had switched between four to five jobs, and was always looking for opportunities to venture into a business. One day, while both were engaged in a friendly conversation, Nirv asked Akin, "This thought has occurred to me many a time, but I have failed to understand what exactly you want to do in life."

Akin haughtily replied, "All I need to do is explore the avenue of business, start a new venture, work hard to establish it, earn lots of money and settle down."

Hearing Akin's plan, Nirv became a little worried and said, "Even if everything falls in place as planned, by the time you achieve all this, you would be nearing sixty. You would have achieved everything, but then what?"

Truly there is no wealth greater —than Contentment in human life

Akin replied, "Then what! I will live a life of contentment and peace."

Laughing Nirv replied, "You can do that today, by sticking to one job. Why do you need to wait for thirty years and take such a huge risk?"

Neither did Akin have an answer for this, nor would you. For a sensible person, a mere hint is enough. And, who is more sensible than you, right?

In summation, the immediate benefit of contentment is that a person will become happy right here, right now. The second benefit will be, his mindset will always remain positive. And you all are already aware, how important a positive state of mind is, for taking the right decision. Now, it is not necessary to reiterate the fact that it is the decisions of an individual that determine the direction and the dimension of his life, as well as the predisposition of the individual. Moreover, only a content person can experience happiness and peace which is the ultimate goal of human life. What is of greater significance is the fact that a content individual does not have to backtrack or face any setback. In addition, only a content individual can enjoy what he has at present. So, I hope you will embrace this supreme quality of contentment which is potent with the power to instantaneously eliminate all the problems from your life and help you scale newer peaks of success. Welcome contentment into your life today itself and set out on the path of success!

The Summary

To summarise, there are only two purposes of human life, to live joyously and to scale the summit of success. Although, the purpose is clear, barely a few in millions become happy and successful. As for the rest, they are not only discontent with their life in its present state, but are also sceptical about their future. However, to make their lives successful, people have usually explored each and every avenue of support, right from their family to society, friends to government; even religion and education have been exhausted, but happiness and success still been eludes them. The irony is, for ages, human beings have been persistently engaged in achieving success and discovering happiness with the help of the same age-old principles and practices.

And this is where every individual is committing a grave mistake. In the quest to build a good life for themselves, the 'brilliant' human beings are relying on the same age-old practices that have been proven ineffective for thousands of years. Also, they have failed to realise the fact that human life gets influenced by not one, but many forces. On one hand a person's brain desires one thing and on the other his DNA, genes and body are singing a different tune altogether. Over and above that, the two mutually opposing yet powerful forces, 'Nature' and 'society' are not sparing him either. And the irony is, I, meaning, their mind affects his life the most, yet, he knows very little about me.

As for me, I am completely independent and my system of functioning is indeed complicated. And the most noteworthy point here is, despite that, I always function in accordance with my own laws. Meaning, it is certainly possible for you to comprehend me and my functioning and deal with me accordingly. My peculiarity is that on one hand, I am the centre of numerous powers and on the other, several negativities also lie hidden within me. Now, be that as it may, but without the knowledge and understanding of my negativities, or the ways to deal with them, a person can neither get rid of his sorrows, nor can he utilise my powers to scale the peaks of success.

The most significant fact to be grasped is, the various psychological solutions that I have suggested to ward off man's sorrows such as living in the present, saving yourself from the trap of complexes, lowering the bar of your involvement and expectations and so on, are the attributes that are already existent in abundance in children. And this is the reason why a child is generally not worried or frustrated. On the other hand, if you observe closely, you will be surprised to know that to achieve success, all the qualities that I have suggested, such as self-confidence, concentration, creativity, enthusiasm, the development of your inner personality, applying intelligence to the point and so on, exist in children in abundance.

248

You all must have carefully observed children many a times. You must have noticed that they can play with the same toy for hours at a stretch. Let alone toys, they do not get fed up even while playing with mud and water. What can be said about their level of absorption and engrossment in playing! Even the most meditative person will be no match for them! In other words, they do not lack concentration - the most amazing quality that helps your life and energy grow exponentially. This is the reason why most children live in a Super Conscious state of mind. Enthusiasm, self-confidence and firmness are the inherent attributes of this state of mine. You must have also noticed that if children become obstinate about something, then they do not leave you with any option but to surrender to them. Their firmness is unparalleled. And we have all seen their enthusiasm! Even though they fail fifty times in their attempt to walk and keep getting hurt, they never give up until they finally learn how to walk. At the same time, the power of acceptance - the elixir that eliminates all your sorrows is also abundantly present in them. It is not in their nature to mourn or lament over a loss; be it the breaking of a toy or getting hurt, they whine over it for a while, and then, immediately focus on something new and get engrossed in it.

Science states that approximately eighty per cent of a child's brain is developed by the time he reaches the age of four-five. In a way, science is correct, but only to some extent. Since science is completely ignorant of my invisible existence, it considers even my Super Conscious state as an attribute of the brain. But it is wrong. Till four-five years of age, a child's brain has not substantially developed, but because children dwell in the Super Conscious state of mine, my intrinsic attributes manifest in them. The sound progress of a child clearly implies that this state of mine has remained intact. And because a powerful brain and a Super Conscious Mind cannot co-exist, as the child grows and the brain begins to develop, he is slowly compelled to slip from the Super Conscious state to the conscious state of mine. Here, let me make it clear once again, that unless you understand the distinction between me and the brain, all efforts on my part will prove to be of no use to you. Until you clearly grasp the difference between both our systems and areas of functioning, or until you recognise our separate existence or acknowledge them as separate entities, neither will you be able to take advantage of all that I have stated, nor will you be able to miraculously transform your life. Therefore, it is imperative for you to read over and over again the difference between me and the brain which I have already explained earlier. And please ensure you do so!

Now the question you need to ask yourself is, how does the child, who is living with all the qualities of the Super Conscious state of mind - with which, he is capable of reaching the unprecedented heights of success in life - lose them as he grows up? Of course, it is because of the strengthening of his brain. And how does the brain get strengthened? It becomes strong because of wrong teachings and his ignorance about me. Therefore, whenever you become serious about setting your life on the path to progress, first try to regain your 'child-like' state of mind. Because without acquiring the qualities of the Super Conscious state of mind, even if you try and test numerous other solutions, happiness and success will never set foot into your life. And this is the reason why all the psychological treatments related to my system of functioning, seem to take you backwards. They are meant to take you backwards because you have to go through the process of unlearning and once again start living in your Super Conscious state of mind. And as for your next course of action, once this state is regained, it is a different subject altogether. Let us not discuss about it right now. So far, I have briefed you about the solutions with the help of which you can once again start living in your Super Conscious Mind.

In short, it is my earnest request, please do not interfere or experiment much with children. All you family members, teachers, society, religious heads and self-professed caretakers of society, please understand and learn how to take children beyond the Super Conscious state of mind. You must understand that if you yourself are ignorant about it, and are still compelling them to walk on the path suggested by you, then you are doing is nothing, but misguiding them. It is only because of your advice and tutoring that the child loses his precious Super Conscious state, and is forced to live in the conscious state of mine. Sorrows, worries, frustration, miseries and restlessness are all the intrinsic characteristics of the conscious state of mine. Speaking in words filled with compassion, it is only because of the unwarranted obligation thrust upon by one ignorant human being on another, that mankind as a whole is in such a dire state today.

I assert that all the people who are happy and successful in life today, regardless of the extent of happiness and success, are because they have either retained the qualities of their Super Conscious state of mind of their childhood, or their parents or a wise teacher or someone else has helped them retain the same, as they grew up. If you make a list of thousands of happy and successful people, you will find them to be the ones whose Super Conscious state of mind was active even when they had grown up. Definitely, there are many amongst them who have regained their Super Conscious state with the help of their own intelligence and understanding, even after losing it. Ultimately, it is the attributes of their Super Conscious Mind, namely concentration, self-confidence and enthusiasm that have led them to the pinnacle of success. Hence, it is my humble request that please impart only those teachings to children that would help them transcend or at least retain their state of Super Conscious Mind. Using experience as a tool, allow the numerous powers of their mind to blossom, and facilitate the simultaneous development of the brain. And if you do not know how to do so, then at least, do not compel them to do anything against their wishes and do not impose compulsions on their life.

Last but not the least; let me reveal a secret to you. If you perceive life in its true sense, you will observe that I am the one around whom your entire life revolves. And the spectrum of both my complexities as well as my powers, is extremely wide. Hence, at present I have restricted my discussion solely to achieving the Super Conscious state of mind, which is not even one tenth of my potential. I am brimming with such amazing powers that once you tap them, you can become the master of not only your life, but of everyone else's too.

Since this is my first effort at unveiling myself, let us go step-by-step. I promise you, that very soon I will hold your hand and take you on the journey beyond my Super Conscious state.

Thank you!

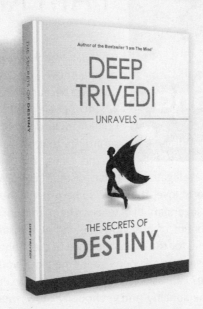

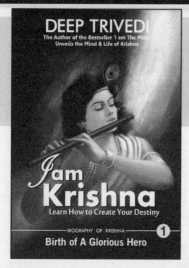

Learn From Me How To
Create Your Own Destiny
I Am Krishna!

I Am Krishna! Is there anyone who has not heard of me? No...but do people know who I really am? I ask this question because I am the only one about whom people still hold contradictory opinions. On one hand, there are some scriptures that state that I am the God of the Gods, on the other, there are scriptures that have relegated me to languishing in hell. While some perceive me as the epitome of love, there are some others who do not hesitate to brazenly call me a legendary eve-teaser. There are those who consider me the greatest proponent of non-violence, and at the same time, there are many who blame me for the brutal violence of the Mahabharata war.

Don't these contradictions about me pique your curiosity to know and understand me? I am asking this question because on the face of it, I am the most popular personality, and yet nobody knows much about me. Many a time, I am amazed by this and wonder why it is so. The stories of my birth and childhood are well-known, as is the fact that I had to struggle a lot in my childhood. But then, when and how did I become the king of a golden city like Dwarka? Everyone knows how deep and intense my love was for Radha. In fact, people addressed me as 'Radha's Kishen'. Then why did Krishna and Radha part ways forever? Why does no one want to know and understand all this? Every time there is mention of me, only the beautiful part of my life is discussed, whereas not only my childhood, but my entire life was spent under the looming shadow of death. But I was Krishna after all; death did not dare approach without my express permission. Then why does no one discuss my great abilities to cope with the struggles? My entire childhood was spent grappling with my impoverished existence. My entire life was spent evading death. All kinds of accusations were leveled against me throughout my life. Draupadi blamed me for the death of her sons, and even Gandhari accused me of being responsible for the death of her sons. As a matter of fact, even my dear wife Satyabhama accused me of stealing her father Satrajit's precious Syamantaka Mani. My dearest and most beloved brother Balarama not only accused me of stealing the Syamantaka Mani, but also of killing an innocent Shatdhanva. Even life itself was no exception in showing me all its possible colours. My eldest son Pradyuman was kidnapped by a demon named Shambhasur as soon as he was born. And by the time he returned, he had already married a demoness, Mayavati, who was much older than him. What more? So many of my sons and grandsons were slain right before my eyes as they fought each other in the tragedy faced by the inhabitants of Dwarka infamously known as the Yadavasthali. That is why I say, I may be the most popular personality, but of what use is that, when you know nothing about me, my personality and my life?

However, no crisis in my life could ever wipe the smile off my face. I emerged victorious in every struggle that I faced in my life—familial, societal, economic or psychological. That is why, I am known as Jai Shri Krishna. Never did I weep, nor did I ever become despondent, as I was a firm believer of Karma. And I had carved my destiny with my karma alone. I played the flute even as death hovered over my head. Whether it was the Mahabharat or the Yadavasthali, to me they were nothing but a Raasa that I simply played along.

I was an achiever, and such a legendary achiever, that no one like me has ever been born. I am the only one in history to reach the highest level of wisdom, concentration, action and devotion. I am the first one to stop the worship of Indra (considered the God of rain) and raise my voice against superstition. I am the first to become a king in spite of not being born as a prince. I am the first one to give women equal status in all walks of life. I am the undisputed master of Psychology, and the Bhagavad Gita I enunciated is existent proof of this. I am the first one to establish a link between wisdom and Science. I am the first one to discuss the laws of the mind, life and Nature. I am the one to have had the privilege of being married to seven princesses in spite of being raised as a cowherd. All these achievements were the outcome of my great deeds. And to tell you the truth, it is this prodigious talent of mine which is the real 'me'. Whether it is my mind, my life, or the Bhagavad Gita, there is nothing more precious for a human being than these. You too wish to lead a successful, luxurious life filled with pleasure and comforts like me. Problems and struggles are inevitable in life. They existed in my life, and will always exist in your life too. The only difference is, I had overcome them all and scaled the peak of success, whereas you have conceded defeat in your fight against the problems and struggles of life. I had carved a destiny for myself with my perseverance and my deeds, and if you want, you too can learn from my life and carve out your own destiny as you desire. And this is the essence of what I had said in the Bhagavad Gita, 'Your life is linked to your deeds... and you are the creator of your own destiny'.

So delve deeper into my life, my personality and my psychological journey, and gain the ability to carve out your own destiny as per your wish. Because as you continue reading about my life, you will begin to understand the profundity of the mind, the heights one can achieve in life, the truth about destiny along with all the laws of Time and Nature. And once you grasp all this, who can stop you from carving out your own destiny?

I have just one request. Do not belittle my great achievements by linking them to destiny. Do not push me away from you by making me larger-than-life or turning me into a performer of miracles. Instead, discover my true personality and let me reside in your heart.

Graphic Books

In every child there lies a potential to become successful and great. Everyone does not have to necessarily struggle in life. The problem is how should a child identify his talent and nurture it. The question is whether the child is flowing in tune with nature or not. The question is, has the child been provided the right upbringing or not?

To know this and many more interesting facts and facets of psychology to make your child successful, read interesting graphic books penned by Deep Trivedi

The Story of Steve Jobs
Mischief Maker to Path Breaker

Naughtiness to Greatness
AI to Edison

The Story of a Lion's Cub
Haughty to Daunty

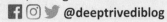